CREATIVE
HOMEOWNER®

Big Ideas for Small Spaces

AFFORDABLE
HOME PLANS

CREATIVE HOMEOWNER®, Upper Saddle River, New Jersey

COPYRIGHT © 2005

CRE▲TIVE
HOMEOWNER®

A Division of Federal Marketing Corp.
Upper Saddle River, NJ

VP/Publisher: Brian H. Toolan
VP/Editorial Director: Timothy O. Bakke
Production Manager: Kimberly H. Vivas

Home Plans Editor: Kenneth D. Stuts
Home Plans Designer Liaison: Maureen Mulligan

Design and Layout: Arrowhead Direct (David Kroha, Cindy DiPierdomenico, Judith Kroha)

Cover Design: David Geer

Current Printing (last digit)
10 9 8 7 6 5 4 3 2 1

Affordable Home Plans
Library of Congress Control Number: 2005924173
ISBN: 1-58011-273-0

CREATIVE HOMEOWNER®
A Division of Federal Marketing Corp.
24 Park Way
Upper Saddle River, NJ 07458
www.creativehomeowner.com

Printed In China

Note: The homes as shown in the photographs and renderings in this book may differ from the actual blueprints. When studying the house of your choice, please check the floor plans carefully.

PHOTO CREDITS

Front cover: *top* plan 211003, page 158; *bottom row left to right* plan 151010, page 36; plan 131030, pages 258–259; plan 131030, pages 258–259; plan 401029, pages 222–223 **back cover:** *top* plan 121064, page 160; *center* plan 151008, page 158; *bottom left* plan 351001, page 154; *bottom center* plan 401029, page 222; *bottom right* plan 131030, page 258 **page 1:** plan 151010, page 36 **page 3:** *top* plan 121009, page 36; *center* plan 151034, page 215; *bottom* plan 161002, page 157 **pages 4–6:** David Geer **page 7:** plan 401029, pages 222–223 **pages 62–63:** courtesy of Kraftmaid Cabinetry **page 64:** *both* courtesy of Wellborn Cabinets **page 65:** courtesy of Kraftmaid Cabinetry **page 66:** courtesy of Wellborn Cabinets **page 67:** *top left* courtesy of Merillat; *top right* courtesy of Wellborn Cabinets; *bottom left* courtesy of Merillat Industries **page 104:** *top* courtesy of American Olean; *bottom* courtesy of Villeroy & Boch **page 105:** *top* courtesy of Wilsonart; *bottom* courtesy of Kraftmaid Cabinetry **pages 106–107:** *left* courtesy of Silestone; *top center* courtesy of Wilsonart; *top right and bottom right* courtesy of Armstrong **page 108:** courtesy of Kraftmaid Cabinetry **page 109:** *top* courtesy of York Wallcoverings; *bottom* courtesy of Villeroy & Boch **page 110:** *top* courtesy of Armstrong; *bottom* courtesy of Merillat **page 111:** courtesy of Villeroy & Boch **page 147:** *top* courtesy of Weber; *bottom right* courtesy of Frontgate; *bottom left* courtesy of Broilmaster **page 148:** courtesy of Sub-Zero **page 149:** courtesy of Malibu Lighting/Intermatic **pages 150–151:** *top left* courtesy of Malibu lighting/Intermatic; *center* Marvin Slobin/courtesy of California Redwood Association; *bottom* courtesy of Southern Forest Products Assoc. **pages 184–195:** *all* illustrations by Steve Buchanan/CH **page 228:** *both* gidesigns.net **pages 229–230:** courtesy of Trellis Structures **page 231:** *all* courtesy of Elyria Fence Co. **pages 232–233:** *left* David Freeman, Spectra Studios/CH; *center* courtesy of Trellis Structures **pages 234–237:** *all* David Freeman, Spectra Studios/CH **page 238:** courtesy of California Redwood Association **page 239:** *both* courtesy of Intermatic **page 279:** plan 121001, page 169

Contents

Getting Started

aybe you can't wait to bang the first nail. Or you may be just as happy leaving town until the windows are cleaned. The extent of your involvement with the construction phase is up to you. Your time, interests, and abilities can help you decide how to get the project from lines on paper to reality. But building a house requires more than putting pieces together. Whoever is in charge of the process must competently manage people as well as supplies, materials, and construction. He or she will have to

- Make a project schedule to plan the orderly progress of the work. This can be a bar chart that shows the time period of activity by each trade.
- Establish a budget for each category of work, such as foundation, framing, and finish carpentry.
- Arrange for a source of construction financing.
- Get a building permit and post it conspicuously at the construction site.
- Line up supply sources and order materials.
- Find subcontractors and negotiate their contracts.
- Coordinate the work so that it progresses smoothly with the fewest conflicts.
- Notify inspectors at the appropriate milestones.
- Make payments to suppliers and subcontractors.

You as the Builder

You'll have to take care of every logistical detail yourself if you decide to act as your own builder or general contractor. But along with the responsibilities of managing the project, you gain the flexibility to do as much of your own work as you want and subcontract out the rest. Before taking this path, however, be sure you have the time and capabilities. Do you also have the

time and ability to schedule the work, hire and coordinate subs, order materials, and keep ahead of the accounting required to manage the project successfully? If you do, you stand to save the amount that a general contractor would charge to take on these responsibilities, normally 15 to 30 percent of the construction cost. If you take this responsibility on but mismanage the project, the potential savings will erode and may even cost you more than if you had hired a builder in the first place. A subcontractor might charge extra for hav-

Acting as the builder, above, requires the ability to hire and manage subcontractors.

Building a home, opposite, includes the need to schedule building inspections at the appropriate milestones.

ing to return to the site to complete work that was originally scheduled for an earlier date. Or perhaps because you didn't order the windows at the beginning, you now have to pay for a recent cost increase. (If you had hired a builder in the first place he or she would absorb the increase.)

Hiring a Builder to Handle Construction

A builder or general contractor will manage every aspect of the construction process. Your role after signing the construction contract will be to make regular progress payments and ensure that the work for which you are paying has been completed. You will also consult with the builder and agree to any changes that may have to be made along the way.

Leads for finding builders might come from friends or neighbors who have had contractors build, remodel, or add to their homes. Real-estate agents and bankers may have some names handy but are more likely familiar with the builder's ability to complete projects on time and budget than the quality of the work itself.

The next step is to narrow your list of candidates to three or four who you think can do a quality job and work harmoniously with you. Phone each builder to see whether he or she is interested in being considered for your project. If so, invite the builder to an interview at your home. The meeting will serve two purposes. You'll be able to ask the candidate about his or her experience, and you'll be able to see whether or not your personalities are compatible. Go over the plans with the builder to make certain that he or she understands the scope of the project. Ask if they have constructed similar houses. Get references, and check the builder's standing with the Better Business Bureau. Develop a short list of builders, say three, and ask them to submit bids for the project.

Contracts

Lump-Sum Contracts

A lump-sum, or fixed-fee, contract lets you know from the beginning just what the project will cost, barring any changes made because of your requests or unforeseen conditions. This form works well for projects that promise few surprises and are well defined from the outset by a complete set of contract documents. You can enter into a fixed-price contract by negotiating with a single builder on your short list or by obtaining bids from three or four builders. If you go the latter route, give each bidder a set of documents and allow at least two weeks for them to submit their bids. When you get the bids, decide who you want and call the others to thank them for their efforts. You don't have to accept the lowest bid, but it probably makes sense to do so since you have already honed the list to builders you trust. Inform this builder of your intentions to finalize a contract.

Cost-Plus-Fee Contracts

Under a cost-plus-fee contract, you agree to pay the builder for the costs of labor and materials, as verified by receipts, plus a fee that represents the builder's overhead and profit. This arrangement is sometimes referred to as "time and materials." The fee can range between 15 and 30 percent of the incurred costs. Because you ultimately pick up the tab—whatever the costs—the contractor is never at risk, as he is with a lump-sum contract. You won't know the final total cost of a cost-plus-fee contract until the project is built and paid for. If you can live with that uncertainty, there are offsetting advantages. First, this form allows you to accommodate unknown conditions much more easily than does a lump-sum contract. And rather than being tied down by the project documents, you will be free to make changes at any point along the way. This can be a trap, though. Watching the project take shape will spark the desire to add something or do something differently. Each change costs more, and the accumulation can easily exceed your budget. Because of the uncertainty of the final tab and the built-in advantage to the contractor, you should think twice before entering into this form of contract.

Contract Content

The conditions of your agreement should be spelled out thoroughly in writing and signed by both parties, whatever contractual arrangement you make with your builder. Your contract should include provisions for the following:

- The names and addresses of the owner and builder.
- A description of the work to be included ("As described in the plans and specifications dated . . .").
- The date that the work will be completed if time is of the essence.
- The contract price for lump-sum contracts and the builder's allowed profit and overhead costs for changes.
- The builder's fee for cost-plus-fee contracts and the method of accounting and requesting payment.
- The criteria for progress payments (monthly, by project milestones) and the conditions of final payment.
- A list of each drawing and specification section that is to be included as part of the contract.
- Requirements for guarantees. (One year is the standard period for which contractors guarantee the entire project, but you may require specific guarantees on

When submitting bids, all of the builders should base their estimates on the same specifications. Once the work begins, communicate with your builder to keep the work proceeding smoothly.

Inspect your newly built home, if possible, before the builder closes it up and finishes it.

certain parts of the project, such as a 20-year guarantee on the roofing.)
- Provisions for insurance.
- A description of how changes in the work orders will be handled.

The builder may have a standard contract that you can tailor to the specifics of your project. These contain complete specific conditions with blanks that you can fill in to fit your project and a set of "general conditions" that cover a host of issues from insurance to termination provisions. It's always a good idea to have an attorney review the draft of your completed contract before signing it.

Working with Your Builder

The construction phase officially begins when you have a signed copy of the contract and copies of any insurance required from the builder. It's not unheard of for a builder to request an initial payment of 10 to 20 percent of the total cost to cover mobilization costs, those costs associated with obtaining permits and getting set up to begin the actual construction. If you agree to this, keep a careful eye on the progress of the work to ensure that the total paid out at any one time doesn't get too far out of sync with the actual work completed.

What about changes? From here on, it's up to you and your builder to proceed in good faith and to keep the channels of communication open. Even so, changes of one sort or another beset every project, and they usually add to its cost.

Light at the End of the Tunnel.

The builder's request for a final inspection marks the end of the construction phase—almost. At the final inspection meeting, you and the builder will inspect the work, noting any defects or incomplete items on a "punch list." When the builder tidies up the punch list items, you should reinspect. Sometimes, builders go on to another job and take forever to clean up the last few details, so only after all items on the list have been completed satisfactorily should you release the final payment, which often accounts for the builder's profit.

Some Final Words

Having a positive attitude is important when undertaking a project as large as building a home. A positive attitude can help you ride out the rigors and stress of the construction process.

Stay Flexible. Expect problems, because they certainly will occur. Weather can upset the schedule you have established for subcontractors. A supplier may get behind on deliveries, which also affects the schedule. An unexpected pipe may surprise you during excavation. Just as certain, every problem that comes along has a solution if you are open to it.

Be Patient. The extra days it may take to resolve a construction problem will be forgotten once the project is completed.

Express Yourself. If what you see isn't exactly what you thought you were getting, don't be afraid to look into changing it. Or you may spot an unforeseen opportunity for an improvement. Changes usually cost more money, though, so don't make frivolous decisions.

Finally, watching your home go up is exciting, so stay upbeat. Get away from your project from time to time. Dine out. Take time to relax. A positive attitude will make for smoother relations with your builder. An optimistic outlook will yield better-quality work if you are doing your own construction. And though the project might seem endless while it is under way, keep in mind that all the planning and construction will fade to a faint memory at some time in the future, and you will be getting a lifetime of pleasure from a home that is just right for you.

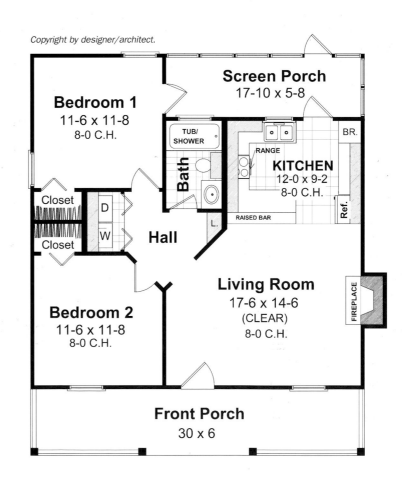

Plan #351013

Dimensions: 30' W x 36' D

Levels: 1

Square Footage: 800

Bedrooms: 2

Bathrooms: 1

Foundation: Crawl space or basement

Materials List Available: Yes

Price Category: A

The design and layout of this home bring back the memories of days gone by and places in which we feel comfortable.

Features:

- Living Room: When you enter this room from the front porch, you can feel the warmth from its fireplace.

- Kitchen: This kitchen features a raised bar and is open to the living room.

- Bedrooms: Two equally sized bedrooms share a common bathroom located in the hall.

- Screened Porch: Located in the rear of the home and accessible from bedroom 1 and the kitchen, this area is for relaxing.

Screen Porch
17-10 x 5-8

Bedroom 1
11-6 x 11-8
8-0 C.H.

TUB/SHOWER

BR.

RANGE

KITCHEN
12-0 x 9-2
8-0 C.H.

Ref.

Bath

Closet

Closet

D

W

L.

RAISED BAR

Hall

Living Room
17-6 x 14-6
(CLEAR)
8-0 C.H.

FIREPLACE

Bedroom 2
11-6 x 11-8
8-0 C.H.

Front Porch
30 x 6

Plan #391008

Dimensions: 50' W x 40' D
Levels: 1
Square Footage: 1,312
Bedrooms: 3
Bathrooms: 2
Foundation: Crawl space, slab, or basement
Materials List Available: Yes
Price Category: B

Here's the sum of brains and beauty, which will please all types of families, from starters and nearly empty nesters to those going golden.

Features:

- Entry: This restful fresh-air porch and formal foyer bring you graciously toward the great room, with its fireplace and vaulted ceiling.

- Dining Room: This adjacent dining room features sliding doors to the deck and smooth open access to the U-shaped kitchen.

- Laundry Room: The laundry area has its own separate landing from the garage, so it's conveniently out of the way.

- Master Suite: This master suite with tray ceilings features nearly "limitless" closet space, a private bath, and large hall linen closet.

- Bedrooms: The two secondary bedrooms, also with roomy closets, share a full bath. Bedroom 3 easily becomes a home office with direct foyer access and a window overlooking the porch.

Images provided by designer/architect.

Copyright by designer/architect.

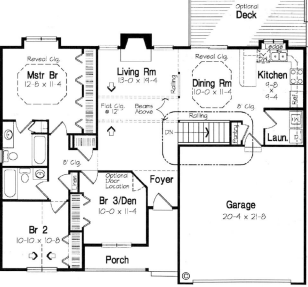

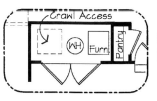

Crawl Space Option

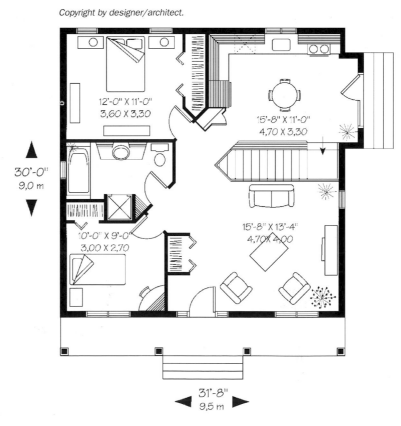

Plan #181216

Dimensions: 31'8" W x 30' D

Levels: 1

Square Footage: 910

Bedrooms: 2

Bathrooms: 1

Foundation: Basement

Materials List Available: Yes

Price Category: A

Images provided by designer/architect.

Copyright by designer/architect.

A lot of creativity goes into creating this comfortable home. It begins with a Creole-style covered front porch that lines up across the entire front of the house, beckoning folks to laze awhile in the cool summer shade.

Features:

- **Front Door:** This entry door has something special—transom and sidelight windows to brighten the interior with natural light.

- **Family Room:** This large and open room eases to other important rooms—including the great-sized kitchen.

- **Kitchen:** This large eat-in kitchen has hearty cabinet and counter space.

- **Bedrooms:** A roomy full bathroom pampers two full-sized bedrooms, which are enhanced by unusual windows and excellent closet space.

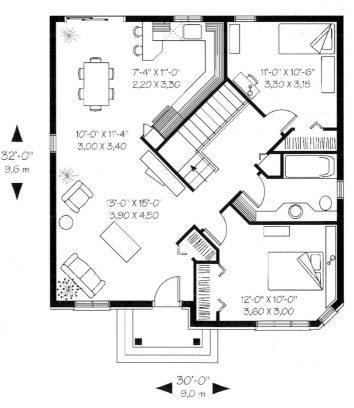

Plan #181215

Dimensions: 30' W x 32' D

Levels: 1

Square Footage: 929

Bedrooms: 2

Bathrooms: 1

Foundation: Basement

Materials List Available: Yes

Price Category: A

Whether just starting out or wrapping it up for the Golden Years, this generous one-level is perfect for two-plus. A peaked roofline, Palladian window, and covered front porch are a visual delight.

Features:

- Entry: An open interior branches out from the entry hall to the family room, where a cathedral ceiling soars to 10'-6¾".

- Dining Room: This room, which adjoins the family room, also embraces openness.

- Kitchen: This cordial kitchen features a breakfast counter for two and sprawling space for food preparation.

- Bedrooms: A full bathroom is nestled between two large bedrooms. Bedroom 1 enjoys a front and side view. Bedroom 2 has an intimate backyard vista.

7'-4" X 11'-0"
2,20 X 3,30

11'-0" X 10'-6"
3,30 X 3,15

10'-0" X 11'-4"
3,00 X 3,40

13'-0" X 15'-0"
3,90 X 4,50

12'-0" X 10'-0"
3,60 X 3,00

32'-0"
9,6 m

30'-0"
9,0 m

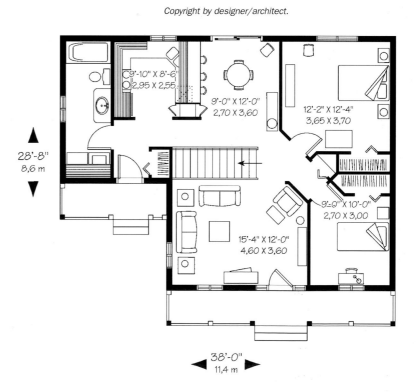

Plan #181218

Dimensions: 38' W x 28'8" D

Levels: 1

Square Footage: 946

Bedrooms: 2

Bathrooms: 1

Foundation: Basement

Materials List Available: No

Price Category: A

Images provided by designer/architect.

Copyright by designer/architect.

With a showcase front porch trimmed by quaint railings and carved brackets, this design uses all of its space beautifully and practically.

Features:

- **Living room:** This company-loving room waits just inside the entrance.

- **Kitchen:** This creative U-shaped kitchen has a bounty of counter and cabinet space as well as a breakfast counter that stretches into the dining area and doubles as a serving board.

- **Utility Areas:** The full bathroom is paired with the laundry area, and a side door near the kitchen leads to a smaller covered porch.

- **Bedrooms:** Two spacious bedrooms sit comfortably beside each other.

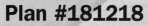

9'-10" X 8'-6"
2,95 X 2,55

9'-0" X 12'-0"
2,70 X 3,60

12'-2" X 12'-4"
3,65 X 3,70

9'-0" X 10'-0"
2,70 X 3,00

15'-4" X 12'-0"
4,60 X 3,60

28'-8"
8,6 m

38'-0"
11,4 m

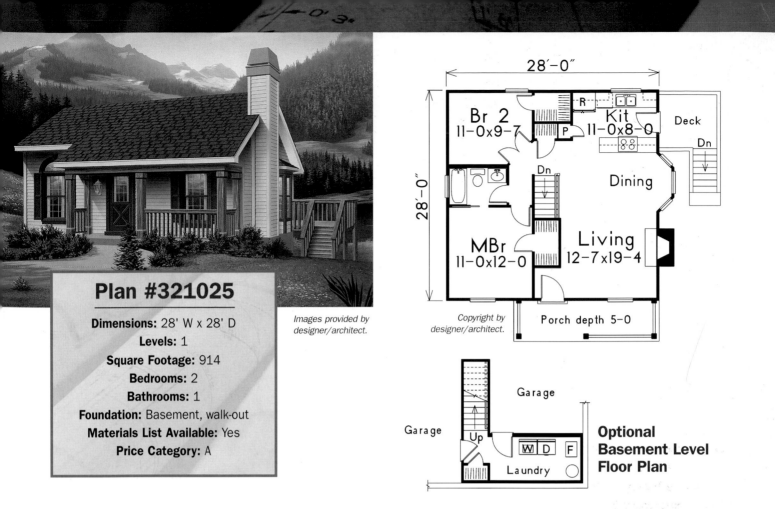

Plan #321025

Dimensions: 28' W x 28' D

Levels: 1

Square Footage: 914

Bedrooms: 2

Bathrooms: 1

Foundation: Basement, walk-out

Materials List Available: Yes

Price Category: A

Images provided by designer/architect.

Br 2 11-0x9-7

Kit 11-0x8-0

Deck

Dn

Dining

Living 12-7x19-4

MBr 11-0x12-0

Dn

R

P

28'-0"

28'-0"

Porch depth 5-0

Copyright by designer/architect.

Garage

Garage

Up

W D F

Laundry

Optional Basement Level Floor Plan

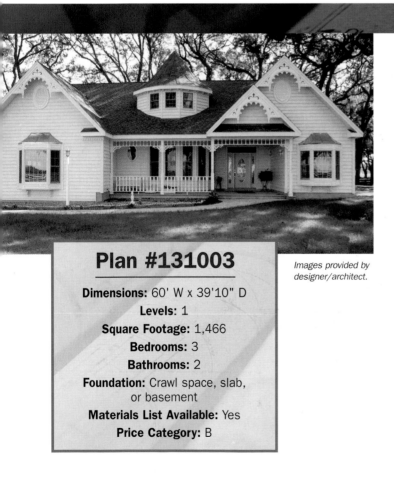

Plan #131003

Dimensions: 60' W x 39'10" D

Levels: 1

Square Footage: 1,466

Bedrooms: 3

Bathrooms: 2

Foundation: Crawl space, slab, or basement

Materials List Available: Yes

Price Category: B

Images provided by designer/architect.

Copyright by designer/architect.

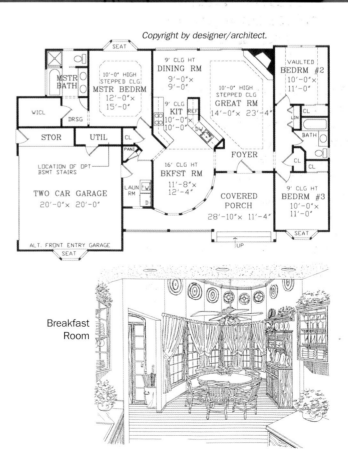

MSTR BATH

MSTR BEDRM 12'-0"x 15'-0"

10'-0" HIGH STEPPED CLG

WICL

DRSG

STOR

UTIL

CL

DINING RM 9'-0"x 9'-0"

9' CLG HT

9' CLG KIT 10'-0"x 10'-0"

GREAT RM 14'-0" x 23'-4"

10'-0" HIGH STEPPED CLG

VAULTED BEDRM #2 10'-0"x 11'-0"

CL

LIN

BATH

CL

PANI

LOCATION OF OPT BSMT STAIRS

TWO CAR GARAGE 20'-0"x 20'-0"

LAUN RM

16' CLG HT BKFST RM 11'-8"x 12'-4"

FOYER

COVERED PORCH 28'-10"x 11'-4"

9' CLG HT BEDRM #3 10'-0"x 11'-0"

SEAT

ALT. FRONT ENTRY GARAGE

SEAT

UP

Breakfast Room

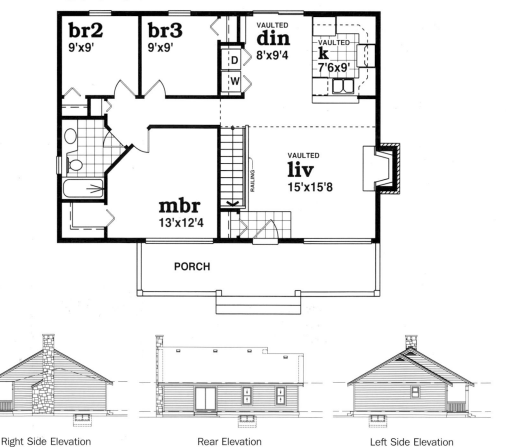

Plan #401043

Dimensions: 38' W x 32' D

Levels: 1

Square Footage: 988

Bedrooms: 3

Bathrooms: 1

Foundation: Basement

Materials List Available: Yes

Price Category: A

Images provided by designer/architect.

Copyright by designer/architect.

This economical, compact home is the ultimate in efficient use of space.

Features:

- **Porch:** The front entry is sheltered by this casual country porch, which also protects the living room windows.

- **Living Room:** This central living room features a cozy fireplace and outdoor access to the front porch.

- **Kitchen:** This U-shaped kitchen serves both a dining area and a breakfast bar. Sliding glass doors lead from here to the rear yard.

- **Master Bedroom:** This room has a walk-in closet and shares a full bathroom with the secondary bedrooms.

- A single or double garage may be built to the side or to the rear of the home.

br2 9'x9'

br3 9'x9'

VAULTED din 8'x9'4

VAULTED k 7'6"x9'

D

W

VAULTED liv 15'x15'8

RAILING

mbr 13'x12'4

PORCH

Right Side Elevation

Rear Elevation

Left Side Elevation

Plan #351014

Dimensions: 30' W x 38'4" D
Levels: 1
Square Footage: 1,000
Bedrooms: 2
Bathrooms: 2
Foundation: Crawl space or slab
Materials List Available: Yes
Price Category: B

This small home has many great features.

Features:

- Living Room: This gathering area boasts a fireplace with gas logs and plenty of built-ins.

- Kitchen: This large kitchen features a raised bar that's open to the living room and another raised bar that's open to the breakfast area.

- Bedrooms: These two bedrooms are much larger than you would expect for a home of this size.

- Bathrooms: The main bath, with access from bedroom 1, has a 42 x 60-in. jetted tub. The second bath is located off the hall near bedroom 2.

Images provided by designer/architect.

Copyright by designer/architect.

Plan #351016

Dimensions: 52' W x 38'4" D

Levels: 1

Square Footage: 1,002

Bedrooms: 2

Bathrooms: 2

Foundation: Crawl space or slab

Materials List Available: Yes

Price Category: B

Images provided by designer/architect.

This design includes many popular features, including a two-car garage.

Features:

- **Living Room:** This room welcomes you into the cozy home. It features a gas fireplace with built-in shelves on each side.

- **Kitchen:** This kitchen boasts two raised bars. One is open to the breakfast area and the other is open to the living room.

- **Bedrooms:** These two bedrooms have large closets, and bedroom 1 has direct access to the bathroom, which features a jetted tub.

- **Garage:** This two-car garage has a storage area, plus room for two nice-sized cars.

Copyright by designer/architect.

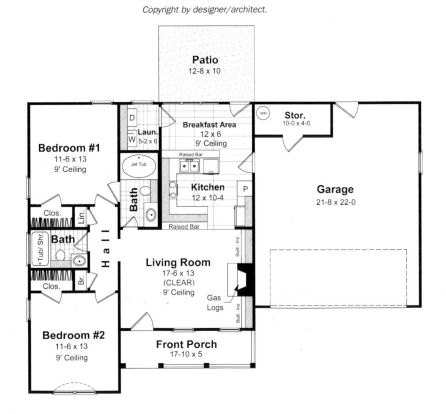

Plan #151218

Dimensions: 48' W x 30'6" D

Levels: 1

Square Footage: 1,008

Bedrooms: 2

Bathrooms: 2

Foundation: Crawl space or slab

Materials List Available: No

Price Category: B

Images provided by designer/architect.

This economical home may be just what you're looking for!

Features:

- Great Room: This gathering room has a vaulted ceiling.

- Kitchen: This kitchen boasts an abundant amount of cabinets, and counter space is open to the dining room.

- Master Suite: This retreat area features a large walk-in closet and a private bathroom.

- Bedroom: The second bedroom has its own door into the hall bathroom.

- Carport: This area has room for one car, plus there is a storage area.

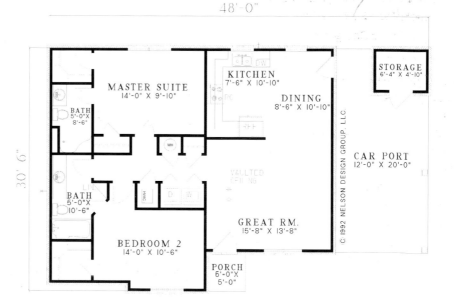

Copyright by designer/architect.

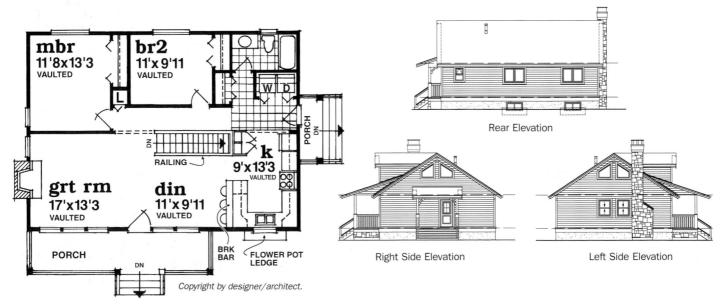

Plan #401047

Dimensions: 38' W x 34' D

Levels: 1

Square Footage: 1,064

Bedrooms: 2

Bathrooms: 1

Foundation: Basement

Materials List Available: Yes

Price Category: B

Images provided by designer/architect.

This farmhouse design squeezes space-efficient features into its compact design. Twin dormer windows flood the vaulted interior with natural light and accentuate the high ceilings.

Features:

- Porch: This cozy front porch opens into a vaulted great room and its adjoining dining room.

- Great Room: A warm hearth in this gathering place for the family adds to its coziness.

- Kitchen: This U-shaped kitchen has a breakfast bar open to the dining room and a sink overlooking a flower box. Nearby side-door access is found in the handy laundry room.

- Bedrooms: Vaulted bedrooms are positioned along the back of the plan. They contain wall closets and share a full bathroom with a soaking tub.

- Future Expansion: An open-rail staircase leads to the basement, which can be developed into living or sleeping space at a later time, if needed.

mbr
11'8x13'3
VAULTED

br2
11'x9'11
VAULTED

W D

PORCH
DN

grt rm
17'x13'3
VAULTED

DN
RAILING

k
9'x13'3
VAULTED

din
11'x9'11
VAULTED

PORCH

DN

BRK BAR

FLOWER POT LEDGE

Copyright by designer/architect.

Rear Elevation

Right Side Elevation

Left Side Elevation

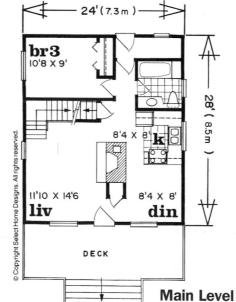

Plan #401005

Dimensions: 24' W x 36' D
Levels: 2
Square Footage: 1,073
Main Level Sq. Ft.: 672
Upper Level Sq. Ft.: 401
Bedrooms: 3
Bathrooms: 1½
Foundation: Basement
Materials List Available: Yes
Price Category: B

Scalloped fascia boards in the steep gable roof and the fieldstone chimney detail enhance this chalet.

Features:

- **Outdoor Living:** The front-facing deck and covered balcony are ideal outdoor living spaces.

- **Living Room:** The fireplace is the main focus in this living room, separating it from the dining room.

- **Bedrooms:** One bedroom is found on the first floor; two additional bedrooms and a full bath are upstairs.

- **Storage:** You'll find three large storage areas on the second floor.

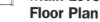

Main Level Floor Plan

br3 10'8 X 9'

8'4 X 8' k

liv 11'10 X 14'6

din 8'4 X 8'

DECK

24' (7.3 m)

28' (8.5 m)

Upper Level Floor Plan

STORAGE

br2 13'8 X 9'

STORAGE

STORAGE

mbr 13'8 X 10'

BALCONY

Rear Elevation

Left Side Elevation

www.ultimateplans.com

Plan #181235

Dimensions: 22' W x 26'4" D
Levels: 2
Square Footage: 1,077
Main Level Sq. Ft.: 550
Upper Level Sq. Ft.: 527
Bedrooms: 3
Bathrooms: 1
Foundation: Basement
Materials List Available: Yes
Price Category: B

Everything about this design is made for sharing, from the wraparound porch and balcony to the interior.

Features:

- **Main Level:** This level showcases the family room with fireplace and the generous eat-in island kitchen.

- **Second Level:** This level provides three spacious bedrooms, a perfect setup for a vacation home.

- **Master Bedroom:** This room enjoys lots of space, natural light. and a private balcony.

- **Bedrooms:** The two secondary bedrooms enjoy backyard views and just the right amount of closets.

Main Level Floor Plan

Upper Level Floor Plan

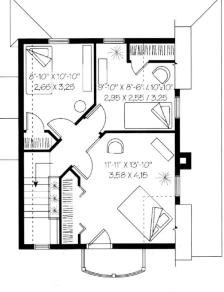

11'-8" X 11'-0"
3,50 X 3,30

26'-4"
7,9 m

15'-4" X 14'-0"
4,60 X 4,20

22'-0"
6,6 m

8'-10" X 10'-10"
2,65 X 3,25

9'-10" X 8'-6" / 10'-10"
2,95 X 2,55 / 3,25

11'-11" X 13'-10"
3,58 X 4,15

order direct: 1-800-523-6789

Plan #321040

Dimensions: 35' W x 40'8" D

Levels: 1

Square Footage: 1,084

Bedrooms: 2

Bathrooms: 2

Foundation: Basement

Materials List Available: Yes

Price Category: B

Images provided by designer/architect.

Copyright by designer/architect.

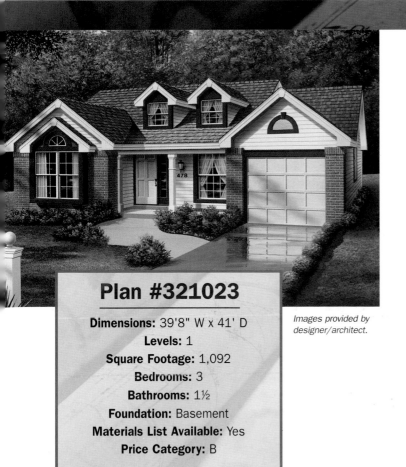

Plan #321023

Dimensions: 39'8" W x 41' D

Levels: 1

Square Footage: 1,092

Bedrooms: 3

Bathrooms: 1½

Foundation: Basement

Materials List Available: Yes

Price Category: B

Images provided by designer/architect.

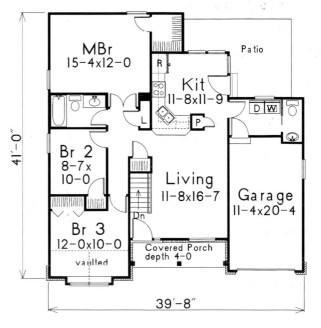

Copyright by designer/architect.

Plan #401041

Dimensions: 38' W x 31' D

Levels: 1

Square Footage: 1,108

Bedrooms: 3

Bathrooms: 2

Foundation: Basement

Materials List Available: Yes

Price Category: B

Craftsman styling and a welcoming porch create marvelous curb appeal for this design. A compact footprint allows economy in construction.

Features:

• **High Ceiling:** This volume ceiling in the living and dining rooms and the kitchen make the home live larger than its modest square footage suggests.

• **Kitchen:** This area features generous cabinet space and flows directly into the dining room to create a casual country feeling. (Note the optional buffet.)

• **Master Bedroom:** This room offers a walk-in closet, a full bath, and a bumped-out window overlooking the rear yard.

• **Expansion:** The lower level provides room for an additional bedroom, den, family room, and full bath.

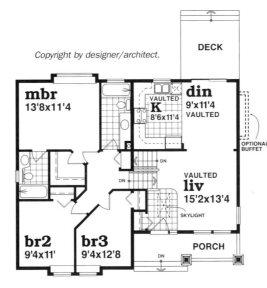

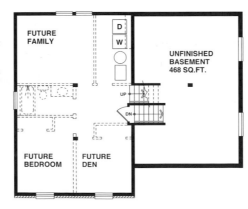

Optional Basement Level Floor Plan

front Elevation

Rear Elevation

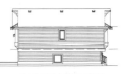
Left Side Elevation

Right Side Elevation

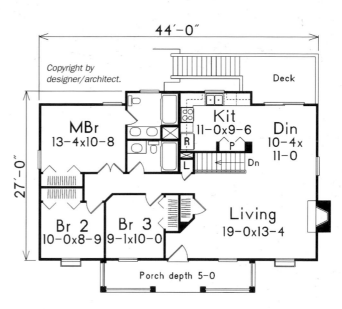

Plan #321022

Dimensions: 44' W x 27' D

Levels: 1

Square Footage: 1,140

Bedrooms: 3

Bathrooms: 2

Foundation: Basement

Materials List Available: Yes

Price Category: B

Images provided by designer/architect.

SMARTtip

Basement Moldings

Keep moldings simple in a basement with lower ceilings. Elaborate moldings around the ceiling or floor can shorten the height of the room.

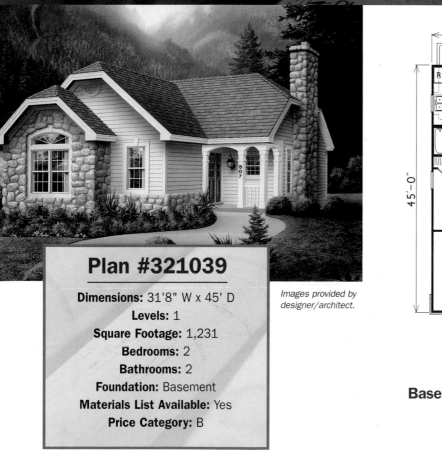

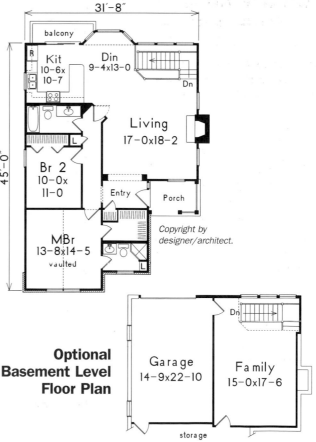

Plan #321039

Dimensions: 31'8" W x 45' D

Levels: 1

Square Footage: 1,231

Bedrooms: 2

Bathrooms: 2

Foundation: Basement

Materials List Available: Yes

Price Category: B

Images provided by designer/architect.

Optional Basement Level Floor Plan

Plan #371047

Dimensions: 58'6" W x 38' D

Levels: 1

Square Footage: 1,222

Bedrooms: 3

Bathrooms: 2

Foundation: Slab

Materials List Available: No

Price Category: B

Images provided by designer/architect.

Copyright by designer/architect.

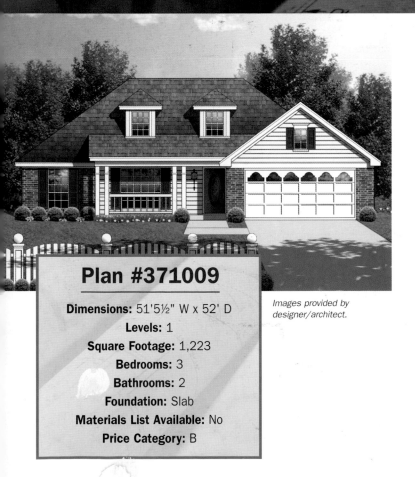

Plan #371009

Dimensions: 51'5½" W x 52' D

Levels: 1

Square Footage: 1,223

Bedrooms: 3

Bathrooms: 2

Foundation: Slab

Materials List Available: No

Price Category: B

Images provided by designer/architect.

Copyright by designer/architect.

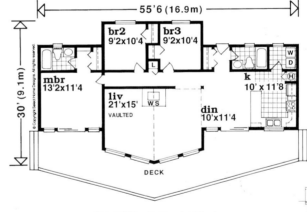

Plan #401020

Dimensions: 55'6" W x 30' D
Levels: 1
Square Footage: 1,230
Bedrooms: 3
Bathrooms: 2
Foundation: Basement
Materials List Available: Yes
Price Category: B

Images provided by designer/architect.

This is a grand vacation or retirement home, designed for views and the outdoor lifestyle. The full-width deck complements the abundant windows in the rooms that face it.

Features:

- Living Room: This area, with a vaulted ceiling, a fireplace, and full-height windows overlooking the deck, is made for gathering.

- Dining Room: This room is open to the living room; it has sliding glass doors that lead to the outdoors.

- Kitchen: This room has a pass-through counter to the dining room and is U-shaped in design.

- Bedrooms: Two family bedrooms in the middle of the plan share a full bath.

- Master Suite: This area has a private bath and deck views.

Copyright by designer/architect.

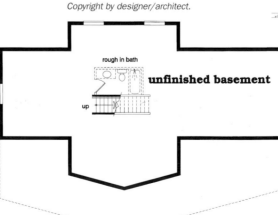

Optional Basement Level Floor Plan

Left Side Elevation

Rear Elevation

Right Side Elevation

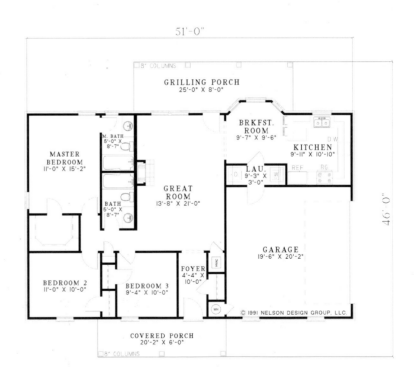

Plan #151213

Dimensions: 51' W x 46' D

Levels: 1

Square Footage: 1,231

Bedrooms: 3

Bathrooms: 2

Foundation: Crawl space or slab

Materials List Available: No

Price Category: B

Images provided by designer/architect.

This cute brick ranch home is a great place to live.

Features:

- Foyer: This area welcomes you home with a handy coat closet.

- Great Room: A cozy fireplace and entry to the grilling porch make this gathering area special.

- Kitchen: This fully equipped kitchen is open into the breakfast room with a bay window looking out to the backyard.

- Master Bedroom: This master bedroom has a large walk-in closet and a private bathroom.

- Garage: In addition to two cars, there is room for storage.

Copyright by designer/architect.

Plan #181227

Dimensions: 24' W x 29' D
Levels: 2
Square Footage: 1,248
Main Level Sq. Ft.: 624
Upper Level Sq. Ft.: 624
Bedrooms: 3
Bathrooms: 1½
Foundation: Basement
Materials List Available: Yes
Price Category: B

Images provided by designer/architect.

Architecturally rich, this striking design boasts ribbon and Palladian windows as well as a pavilion effect.

Features:

- **Open Layout:** A central staircase divides this otherwise fully open and contemporary layout.
- **Kitchen:** This large kitchen, with ample counter and cabinetry, keeps the laundry facilities and powder room close at hand.
- **Casual living:** An open living and dining room celebrates casual living and personal style.
- **Master Bedroom:** This bedroom, with its wall-length closet, overlooks the front porch through wide ribbon windows.
- **Bedrooms:** The two secondary bedrooms and a bright full bathroom are also nestled comfortably on the second level.

Main Level Floor Plan

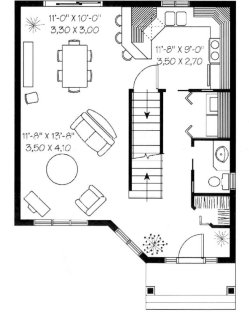

Upper Level Floor Plan

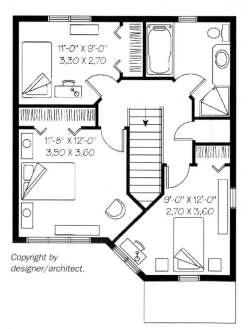

Copyright by designer/architect.

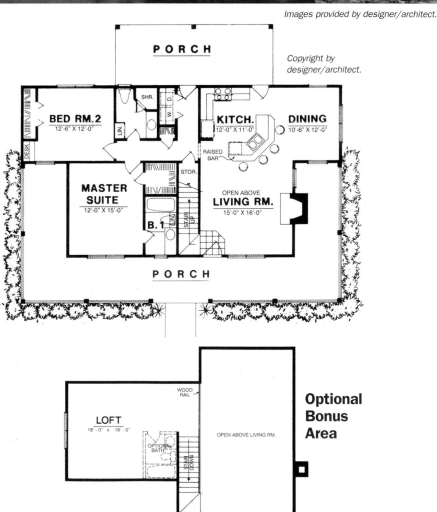

Plan #371005

Dimensions: 52'6" W x 45'8" D

Levels: 1½

Square Footage: 1,250

Bedrooms: 2

Bathrooms: 2

Foundation: Crawl space, slab, or basement

Materials List Available: No

Price Category: B

Images provided by designer/architect.

Copyright by designer/architect.

This quaint country home feels much larger because of the cathedral ceiling in the living room and an upstairs loft. This is the perfect vacation getaway or a home for a small family.

Features:

- Front Porch: This large front porch is perfect for relaxing and entertaining.

- Living Room: This room is an open area and is great for having guests over.

- Loft: This area overlooks the living room and has an optional bath.

- Master Suite: This area has a large walk-in closet and its own private bath.

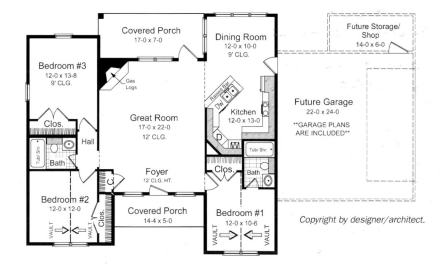

Plan #351018

Dimensions: 40'8" W x 38'6" D
Levels: 1
Square Footage: 1,251
Bedrooms: 3
Bathrooms: 2
Foundation: Crawl space or slab
Materials List Available: Yes
Price Category: B

Images provided by designer/architect.

This traditional home has great curb appeal and a great floor plan.

Features:

- Ceilings: All ceilings are a minimum of 9-ft. high.

- Great Room: This entertainment area, with a 12-ft.-high ceiling, features a gas fireplace and has views of the front yard through round-top windows and doors.

- Kitchen: This kitchen fulfills all the needs of the active family, plus it has a raised bar.

- Dining Room: Being adjacent to the kitchen allows this room to be practical as well as beautiful by means of the numerous windows overlooking the porch and backyard.

- Bedrooms: Vaulted ceilings in two of the three bedrooms provide a feeling of spaciousness. One bedroom has its own bathroom.

Copyright by designer/architect.

Front View

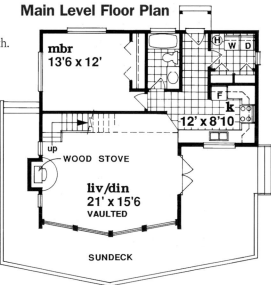

Plan #401019

Dimensions: 34' W x 32' D
Levels: 1½
Square Footage: 1,256
Main Level Sq. Ft.: 898
Upper Level Sq. Ft.: 358
Bedrooms: 3
Bathrooms: 1½
Foundation: Crawl space
Materials List Available: Yes
Price Category: B

A surrounding sun deck and expansive window wall capitalize on vacation-home views in this design. The full-height windows flood the living and dining rooms with abundant natural light and bring attention to the high vaulted ceilings.

Features:

- Living Room: A woodstove in this room warms cold winter nights.

- Kitchen: This efficient U-shaped kitchen has ample counter and cupboard space. Behind it is a laundry room and rear entrance.

- Master Bedroom: Located on the first floor, this main bedroom has a large wall closet.

- Bedrooms: Two family bedrooms are on the second floor and have use of a half-bath.

Images provided by designer/architect.

Main Level Floor Plan

mbr 13'6 x 12'

H W D

F

k

12' x 8'10

up

WOOD STOVE

liv/din 21' x 15'6 **VAULTED**

SUNDECK

Upper Level Floor Plan

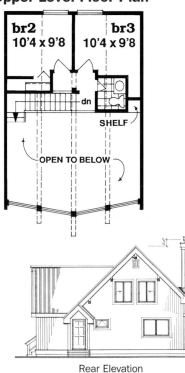

br2 10'4 x 9'8

br3 10'4 x 9'8

dn

SHELF

OPEN TO BELOW

Copyright by designer/architect.

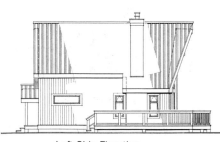

Left Side Elevation

Rear Elevation

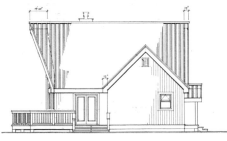

Right Side Elevation

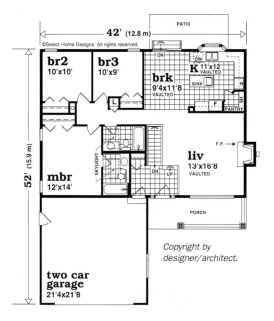

Plan #401031

Dimensions: 42' W x 52' D
Levels: 1
Square Footage: 1,260
Bedrooms: 3
Bathrooms: 2
Foundation: Basement
Materials List Available: Yes
Price Category: B

Images provided by designer/architect.

This economical-to-build bungalow works well as a small family home or a retirement cottage. The covered porch leads to a vaulted living room with a fireplace.

Features:

• Kitchen: This L-shaped space with a walk-in pantry and an island with a utility sink. An attached breakfast nook has sliding glass doors to a rear patio.

• Master Suite: The master bedroom has a private full bathroom with bright skylight.

• Bedrooms: There are three bedrooms, each with a roomy wall closet, that share a main bathroom with skylight.

• Garage: A two-car garage sits at the front of the plan to protect the bedrooms from street noise.

Copyright by designer/architect.

Rear Elevation

Right Side Elevation

Left Side Elevation

Plan #401007

Dimensions: 25' W x 36'6" D
Levels: 2
Square Footage: 1,286
Main Level Sq. Ft.: 725
Upper Level Sq. Ft.: 561
Bedrooms: 3
Bathrooms: 2
Foundation: Crawl space
Materials List Available: Yes
Price Category: B

Images provided by designer/architect.

This cozy chalet design begins with a railed veranda opening to a living room with a warm fireplace.

Features:

- **Dining Room:** This formal room also has a snack-bar counter that opens to the kitchen.

- **Master Bedroom:** Located on the second floor with a private balcony, this room has its own full bath.

- **Bedrooms:** One bedroom with a roomy wall closet is on the first floor. The second one is on the upper floor.

- **Storage:** Additional storage is found on the second floor.

Main Level Floor Plan

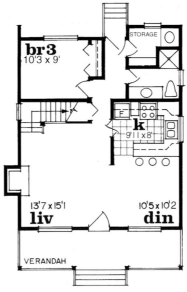

Upper Level Floor Plan

Copyright by designer/architect.

Rear Elevation

Right Side Elevation

Left Side Elevation

order direct: 1-800-523-6789

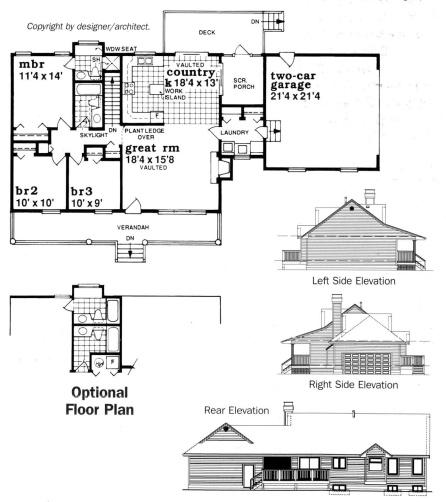

Plan #401024

Dimensions: 70' W x 36' D

Levels: 1

Square Footage: 1,298

Bedrooms: 3

Bathrooms: 2

Foundation: Basement

Materials List Available: Yes

Price Category: B

A front veranda, cedar lattice, and a solid-stone chimney enhance the appeal of this one-story country-style home.

Features:

- **Great Room:** The open plan begins with this great room, which includes a fireplace and a plant ledge over the wall separating the living space from the country kitchen.

- **Kitchen:** This U-shaped kitchen provides an island work counter and sliding glass doors to the rear deck and screened porch.

- **Master Suite:** This area has a wall closet and a private bath with window seat.

DECK

DN

WDW SEAT

mbr 11'4 x 14'

SH

VAULTED **country k** 18'4 x 13'

WORK ISLAND

SCR. PORCH

two-car garage 21'4 x 21'4

F

DN

LAUNDRY

SKYLIGHT

PLANT LEDGE OVER

great rm 18'4 x 15'8 VAULTED

br2 10' x 10'

br3 10' x 9'

VERANDAH

DN

Optional Floor Plan

F

Left Side Elevation

Right Side Elevation

Rear Elevation

Plan #131014

Dimensions: 48' W x 43'4" D
Levels: 1
Square Footage: 1,380
Bedrooms: 3
Bathrooms: 2
Foundation: Crawl space, slab, or basement
Materials List Available: Yes
Price Category: B

Images provided by designer/architect.

Living Room

The exterior of this home looks formal, thanks to its twin dormers, gables, and the bay windows that flank the columned porch, but the inside is contemporary in both design and features.

Features:

- Great Room: Centrally located, this great room has a 10-ft. ceiling. A fireplace, built-in cabinets, and windows that overlook the rear covered porch make it as practical as it is attractive.

- Dining Room: A bay window adds to the charm of this versatile room.

- Kitchen: This U-shaped room is designed to make cooking and cleaning jobs efficient.

- Master Suite: With a bay window, a walk-in closet, and a private bath with an oval tub, the master suite may be your favorite area.

- Additional Bedrooms: Located on the opposite side of the house from the master suite, these rooms share a full bath in the hall.

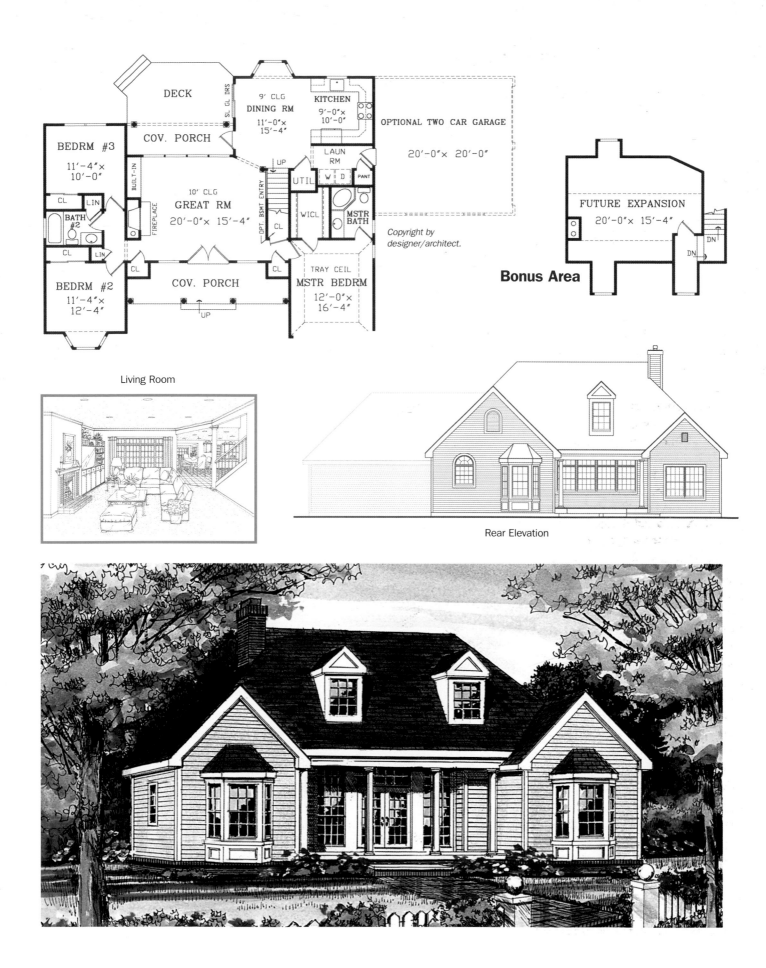

DECK

9' CLG
DINING RM
11'-0" x
15'-4"

KITCHEN
9'-0" x
10'-0"

SL GL DRS

COV. PORCH

OPTIONAL TWO CAR GARAGE
20'-0" x 20'-0"

BEDRM #3
11'-4" x
10'-0"

BUILT-IN

UP

LAUN
RM

CL

LIN

BATH
#2

FIREPLACE

10' CLG
GREAT RM
20'-0" x 15'-4"

DPT. BSMT ENTRY

UTIL

W D

PANT

CL

WICL

MSTR
BATH

CL

LIN

Copyright by
designer/architect.

BEDRM #2
11'-4" x
12'-4"

CL

COV. PORCH

CL

TRAY CEIL
MSTR BEDRM
12'-0" x
16'-4"

UP

FUTURE EXPANSION
20'-0" x 15'-4"

DN

DN

Bonus Area

Living Room

Rear Elevation

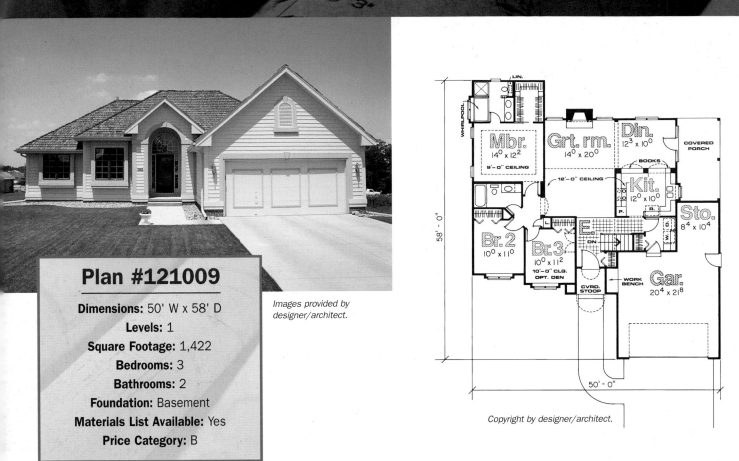

Plan #121009

Dimensions: 50' W x 58' D

Levels: 1

Square Footage: 1,422

Bedrooms: 3

Bathrooms: 2

Foundation: Basement

Materials List Available: Yes

Price Category: B

Images provided by designer/architect.

Copyright by designer/architect.

Plan #151010

Dimensions: 38'4" W x 68'6" D

Levels: 1

Square Footage: 1,379

Bedrooms: 3

Bathrooms: 2

Foundation: Crawl space, slab

Materials List Available: No

Price Category: B

Images provided by designer/architect.

Copyright by designer/architect.

Plan #391036

Dimensions: 28' W x 32' D
Levels: 2
Square Footage: 1,301
Main Level Sq. Ft.: 728
Upper Level Sq. Ft.: 573
Bedrooms: 3
Bathrooms: 2
Foundation: Basement
Materials List Available: Yes
Price Category: B

This home, as shown in the photograph, may differ from the actual blueprints. For more detailed information, please check the floor plans carefully.

Images provided by designer/architect.

This home is a vacation haven, with views from every room, whether it is situated on a lake or a mountaintop.

Features:

- Main Floor: A fireplace splits the living and dining rooms in this area.
- Kitchen: This kitchen flows into the dining room and is gracefully separated by a bar.

- Master Suite: A large walk-in closet, full bathroom, and deck make this private area special.
- Bedroom or Loft: The second floor has this bedroom or library loft, with clerestory windows, which opens above the living room.
- Lower Level: This lower floor has a large recreation room with a whirlpool tub, bar, laundry room, and garage.

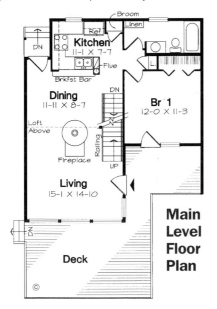

Main Level Floor Plan

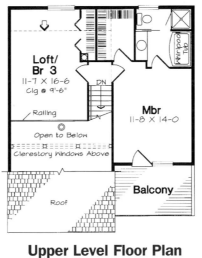

Upper Level Floor Plan

Copyright by designer/architect.

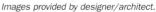

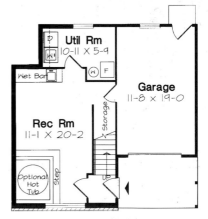

Lower Level Floor Plan

Plan #181219

Dimensions: 30' W x 26' D
Levels: 2
Square Footage: 1,311
Main Level Sq. Ft.: 791
Upper Level Sq. Ft.: 520
Bedrooms: 2
Bathrooms: 1½
Foundation: Basement
Materials List Available: Yes
Price Category: B

Images provided by designer/architect.

The double bay windows and arched entry with a fanlight window play up the classic cottage look and feel of this home.

Features:

- **Home Office:** Work-from-home professionals will appreciate this smart work space located near the front entrance.
- **Family Room:** This family room opens to the dining room and kitchen to share its hearty fireplace.
- **Kitchen:** This kitchen, with it built-in lunch counters, partners with the dining area for a wide-open look.
- **Laundry Room:** This large laundry room with exterior side entry is positioned beside the centralized kitchen for convenience.
- **Bedrooms:** Upstairs, two bedrooms with ample closets and one full bathroom provide plenty of personal space and comfort.

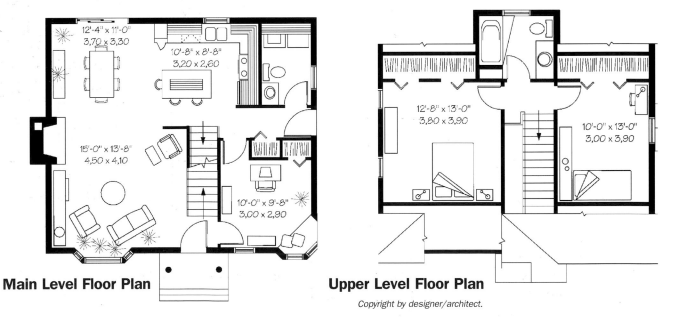

Main Level Floor Plan

12'-4" x 11'-0"
3,70 x 3,30

10'-8" x 8'-8"
3,20 x 2,60

15'-0" x 13'-8"
4,50 x 4,10

10'-0" x 9'-8"
3,00 x 2,90

Upper Level Floor Plan

12'-8" x 13'-0"
3,80 x 3,90

10'-0" x 13'-0"
3,00 x 3,90

Copyright by designer/architect.

Plan #131004

Dimensions: 59'4" W x 35'8" D

Levels: 1

Square Footage: 1,097

Bedrooms: 3

Bathrooms: 2

Foundation: Crawl space, slab, or basement

Materials List Available: Yes

Price Category: B

Images provided by designer/architect.

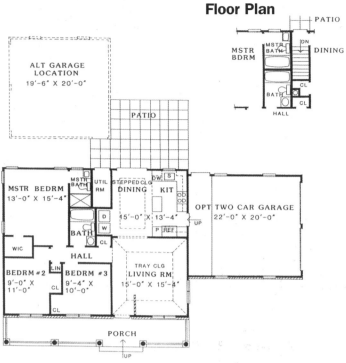

Alternate Basement Floor Plan

Plan #391006

Dimensions: 66' W x 69' D

Levels: 1

Square Footage: 1,456

Bedrooms: 3

Bathrooms: 2

Foundation: Basement

Materials List Available: Yes

Price Category: B

Images provided by designer/architect.

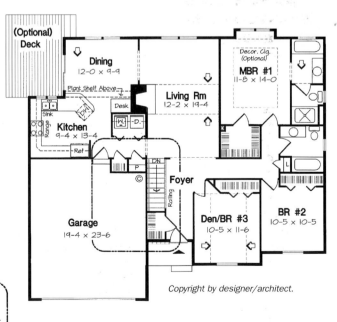

Copyright by designer/architect.

Crawl Space/Slab Option

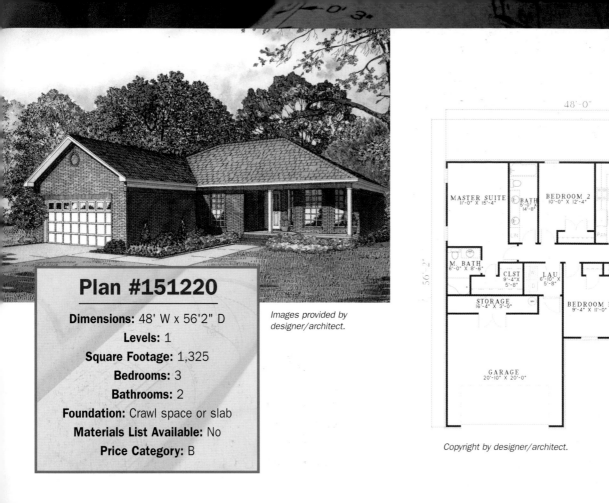

Plan #151220

Dimensions: 48' W x 56'2" D

Levels: 1

Square Footage: 1,325

Bedrooms: 3

Bathrooms: 2

Foundation: Crawl space or slab

Materials List Available: No

Price Category: B

Images provided by designer/architect.

Copyright by designer/architect.

Plan #181232

Dimensions: 33' W x 26' D

Levels: 2

Square Footage: 1,325

Main Level Sq. Ft.: 741

Upper Level Sq. Ft.: 584

Bedrooms: 3

Bathrooms: 2½

Foundation: Basement or walkout

Materials List Available: Yes

Price Category: B

Images provided by designer/architect.

Main Level Floor Plan

Upper Level Floor Plan

Copyright by designer/architect.

Lower Level Floor Plan

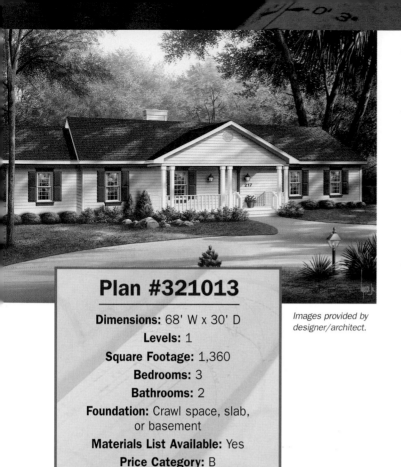

Images provided by designer/architect.

Plan #321013

Dimensions: 68' W x 30' D

Levels: 1

Square Footage: 1,360

Bedrooms: 3

Bathrooms: 2

Foundation: Crawl space, slab, or basement

Materials List Available: Yes

Price Category: B

SMARTtip

Glass Doors and Fire Safety

Professionals recommend keeping glass doors open while a fire is burning. When the doors are left completely open, the burning flame has a more realistic appearance and the glass doesn't become soiled by swirling ashes. When the doors are closed, heat from a large hot fire can break the glass.

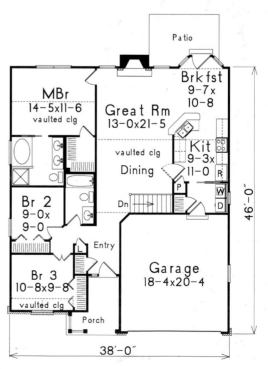

Plan #321033

Dimensions: 38' W x 46' D

Levels: 1

Square Footage: 1,268

Bedrooms: 3

Bathrooms: 2

Foundation: Basement

Materials List Available: Yes

Price Category: B

Images provided by designer/architect.

Plan #371006

Dimensions: 49'7" W x 48'6" D

Levels: 1

Square Footage: 1,374

Bedrooms: 3

Bathrooms: 2

Foundation: Crawl space, slab, or basement

Materials List Available: No

Price Category: B

Images provided by designer/architect.

This elegant brick-and-siding country home brings affordable living to a new level. The three bedrooms and two baths makes the most of the floor space.

Features:

- Master Suite: This large master suite has a large master bath with two walk-in closets.

- Dining Room: This formal room is located just off the entry.

- Living Room: This large but comfortable room has a cozy fireplace.

- Kitchen: This spacious kitchen with a breakfast nook has a view of the backyard.

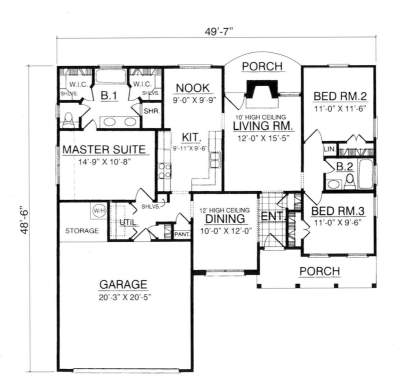

Copyright by designer/architect.

Plan #371028

Dimensions: 50'2" W x 47' D

Levels: 1

Square Footage: 1,376

Bedrooms: 3

Bathrooms: 2

Foundation: Slab

Materials List Available: No

Price Category: B

Images provided by designer/architect.

An efficient and affordable floor plan comes to life in this traditional brick home. This is the perfect home for anyone just starting out or for the "empty-nester."

Features:

- **Living Room:** This open room boasts a media center and cozy fireplace.

- **Dining Room:** The living room leads to this spacious room with a beautiful bay window that looks out into the backyard.

- **Kitchen:** This kitchen has a raised bar and a pantry.

- **Bedrooms:** The two other bedrooms share a convenient bath.

Copyright by designer/architect.

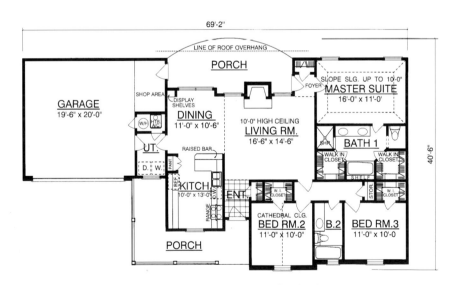

Plan #371029

Dimensions: 69'2" W x 40'6" D

Levels: 1

Square Footage: 1,394

Bedrooms: 3

Bathrooms: 2

Foundation: Crawl space

Materials List Available: No

Price Category: B

Images provided by designer/architect.

This charming country home brings affordability and luxury together.

Features:

- **Living Room:** This spacious room opens to the dining room for easy entertaining.

- **Dining Room:** This room has display shelves and a view of the backyard.

- **Kitchen:** This kitchen has a raised bar and a pantry.

- **Master Suite:** This large getaway boasts his and her walk-in closets, a soaking tub, and a shower.

- **Bedrooms:** The two other bedrooms have walk-in closets and share a convenient bathroom.

Copyright by designer/architect.

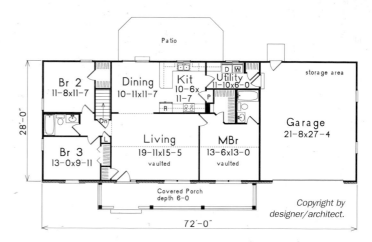

Patio

Br 2
11-8x11-7

Dining
10-11x11-7

Kit
10-6x
11-7

Utility
11-10x6-0

storage area

28'-0"

Living
19-11x15-5
vaulted

Br 3
13-0x9-11

MBr
13-6x13-0
vaulted

Garage
21-8x27-4

Covered Porch
depth 6-0

72'-0"

Copyright by designer/architect.

Plan #321002

Dimensions: 72' W x 28' D

Levels: 1

Square Footage: 1,400

Bedrooms: 3

Bathrooms: 2

Foundation: Crawl space, basement

Materials List Available: Yes

Price Category: B

Images provided by designer/architect.

SMARTtip

Fabric Draping Ability

Test a fabric's draping ability by looking at a large piece in a fabric store. Gather at least two to three yards of material, holding one end in your hand. Check how it drapes. Does it fall into folds easily? Also look at the pattern when it is gathered. Does the design become lost in the folds? Ask a salesclerk or a friend to hold the fabric, and look at it from a few feet away.

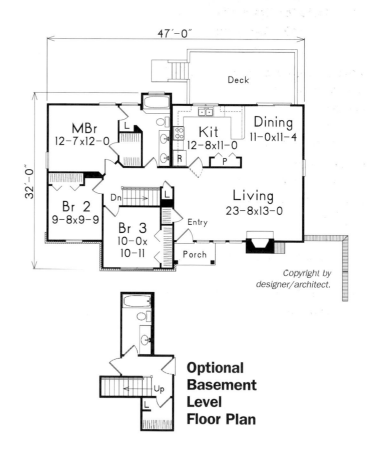

47'-0"

Deck

MBr
12-7x12-0

Kit
12-8x11-0

Dining
11-0x11-4

32'-0"

Br 2
9-8x9-9

Dn

Living
23-8x13-0

Br 3
10-0x
10-11

Entry

Porch

Copyright by designer/architect.

Optional Basement Level Floor Plan

Up

Plan #321024

Dimensions: 47' W x 32' D

Levels: 1

Square Footage: 1,403

Bedrooms: 3

Bathrooms: 1-2

Foundation: Daylight basement

Materials List Available: Yes

Price Category: B

Images provided by designer/architect.

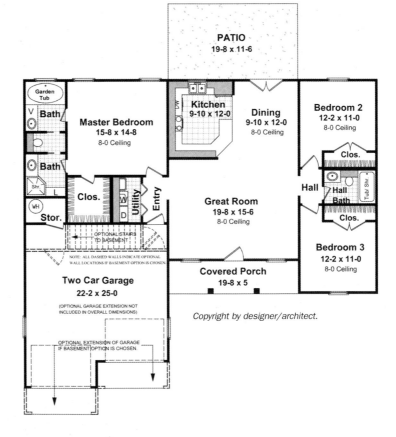

Plan #351009

Dimensions: 54' W x 47' D

Levels: 1

Square Footage: 1,400

Bedrooms: 3

Bathrooms: 2

Foundation: Crawl space, slab, or basement

Materials List Available: Yes

Price Category: B

Images provided by designer/architect.

This design offers a great value in space planning by using the open concept, with split bedrooms, in a layout that is easy to build.

Features:

- Ceilings: All ceilings are a minimum of 9-ft. high.

- Great Room: This large gathering area provides room for family activities as well as being open to the kitchen and dining area.

- Master Suite: This oversized private area provides a great bathroom arrangement for busy couples as well as a large walk-in closet.

- Bedrooms: The split bedroom layout provides zoned privacy and improved noise control.

- Patio: This area is the perfect place to enjoy the afternoons grilling out or relaxing with friends and family.

Copyright by designer/architect.

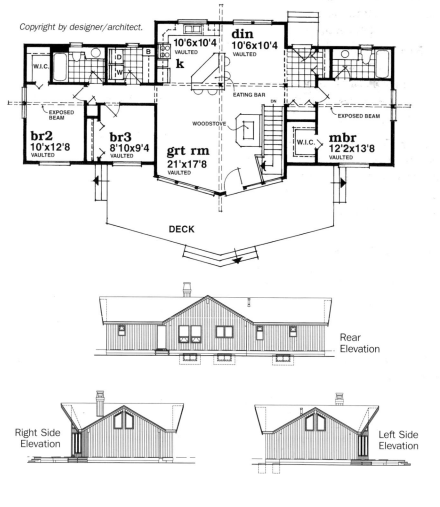

Plan #401033

Dimensions: 62' W x 29' D

Levels: 1

Square Footage: 1,405

Bedrooms: 3

Bathrooms: 2

Foundation: Basement

Materials List Available: Yes

Price Category: B

This three-bedroom leisure home is perfect for the family that spends casual time out of doors. An expansive wall of glass gives a spectacular view from the great room and accentuates the high vaulted ceilings throughout the design.

Features:

- **Great Room:** This room is warmed by a hearth and is open to the dining room and L-shaped kitchen.

- **Kitchen:** A triangular snack bar graces this kitchen and provides space for casual meals.

- **Bedrooms:** The bedrooms are split, with the master bedroom on the right side of the plan and family bedrooms on the left.

Images provided by designer/architect.

Copyright by designer/architect.

Rear Elevation

Right Side Elevation

Left Side Elevation

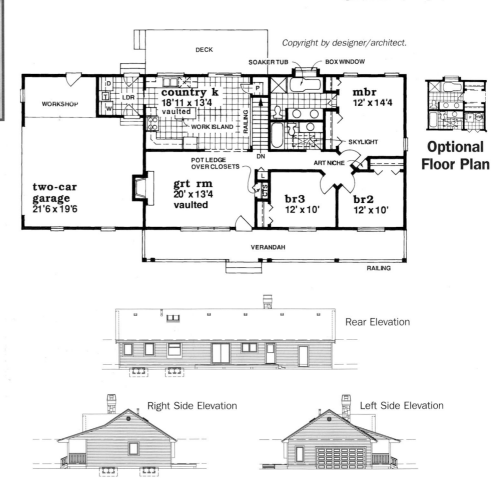

Plan #401025

Dimensions: 70' W x 34' D

Levels: 1

Square Footage: 1,408

Bedrooms: 3

Bathrooms: 2

Foundation: Basement

Materials List Available: Yes

Price Category: B

An eyebrow dormer and a large veranda give guests a warm country greeting outside, while inside vaulted ceilings lend a sense of spaciousness to this three-bedroom home.

Features:

- Front Entry: A broad veranda shelters this area.

- Kitchen: This bright country kitchen boasts an abundance of counter space and cup boards, a walk-in pantry, and an island workstation.

- Built-in Amenities: A number of built-ins adorn the interior, including a pot shelf over the entry coat closet, an art niche, and a skylight.

- Master Suite: A box-bay window and a spa-style tub highlight this retreat.

- Garage: The two-car garage provides a work shop area.

Images provided by designer/architect.

Copyright by designer/architect.

Optional Floor Plan

Rear Elevation

Right Side Elevation

Left Side Elevation

Plan #371048

Dimensions: 47' W x 47'6" D

Levels: 1

Square Footage: 1,415

Bedrooms: 3

Bathrooms: 2

Foundation: Slab

Materials List Available: No

Price Category: B

Images provided by designer/architect.

Simple elegance defines this traditional brick home.

Features:

- Living Room: With its sloped ceiling and cozy fireplace, this space is great for entertaining.

- Kitchen: This functional kitchen has a raised bar and is open to the dining area.

- Master Suite: This large retreat has a sloped ceiling and luxurious bathroom with a marble tub and two walk-in closets.

- Bedrooms: The two additional bedrooms share a convenient hall bathroom.

Copyright by designer/architect.

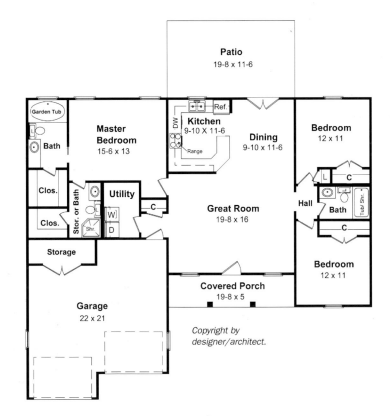

Plan #351019

Dimensions: 54' W x 47' D

Levels: 1

Square Footage: 1,427

Bedrooms: 3

Bathrooms: 3

Foundation: Crawl space or slab (basement for fee)

Materials List Available: Yes

Price Category: B

Images provided by designer/architect.

This fine three-bedroom home, with its open floor plan, may be just what you have been looking for.

Features:

- Great Room: This large room is open to the dining room.

- Kitchen: This fully equipped kitchen has a peninsula counter and is open into the dining room.

- Master Suite: This private area, located on the other side of the home from the secondary bedrooms, features large walk-in closets and bath areas.

- Bedrooms: Two secondary bedrooms have large closets and share a hall bathroom.

Copyright by designer/architect.

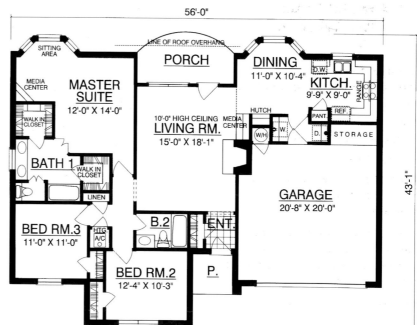

Plan #371010

Dimensions: 56' W x 43'1" D

Levels: 1

Square Footage: 1,429

Bedrooms: 3

Bathrooms: 2

Foundation: Slab

Materials List Available: No

Price Category: B

Images provided by designer/architect.

Copyright by designer/architect.

This warm American Traditional home has all the conveniences.

Features:

- **Living Room:** This large room has 10-ft.-high ceilings, a media center, and a fireplace.

- **Kitchen:** This kitchen boasts a built-in pantry and is open to the dining area, which has a built-in hutch.

- **Master Suite:** This suite boasts a media center, a sitting area, two walk-in closets, and a private bath.

- **Bedrooms:** These two additional bedrooms share a private bathroom.

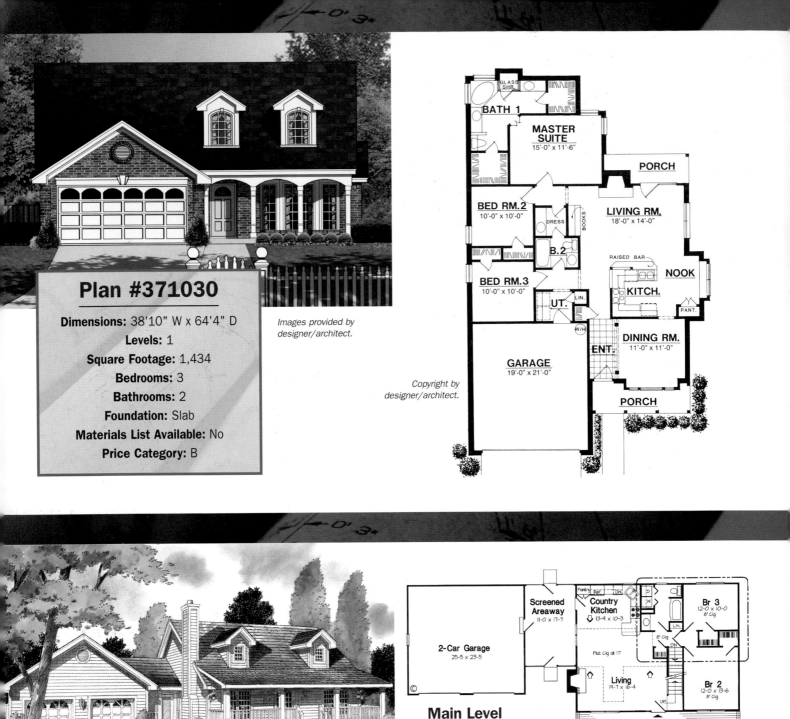

Plan #371030

Dimensions: 38'10" W x 64'4" D

Levels: 1

Square Footage: 1,434

Bedrooms: 3

Bathrooms: 2

Foundation: Slab

Materials List Available: No

Price Category: B

Images provided by designer/architect.

BATH 1

MASTER SUITE
15'-0" x 11'-6"

PORCH

BED RM.2
10'-0" x 10'-0"

DRESS

LIVING RM.
18'-0" x 14'-0"

B.2

BOOKS

BED RM.3
10'-0" x 10'-0"

UT.

LIN.

RAISED BAR

KITCH.

NOOK

PANT.

W/H

ENT.

DINING RM.
11'-0" x 11'-0"

GARAGE
19'-0" x 21'-0"

PORCH

Copyright by designer/architect.

Plan #391027

Dimensions: 73' W x 36' D

Levels: 2

Square Footage: 1,434

Main Level Sq. Ft.: 1,018

Upper Level Sq. Ft.: 416

Bedrooms: 3

Bathrooms: 2

Foundation: Crawl space, slab, or basement

Materials List Available: Yes

Price Category: B

Images provided by designer/architect.

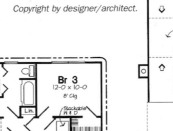

Main Level Floor Plan

2-Car Garage
25-5 x 23-5

Screened Areaway
11-0 x 17-7

Country Kitchen
13-4 x 10-3

Br 3
12-0 x 10-0
8' Clg

Living
14-7 x 16-4

Br 2
12-0 x 13-6
8' Clg

Flat Clg at 11'

Porch

Upper Level Floor Plan

Copyright by designer/architect.

Master Br
12-2 x 15-0
8' clg

Open To Below

Balcony

Flat Clg at 11'

Attic Access

roof below

Basement Level Floor Plan

Br 3
12-0 x 10-0
8' Clg

Stackable W & D

Crawl Space Access

Alternate Foundation Plan

Plan #181223

Dimensions: 27'8" W x 26' D
Levels: 2
Square Footage: 1,440
Main Level Sq. Ft.: 720
Upper Level Sq. Ft.: 720
Bedrooms: 3
Bathrooms: 2
Foundation: Basement
Materials List Available: Yes
Price Category: B

Images provided by designer/architect.

Main Level Floor Plan

Upper Level Floor Plan

Copyright by designer/architect.

Plan #371049

Dimensions: 52' W x 45' D
Levels: 1
Square Footage: 1,440
Bedrooms: 3
Bathrooms: 2
Foundation: Slab
Materials List Available: No
Price Category: B

Images provided by designer/architect.

Copyright by designer/architect.

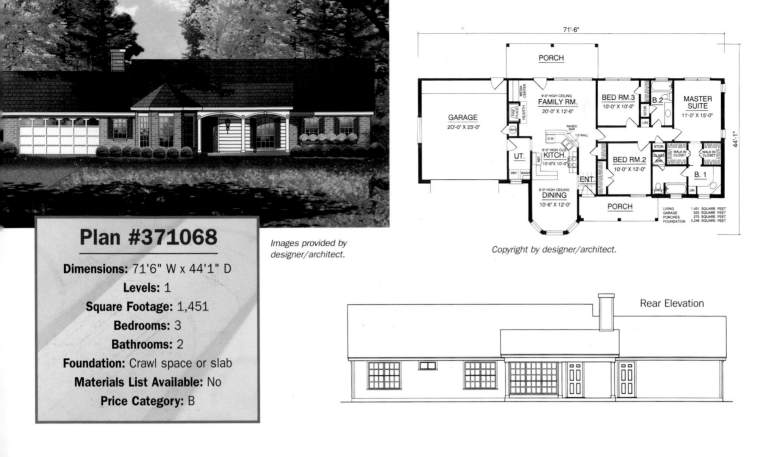

Images provided by
designer/architect.

Copyright by designer/architect.

Plan #371068

Dimensions: 71'6" W x 44'1" D

Levels: 1

Square Footage: 1,451

Bedrooms: 3

Bathrooms: 2

Foundation: Crawl space or slab

Materials List Available: No

Price Category: B

Rear Elevation

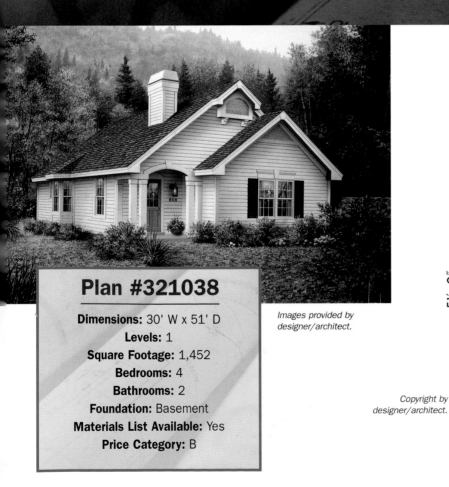

Plan #321038

Dimensions: 30' W x 51' D

Levels: 1

Square Footage: 1,452

Bedrooms: 4

Bathrooms: 2

Foundation: Basement

Materials List Available: Yes

Price Category: B

Images provided by
designer/architect.

Copyright by
designer/architect.

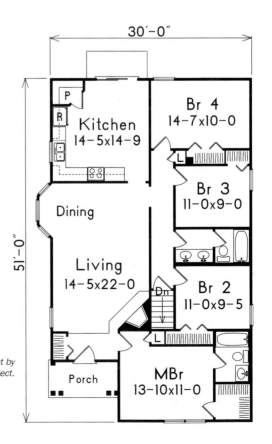

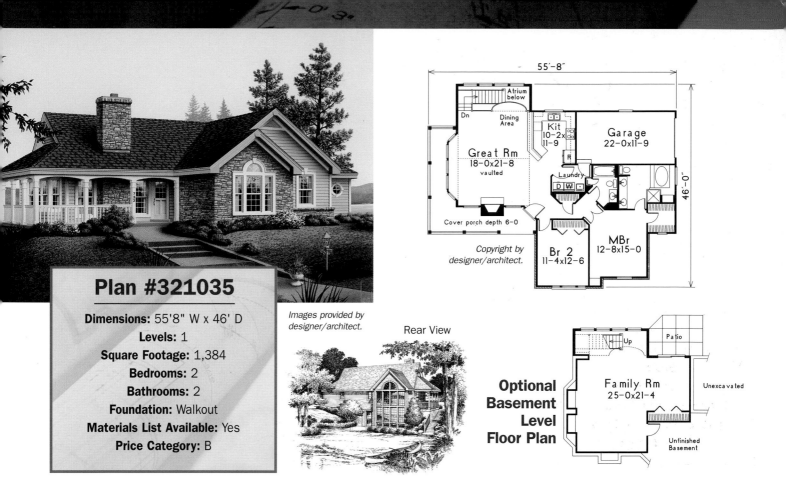

Plan #321035

Dimensions: 55'8" W x 46' D

Levels: 1

Square Footage: 1,384

Bedrooms: 2

Bathrooms: 2

Foundation: Walkout

Materials List Available: Yes

Price Category: B

Images provided by designer/architect.

Rear View

Optional Basement Level Floor Plan

Plan #151212

Dimensions: 47' W x 63'6" D

Levels: 1

Square Footage: 1,462

Bedrooms: 3

Bathrooms: 2

Foundation: Crawl space or slab

Materials List Available: No

Price Category: B

Images provided by designer/architect.

Copyright by designer/architect.

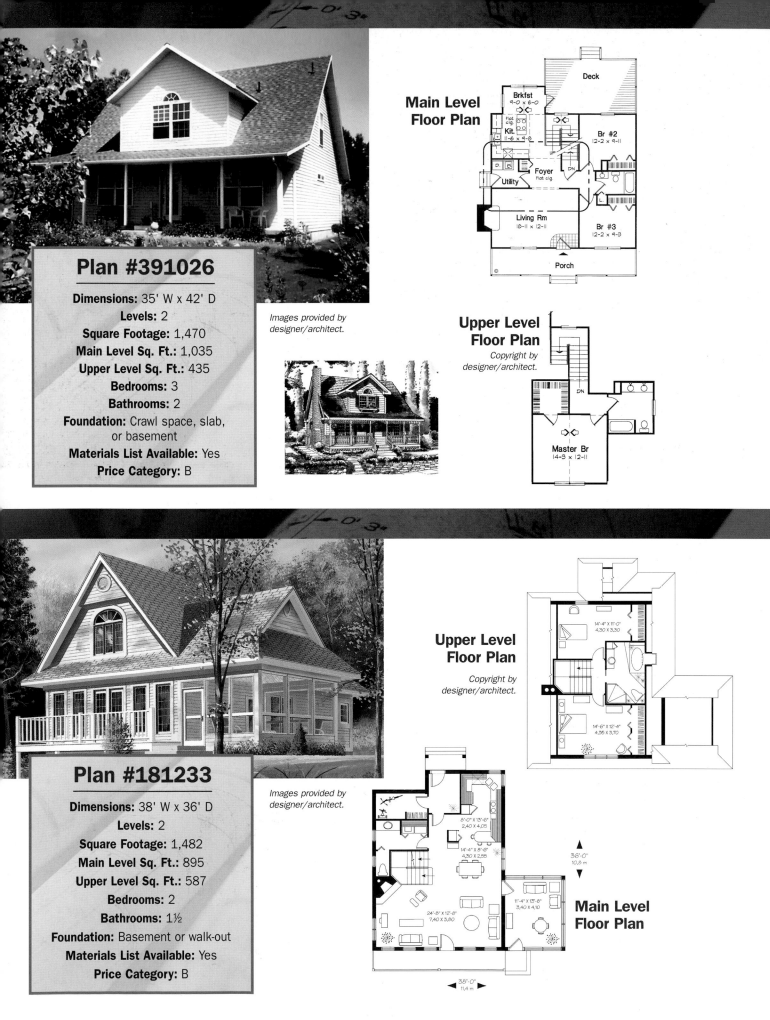

Main Level Floor Plan

Deck

Brkfst
9-0 × 6-0

Kit.
11-6 × 9-8

Br #2
12-2 × 9-11

UP

Foyer
flat clg.

DN

Utility

Living Rm
18-11 × 12-11

Br #3
12-2 × 9-3

Porch

Images provided by designer/architect.

Plan #391026

Dimensions: 35' W x 42' D

Levels: 2

Square Footage: 1,470

Main Level Sq. Ft.: 1,035

Upper Level Sq. Ft.: 435

Bedrooms: 3

Bathrooms: 2

Foundation: Crawl space, slab, or basement

Materials List Available: Yes

Price Category: B

Upper Level Floor Plan

Copyright by designer/architect.

DN

Master Br
14-3 × 12-11

Upper Level Floor Plan

Copyright by designer/architect.

14'-4" X 11'-0"
4,30 X 3,30

14'-6" X 12'-4"
4,35 X 3,70

Plan #181233

Dimensions: 38' W x 36' D

Levels: 2

Square Footage: 1,482

Main Level Sq. Ft.: 895

Upper Level Sq. Ft.: 587

Bedrooms: 2

Bathrooms: 1½

Foundation: Basement or walk-out

Materials List Available: Yes

Price Category: B

Images provided by designer/architect.

8'-0" X 13'-6"
2,40 X 4,05

14'-4" X 8'-6"
4,30 X 2,55

36'-0"
10,8 m

24'-8" X 12'-8"
7,40 X 3,80

11'-4" X 13'-8"
3,40 X 4,10

Main Level Floor Plan

36'-0"
11,4 m

Plan #371069

Dimensions: 33' W x 65' D
Levels: 1
Square Footage: 1,484
Bedrooms: 3
Bathrooms: 2
Foundation: Crawl space or slab
Materials List Available: No
Price Category: B

Cost-effective and charming, this traditional home has a brick-and-siding exterior.

Features:

- Living Room: This large entertainment area has a media center and a cozy fireplace.

- Kitchen: The walk-in pantry and raised bar help the functionality of this large kitchen, which opens into a beautiful dining room.

- Master Suite: This large, private oasis has an expansive and accommodating bathroom with a generously sized marble tub, glass shower, and spacious walk-in closet.

- Bedrooms: The two additional bedrooms have large closets and share a large hall bathroom.

Images provided by designer/architect.

Copyright by designer/architect.

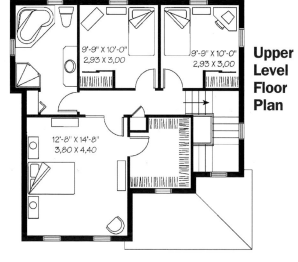

Plan #181226

Dimensions: 28' W x 29'8" D

Levels: 2

Square Footage: 1,485

Main Level Sq. Ft.: 735

Upper Level Sq. Ft.: 750

Bedrooms: 3

Bathrooms: 1½

Foundation: Basement

Materials List Available: Yes

Price Category: B

Images provided by designer/architect.

A gabled roofline and pillared front porch gracefully define the exterior of this great home.

Features:

- **Entry:** This formal entrance features a coat closet, curved staircase, and door to the heart of the home.

- **Living Room:** This room features its own door to offer the option of privacy.

- **Kitchen:** Open to the dining room for an airy and inviting atmosphere, this kitchen also features the functionality of an angled lunch counter.

- **Convenience:** The combination half-bath-and-laundry room is conveniently tucked away but close enough to the dining room for guests' sake.

- **Bedrooms:** The master bedroom and two secondary bedrooms enjoy a lavish bathroom with a shower and a corner tub.

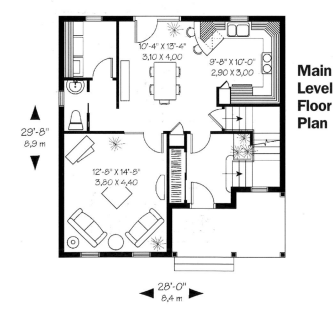

Main Level Floor Plan

10'-4" X 13'-4"
3,10 X 4,00

9'-8" X 10'-0"
2,90 X 3,00

12'-8" X 14'-8"
3,80 X 4,40

29'-8"
8,9 m

28'-0"
8,4 m

Upper Level Floor Plan

9'-9" X 10'-0"
2,93 X 3,00

9'-9" X 10'-0"
2,93 X 3,00

12'-8" X 14'-8"
3,80 X 4,40

Copyright by designer/architect.

Images provided by designer/architect.

Plan #391069

Dimensions: 56' W x 48' D
Levels: 1
Square Footage: 1,492
Bedrooms: 3
Bathrooms: 2
Foundation: Crawl space, slab, or basement
Materials List Available: Yes
Price Category: B

This design opens wide from the living room to the kitchen and dining room. All on one level, even the bedrooms are easy to reach.

Features:

- **Living Room:** This special room features a fireplace and entry to the deck.

- **Dining Room:** This formal room shows off special ceiling effects.

- **Bedrooms:** Bedroom 3 is inspired by a decorative ceiling, and bedroom 2 has double closet doors. There's a nearby bath for convenience.

- **Master Suite:** This private area features a roomy walk-in closet and private bath.

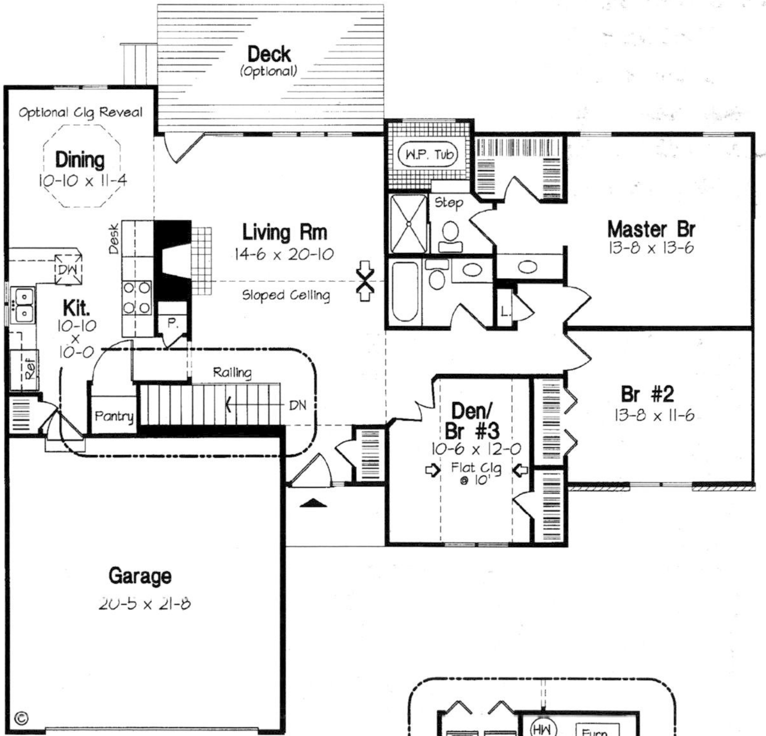

Copyright by designer/architect.

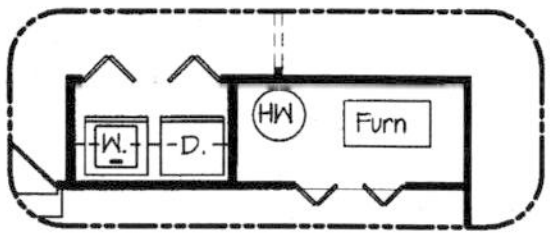

Optional Floor Plan

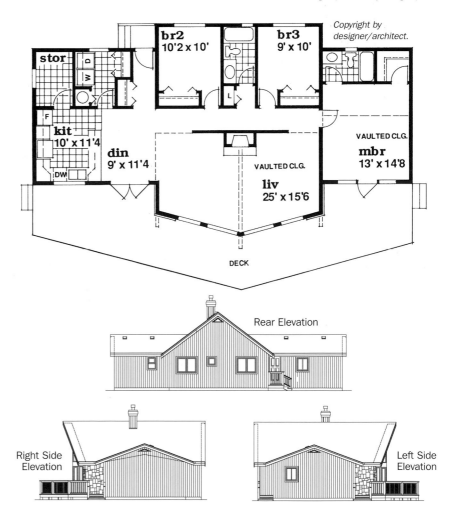

Plan #401022

Dimensions: 77'10" W x 55'8" D

Levels: 1

Square Footage: 1,495

Bedrooms: 3

Bathrooms: 2

Foundation: Basement

Materials List Available: Yes

Price Category: B

This three-bedroom cottage has just the right rustic mix of vertical wood siding and stone accents. Inside, the living is pure resort-style comfort.

Features:

• High Ceilings: Vaulted ceilings are featured throughout the living room and master bedroom.

• Living Room: This room has a fireplace and full-height windows overlooking the deck.

• Dining Room: This room features double-door access to the deck

• Master Bedroom: This principal sleeping area has a single door that opens to the deck.

• Bedrooms: Two family bedrooms share a bathroom that is situated between them.

Images provided by designer/architect.

Copyright by designer/architect.

Rear Elevation

Right Side Elevation

Left Side Elevation

Plan #351021

Dimensions: 61' W x 47'4" D

Levels: 1

Square Footage: 1,500

Bedrooms: 3

Bathrooms: 2

Foundation: Crawl space, slab, or basement

Materials List Available: Yes

Price Category: C

Images provided by designer/architect.

This lovely home provides a functional split-floor-plan layout with many of the features that your family desires.

Features:

- Great Room: This large gathering area, with a vaulted ceiling, has a gas log fireplace.

- Kitchen: This open kitchen layout has plenty of counter space for that growing family.

- Master Suite: This expansive master bedroom and bath has plenty of storage space in its separate walk-in closets.

- Garage: This two-car garage has a storage area.

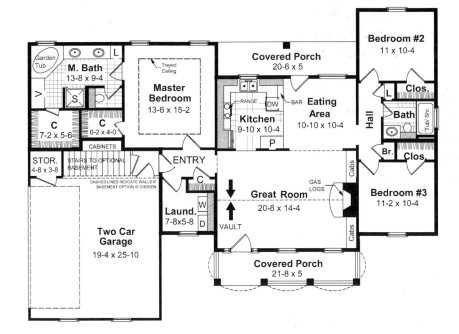

Copyright by designer/architect.

Family Kitchens

From every standpoint, the importance of the kitchen and its design cannot be underestimated. The heart of the home beats in the kitchen. There's the hum of the refrigerator, the whir of the food processor, the crunch of the waste-disposal unit, and the bubbling of dinner simmering on the stove. These are the reassuring sounds of a home in action. The kitchen is also a warehouse, a communications center, a place to socialize, and the hub of family life. According to industry studies, 90 percent of American families eat some or all of their meals in the kitchen. It is also the command center where household bills are paid and vacations are planned. The kitchen is even a playroom at times. Emotions, as well as tasks, reside here. When you were little, this is where you could find mom whenever you needed her. It's where the cookies were kept. When other rooms were cold and empty, the kitchen was a place of warmth and companionship. It is from the kitchen that the family sets off into the day. And it is to the kitchen that they return at nightfall.

The Great Room Concept

Today, the family life that was once contained by the kitchen is spilling into an adjoining great room. Usually a large, open room, great rooms and kitchens are often considered part of the same space. It is here where the family gathers to watch TV, share meals, and do homework. In short, great rooms/kitchens are the new heart of the home and the places where families do most of their living. In most designs, a kitchen and great room are separated by a snack counter, an island, or a large pass-through.

Kitchen Layouts That Work

The basic layout of your kitchen will depend on the home design you choose. Look for aisles that have at least 39 inches between the front of the cabinets and appliances or an opposite-facing island. If it's possible, a clearance of 42 inches is better. And given more available space, a clear-

Large kitchen/great rooms, below, are now considered the true heart of the family home.

In large kitchens, opposite, look for plenty of counter and storage space, but insist on compact, efficient work areas.

ance of 48 to 49 inches is ideal. It means that you can open the dishwasher to load or unload it, and someone will still be able to walk behind you without doing a side-to-side shuffle or a crab walk. It also means that two people can work together in the same area. Any more than 49 inches, and the space is too much and involves a lot of walking back and forth. Fifty-four inches, for example, is too big a stretch. In large kitchens, look for balance; the work areas should have generous proportions, but to be truly efficient they should be compact and well designed.

Food Prep Areas and Surfaces. In many families, much of the food preparation takes place between the sink and the refrigerator. When you think of the work triangle, think of how much and how often you use an appliance. For example, sinks are generally used the most, followed by the refrigerator. The use of the cooktop is a matter of personal habit. Some families use it everyday, others use it sporadically. How close does it really need to be in relation to

the sink and refrigerator? Make your primary work zone the link between the sink and the refrigerator; then make the cooktop a secondary zone that's linked to them.

Cabinets Set the Style

Cabinets are the real furniture of a kitchen, making their selection both an aesthetic and functional choice. They are also likely to account for the largest portion of the budget.

Laminate. There are different brands and grades of plastic laminate, but cabinets made from this material generally are the least expensive you can buy. For the most part, they are devoid of detail and frameless, so don't look for raised panels, moldings, or inlaid beads on plastic laminate cabinets.

Although the surface is somewhat vulnerable (depending on the quality) to scratches and chips, plastic laminate cabinets can be refaced relatively inexpensively. Laminates come in a formidable range of

colors and patterns. Some of the newer speckled and patterned designs, which now even include denim and canvas, not only look great but won't show minor scratches and scars.

Wood. Wood cabinets offer the greatest variety of type, style, and finish. Framed cabinets (the full frame across the face of the cabinets may show between the doors) are popular for achieving a traditional look, but they are slightly less roomy inside. That's because you lose the width of the frame, which can be as much as an inch on each side. Frameless cabinets have full overlay doors and drawer fronts. With frameless cabinets, you gain about 2 inches of interior space per cabinet unit. Multiply that by the number of cabinet doors or drawer units you have, and add it up. It's easy to see that if space is at a premium, choose the frameless or full-overlay type. Besides, most cabinet companies now offer enough frameless styles to give you a traditional look in cabinetry, if that's your style.

Be creative with storage, above. Here a tall cabinet tops a drawer unit that holds dish towels and tablecloths.

A great room, below, works best when a well-defined kitchen area flows effortlessly into the living area.

The Decorative Aspect of Cabinets

While the trend in overall kitchen style is toward more decorative moldings and carvings, the trend in cabinet doors is toward simpler designs. Plain panels, for instance, are now more popular than raised panels. They allow you to have more decoration elsewhere. Ornamentation is effective when it is used to provide a focal point over a hood, fridge, or sink. Instead of installing a single crown profile, you might create a three- or four-piece crown treatment, or add a carving of grapevines, acanthus leaves, or another decorative motif. In the traditional kitchen, add them, but sparingly.

Finishes. Of all of the choices you will need to make regarding wood cabinets, the selection of the finish may be the hardest. Wood can be stained, pickled, painted, or oiled. Your selection will be determined in part by whether you order stock or custom cabinets. Finishing options on stock cabinets are usually limited, and variations are offered as an upgrade. Translation: more money. Try working with the manufacturer's stock cabinets. It not only costs less but also speeds up the process. There is usually a reason why manufacturers offer certain woods in certain choices: it's because those choices work best with other elements in the room.

Wood Stains. Today, stains that are close to natural wood tones are popular, particularly natural wood finishes. Cherry is quickly becoming the number-one wood in the country. Pickled finishes, very popular in the early 1990s, are now looking dated. Some woods, particularly oak, have more grain than others. Some, such as maple, are smoother. And others, such as birch, dent more easily. The quality and inherent characteristics of the wood you choose will help determine whether it is better to stain, pickle, or paint. For staining, you need a good-quality clear wood. Pickling, because it has pigment in the stain, masks more of the grain but is still translucent. Because paint completely covers the grain, painted wood cabinets are usually made of lesser-quality paint-grade wood.

Painted Wood. Paint gives wood a smooth, clean finish. You can paint when you want a change or if the finish starts to show wear. This comes at no small expense, though, because the painter will have to sand the surfaces well before applying several coats of paint. If you choose painted cabinets, be sure to obtain a small can of the exact same paint from your kitchen vendor. There is usually a charge for this, but it allows you to do small touch-ups yourself, ridding your cabinets of particularly hideous scars without a complete repainting. While in theory the color choice for painted cabinets is infinite, manufacturers generally offer four shades of white and a few other standard color options from which to choose.

Pickled Wood. Pickled cabinets fall midway between full-grain natural cabinets and painted ones. Pickling is a combination of stain and paint, allowing some of the grain to show. It subdues the strongest patterns, while it covers over the lesser ones. The degree depends on your choice and on the options available from the manufacturer.

Hardware. Handles are easier to maneuver than knobs. Advocates of universal design, which takes into consideration the capabilities of all people—young and old, with and without physical limitations—recommend them. Knobs do not work easily for children or elderly people with arthritis. A handle with a backplate will keep fingerprints off the cabinet door.

Fitting Cabinets into Your Layout

This calls for attention to the kitchen layout. In specifying cabinets, first let common sense and budget be your guide. Kitchen geography can help you determine how much storage you need and where it should be. Mentally divide your kitchen into zones: food preparation, food consumption, and so on. And don't forget about the nonfood areas. Do you see yourself repotting plants or working on a hobby in the kitchen? You'll need work space and cabinet space for those extra activities.

A kitchen workhorse, the island, is not new to kitchen design. It's as old as the solid, slightly elevated, central table of medieval kitchens in England. But where that table was a work surface, today's island can hold cabinets, a sink, a cooktop, a beverage refrigerator, and it can serve to divide areas of the kitchen.

How Tall Is Too Tall?

Upper cabinets are typically 12 inches deep; base, or lower, cabinets are 24 inches deep. With the exception of a desk unit, standard base cabinets are always the same height, 36 inches. Although most people prefer clean lines and planes as much as possible, some circumstances call for variations in the height of lower cabinets. There may be an often-used area where you want a countertop at which you can work while seated, for example.

Upper cabinets come in two or three standard heights: 30, 36, and 42 inches. The 30-inch ones look short; 36-inch cabinets look standard, and 42-inch ones can look too tall if your ceiling is not unusually high. In general, there is a slight up-charge for 30-inch cabinets and a big jump in price for 42-inch units. Order another size and you will pay double-custom prices. But you don't need to. For greater variation, install upper cabinets at varying heights. The old standard was to install 30-inch upper cabinets under a soffit—the often,

but not always, boxed-in area just under the ceiling and above the wall cabinets. Now, unless you have very tall ceilings, soffits are practically obsolete. Provided you have standard-height, 8-foot ceilings, the way to go now seems to be 36-inch cabinets with the remaining space of 6 inches or so filled with decorative trim up to the ceiling. It is a nicer, more refined look than cabinets that extend all the way to the ceiling, unless you prefer something contemporary and totally sleek and without ornament.

Size and Space. You don't want a massive bank of cabinets, either. Add up the dimensions wherever you're considering wall units. The counter is 36 inches high; backsplashes typically range from 15 to 17 inches. So with 36-inch-high upper cabinets, we're talking 7½ feet in all, 8 feet if you chose 42-inch-high wall units. Your own size can help determine which ones to choose. Determine what's comfortable by measuring your reach. A petite person will lose access to the top third of a cabinet. An inch or two can make a very big difference.

Also, be sure that the small appliances you keep on the countertop fit under the wall cabinets. Having them sit at the front edge of a countertop is an accident waiting to happen. A lot of people who have "appliance garages" discovered this. Whenever they pulled out the appliance, which places it nearer the counter's edge, they watched their mixer or coffeemaker tumble to the floor.

Often people need extra storage, so they extend the cabinets up to the ceiling. This provides the added extra storage space, but it can only be reached by a step stool. An open soffit above the upper cabinets provides just as much space for oversize, infrequently used objects, and it is equally accessible by stepladder. Plus it can be both a display area and perfect home for hard-to-store items: pitchers, trays, salad bowls, vases, collectibles, platters, covered servers, and so forth.

Light, natural wood finishes, left, are a popular cabinet choice.

Just remember to allow plenty of room for air to circulate around the TV.

Kitchen Storage Solutions

There are many storage options that are extremely useful. At the top of the list is a spice drawer or rack attached to an upper cabinet or door. Both drawer and door spice racks are offered as factory options when you order cabinets, or you can retrofit them into existing cabinets. They provide visible access to all spices, so you don't end up with three tins of cinnamon, nine jars of garlic salt, four tiny bottles of vanilla, and no red pepper.

Lazy Susans. These rotating trays make items in the back of corner cabinets accessible. Consider adding inexpensive, plastic lazy Susans in a small upper cabinet. They will make the seasonings and cooking items you use everyday easily accessible.

Pie-cut door attachments can provide the same accessibility as a lazy Susan. Your choice depends on how much and what kind of storage you need. If a corner cabinet is home to sodas, chips, and cooking materials, install a pie-cut. A lazy Susan is more stable, best for pots, bowls, and larger, heavier objects.

The Kitchen Desk

Consider whether you will actually sit at a kitchen desk. Many people don't. Instead, they use it as the family message center and generally stand or perch on a stool. An additional, taller counter simply introduces more clutter to a room that is already overburdened with paraphernalia. And forget a desk-high cabinet, too. Instead use a standard counter-height cabinet to streamline whenever and wherever you can in the room.

Think about outfitting the desk area with a phone and answering machine and a corkboard for notes, your family's social schedule, invitations, and reminders. If you have room, a file drawer makes sense for storing school and business papers that

need to be easy to retrieve. Also, if you don't have a separate study, and there's room, the kitchen may be a place to keep the family computer. Not only will you likely be using it more in the future for household record-keeping, but you can also help the kids with their homework and monitor their Internet use. In those cases, it makes sense to add a desk for comfort.

A Niche for the TV. Many people also want a TV in the kitchen. Plan for it. Who wants to see the back of the set or look at cords stretching across work areas, atop the refrigerator or the stove? Space and an outlet can be built into the lower portion of a well-placed wall cabinet or an open unit.

Pullouts, Rollouts, and Dividers.

Pullout fittings maximize the use of very narrow spaces. There are just two options for these areas: vertical tray-storage units or pullout pantries. You can find a 12-inch-wide base cabinet that is a pullout pantry with storage for canned goods and boxed items.

Pullout racks for cabinets and lid-rack dividers for drawers are also available from some cabinet suppliers. They are handy, but if you have enough cabinet storage space, the best thing is to store pots and pans with the lids on them in a couple of large cabinets.

Rollout cabinets are great and offer a lot of flexibility. They are adjustable to accommodate bulky countertop appliances and

Pullout cutting boards, above left, increase usable counter space.

Accessories for tall, narrow cabinets, left, home in handy for storing cookie sheets and trays.

Decorative molding, above, can enhance any cabinet. Most manufacturers offer a variety of molding options.

stock pots, and they can save a lot of steps and banging around.

You can also divide a base cabinet vertically into separate parts. Some of the vertical spaces are further subdivided horizontally—good places for storing cutting boards, cookie trays, baking tins, and big glass baking dishes.

Other Organizers

Buy cutlery drawers carefully. They are often too big and too clumsy, and they fail to take advantage of the full interior of the drawer. They are as bad as bookshelves spread too far apart. Consider cutlery dividers that are almost no wider than a spoon, with separate sections for teaspoons, cereal spoons, breakfast and dinner knives, lunch forks, dinner forks, and serving pieces. Add to this a section for miscellaneous utensils such as spoons for iced tea, chopsticks, and so on. Drawer dividers should be adjustable in case your needs, or your cutlery, change.

Knife, Towel, and Bread Storage. If you want a place to store knives, use slotted storage on a countertop. Frequently islands have false backs because they are deeper than base cabinets. Slots for knives can be cut into the area of the countertop that covers the void behind the base cabinet.

You can obtain all these storage options at the time you buy your cabinets. But you don't have to and may not even want to until you see how you really end up using your kitchen. A carpenter or handyman can often make them or install off-the-shelf units. Think outside of the box. We get in a rut; it is hard to be objective. Ask friends where they keep their kitchen stuff, and analyze every aspect of how you use your kitchen. Store things at point of use, such as leftover containers and sandwich bags near the refrigerator; mixing bowls and carving knives near the sink.

Plan #321021

Dimensions: 80' W x 42' D

Levels: 1

Square Footage: 1,708

Bedrooms: 3

Bathrooms: 2

Foundation: Crawl space or slab

Materials List Available: Yes

Price Category: C

Images provided by designer/architect.

Copyright by designer/architect.

Plan #321057

Dimensions: 38' W x 39'4" D

Levels: 2

Square Footage: 1,524

Main Level Sq. Ft.: 951

Upper Level Sq. Ft.: 573

Bedrooms: 3

Bathrooms: 2½

Foundation: Basement

Materials List Available: Yes

Price Category: C

Images provided by designer/architect.

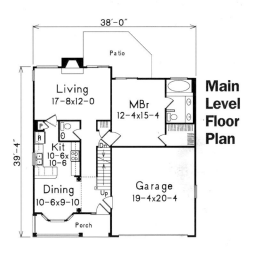

Main Level Floor Plan

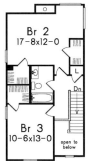

Upper Level Floor Plan

Copyright by designer/architect.

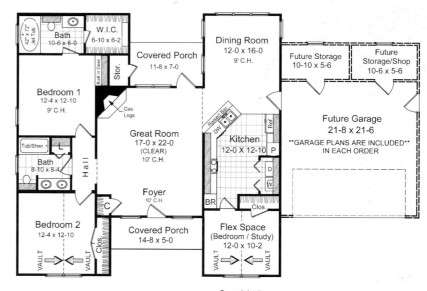

Plan #351022

Dimensions: 64'8" W x 42' D

Levels: 1

Square Footage: 1,503

Bedrooms: 2

Bathrooms: 2

Foundation: Crawl space or slab

Materials List Available: Yes

Price Category: C

Images provided by designer/architect.

This home features an unusual floor plan with both beauty and function.

Features:

- **Great Room:** This gathering area, with a raised ceiling, has a cozy corner gas fireplace and plenty of natural light.

- **Dining Room:** This large dining area is open to the kitchen and the great room.

- **Kitchen:** This kitchen, with an abundance of cabinets and counter space, has a raised bar that's open to the dining room.

- **Flex Space:** This area, just off the kitchen, can be a third bedroom or a study.

Copyright by designer/architect.

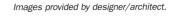

Plan #351030

Dimensions: 64'8" W x 42' D

Levels: 1

Square Footage: 1,503

Bedrooms: 3

Bathrooms: 2

Foundation: Crawl space or slab

Materials List Available: Yes

Price Category: C

Images provided by designer/architect.

This home can be built with or without the garage.

Features:

- Great Room: There is a raised ceiling in this room, which has a gas fireplace and plenty of natural light.

- Kitchen: This kitchen features the popular, sought-after island design and a raised bar that's open to the large dining area.

- Master Suite: This private area features a private bathroom with a walk-in closet.

- Bedrooms: Bedroom 2 has a large closet and access to the hall bathroom. "Flex space" can be used as bedroom 3.

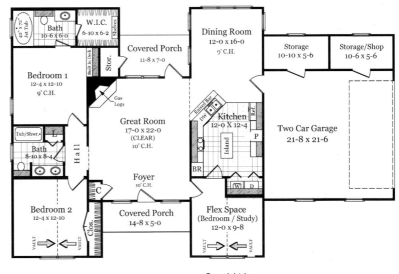

Copyright by designer/architect.

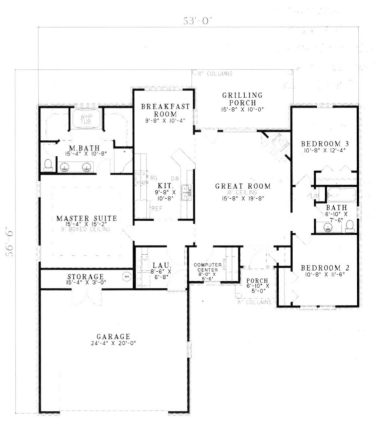

Plan #151215

Dimensions: 53' W x 56'6" D

Levels: 1

Square Footage: 1,519

Bedrooms: 3

Bathrooms: 2

Foundation: Crawl space or slab

Materials List Available: No

Price Category: C

Images provided by designer/architect.

This brick home, with a front-loading garage, is the perfect home for a young family.

Features:

- **Great Room:** This large entertainment area has a corner fireplace and entry to the grilling porch.

- **Kitchen:** Designed with a walk-through layout, this kitchen is open to the breakfast room.

- **Master Suite:** This private area, located on the opposite side of the home from the secondary bedrooms, features a master bathroom with large his and her walk-in closets.

- **Bedrooms:** The two secondary bedrooms share a common bathroom.

Copyright by designer/architect.

Plan #131005

Dimensions: 70' W x 37'4" D
Levels: 1
Square Footage: 1,595
Bedrooms: 3
Bathrooms: 2
Foundation: Crawl space, slab, or basement
Materials List Available: Yes
Price Category: C

With the finest features of an open design in the main living areas, this home gives privacy where you need it. Best of all, it's wheelchair accessible.

Features:

- Foyer: A high ceiling gives this area real presence and serves to blend it seamlessly with the great room and the dining room.

- Great Room: The open design allows you to use this room as an extension of the dining room or, if you wish, furnish it to create a private reading nook or visually separate media center.

- Breakfast Room: Both this room and the adjacent well-appointed kitchen flow into the rest of the living area. However, access to the rear porch, where you can sit out and enjoy the weather while you eat, distinguishes this room.

- Master Suite: Located in the same wing as the other bedrooms, this suite has a separate entrance and features a vaulted ceiling, three closets, and a compartmented bath.

SMARTtip

Create a Courtyard

Create a private walled-garden retreat with fences covered by climbing vines. Add height with trellises, and divide spaces with clipped boxwood hedges. Include an (almost) instant patio by digging away an area of sod and then covering it with a layer of sand and landscaping mesh to discourage weeds. Then cover it with pea gravel, and add a garden bench, statuary, and perhaps an antique or two. The result? European ambiance for even the most nondescript suburban yard.

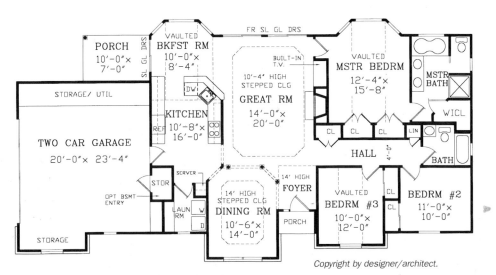

Copyright by designer/architect.

Foyer

Dining Room

Living Room

Great Room

SMARTtip

Natural Trellis

Create a natural rustic trellis that might even, if growing conditions are right, produce its own pretty blooms. Cut and place saplings in the ground as uprights. Then weave old grapevines with smaller saplings for the lattice.

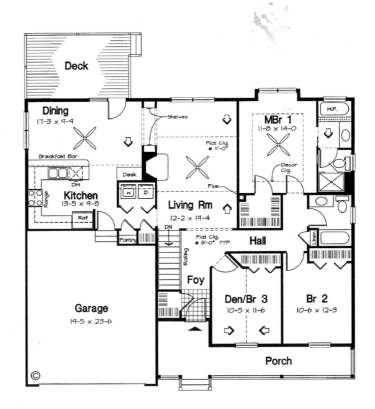

Plan #391039

Dimensions: 50' W x 45'4" D

Levels: 1

Square Footage: 1,539

Bedrooms: 3

Bathrooms: 2

Foundation: Crawl space, slab, or basement

Materials List Available: Yes

Price Category: C

Images provided by designer/architect.

A gabled roofline and easy-going front porch charm the exterior. Practical and pretty touches dramatize the interior.

Features:

- Foyer: This entry hall has a large walk-in closet.

- Kitchen: This kitchen's creative horizontal shape invites plenty of amenities. There is abundant cabinet space and a close-at-hand laundry facility.

- Dining Room: The kitchen's breakfast bar looks cheerfully into this formal room.

- Master Bedroom: A tray ceiling adds to the appeal of this room. The bump-out window seat invites breaks for daydreaming; a large walk-in closet handles wardrobes for two.

- Master Bath: This lavish master bathroom features a window over the tub.

- Bedrooms: The two additional bedrooms have their own unique styling, including excellent closet space and charming windows.

Copyright by designer/architect.

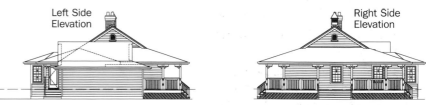

Plan #401008

Dimensions: 87' W x 44' D

Levels: 1

Square Footage: 1,541

Bedrooms: 3

Bathrooms: 2

Foundation: Basement

Materials List Available: Yes

Price Category: C

This popular design begins with a wraparound covered porch made even more charming by turned wood spindles.

Features:

- Great Room: The entry opens directly into this great room, which is warmed by a woodstove.

- Dining Room: This room offers access to a screened porch for outdoor after-dinner leisure.

- Kitchen: This country kitchen features a center island and a breakfast bay for casual meals.

- Bedrooms: Family bedrooms share a full bath that includes a soaking tub.

Images provided by designer/architect.

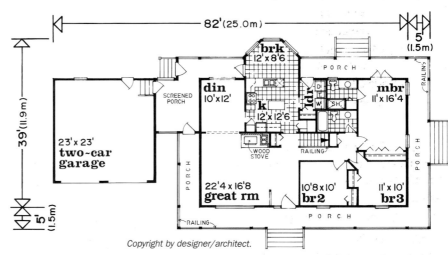

Copyright by designer/architect.

1541 sq. ft.

Rear Elevation

Left Side Elevation

Right Side Elevation

Plan #371050

Dimensions: 50' W x 49'6" D

Levels: 1

Square Footage: 1,542

Bedrooms: 3

Bathrooms: 2

Foundation: Slab

Materials List Available: No

Price Category: C

Images provided by designer/architect.

Simple elegance defines this traditional brick home, which with three bedrooms invites years of growth.

Features:

• Family Room: This large gathering room has a high ceiling and a cozy fireplace.

• Dining Room: The family room flows into this elegant dining area with a bay window.

• Kitchen: This gourmet kitchen with a raised bar looks into the family and dining rooms.

• Master Suite: This large suite has a step-up ceiling. The large master bath features two vanities, a soaking tub, a glass shower enclosure, and two walk-in closets.

• Bedrooms: The two large additional bedrooms share a convenient bathroom.

Copyright by designer/architect.

Images provided by designer/architect.

Plan #401021

Dimensions: 28' W x 39'9" D
Levels: 1½
Square Footage: 1,543
Main Level Sq. Ft.: 1,061
Upper Level Sq. Ft.: 482
Bedrooms: 3
Bathrooms: 2
Foundation: Crawl space
Materials List Available: Yes
Price Category: C

Features:

- Kitchen: This area has a vaulted ceiling, plus a food-preparation island and breakfast bar.
- Laundry Room: Behind the kitchen is this utility room with side-deck access.

- Master Suite: A skylighted staircase leads up to this area and has a walk-in closet and private bath.
- Bedrooms: You'll find two bedrooms and a full bath on the first floor.

A sun deck makes this design popular, and it is even more enhanced by views through an expansive glass wall in the living and dining rooms. These rooms are warmed by a woodstove and enjoy vaulted ceilings.

Main Level Floor Plan

br2 13'4 x 11'
br3 10' x 11'
W D
F VAULTED
up WOOD STOVE
liv 13'6 x 14'6 & 18'3 VAULTED
k 10'4 x 9'9
din 13'6 x 11'9 & 8' VAULTED
dn
SUNDECK

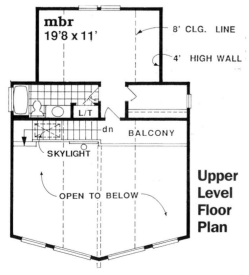

mbr 19'8 x 11'
8' CLG. LINE
4' HIGH WALL
L/T
dn BALCONY
SKYLIGHT
OPEN TO BELOW

Upper Level Floor Plan

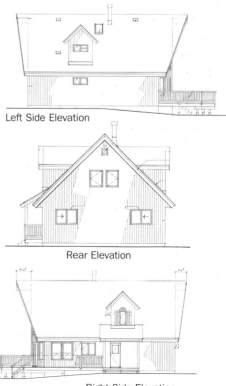

Left Side Elevation

Rear Elevation

Right Side Elevation

Copyright by designer/architect.

Plan #391021

Dimensions: 54' W x 48'4" D

Levels: 1

Square Footage: 1,568

Bedrooms: 3

Bathrooms: 2

Foundation: Crawl space, slab, or basement

Materials List Available: Yes

Price Category: C

Images provided by designer/architect.

A peaked porch roof and luminous Palladian window play up the exterior appeal of this ranch home, while other architectural components dramatize the interior.

Features:

- **Living Room:** There is a soaring ceiling in this living room, where a corner fireplace and built-in bookshelves provide cozy comfort.

- **Dining Room:** Open to the living room, this room features sliders to the wood deck, which makes it conducive to both casual and formal entertaining.

- **Kitchen:** This well-planned kitchen seems to have it all—a built-in pantry, a double sink, and a breakfast bar that feeds into the dining room. The bar provides additional serving space when needed.

- **Master Suite:** This private retreat is situated far from the public areas. A large walk-in closet with a private bath and double vanity add to the suite's intimate appeal.

- **Bedrooms:** The two additional bedrooms boast large closets and bright windows. The generous hall bathroom is located conveniently nearby.

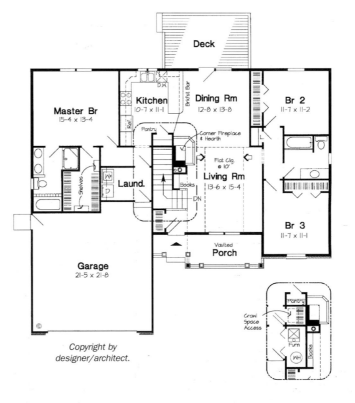

Copyright by designer/architect.

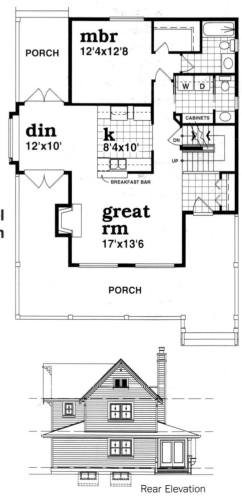

Plan #401044

Dimensions: 34' W x 48' D

Levels: 2

Square Footage: 1,568

Main Level Sq. Ft.: 1,012

Upper Level Sq. Ft.: 556

Bedrooms: 3

Bathrooms: 2½

Foundation: Basement

Materials List Available: Yes

Price Category: C

Images provided by designer/architect.

Features:

- Entry: This recessed front entry leads to the great room, flanked by a breakfast bar and formal dining room with access to both the front and rear porches.

- Great Room: This room is warmed by a fireplace and features a two-story ceiling.

- Master Suite: Located the first level, this sweet retreat has a private bath and walk-in closet.

- Bedrooms: Upstairs, two more bedrooms and a full bathroom complete the plan.

Country comes home to this plan with details such as a metal roof, horizontal siding, multi-pane double-hung windows, and front and rear porches.

Main Level Floor Plan

mbr 12'4x12'8
PORCH
din 12'x10'
k 8'4x10'
W D
CABINETS
DN
UP
BREAKFAST BAR
great rm 17'x13'6
PORCH

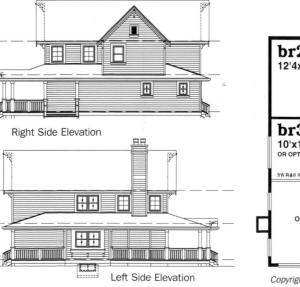

Right Side Elevation

Left Side Elevation

br2 12'4x12'8

br3 10'x10' OR OPTIONAL LOFT

3'6 RAILING

DN

OPEN TO BELOW

Upper Level Floor Plan

Copyright by designer/architect.

Rear Elevation

Plan #391005

Dimensions: 60' W x 40'4" D
Levels: 1
Square Footage: 1,575
Bedrooms: 3
Bathrooms: 2
Foundation: Crawl space, slab, or basement
Materials List Available: Yes
Price Category: C

This single-level layout clearly promises versatility. The floor plan opens easily to public spaces and trails off smoothly for individual privacy—just the way today's families want their living spaces.

Features:

• Curb Appeal: A covered front porch and front-facing garage enhance the home's pretty and practical nature.

• Family Room: Just off the entry hall is this spacious and hospitable gathering room with fireplace.

• Kitchen: This kitchen is adjacent to the living room and enjoys abundant counters and cabinetry. The breakfast area has access to the rear deck.

• Dining Room: This elegant room is open to the family room.

• Master Suite: This suite, at the rear of the house, enjoys a vaulted ceiling, expansive walk-in closet, and full bath with double sinks.

• Bedrooms: The two additional bedrooms share a common bathroom.

Rear Elevation

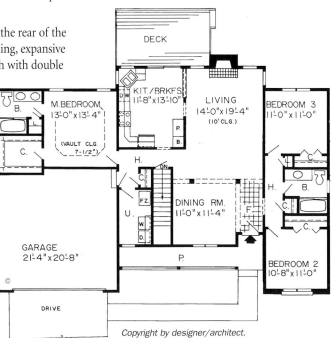

SMARTtip

Kitchen Cabinet Styles

You may not need to purchase expensive kitchen cabinetry to get fine-furniture quality details. Try adding crown molding to the top of basic cabinets and replacing the hardware with reproduction polished-brass door and drawer pulls to achieve a traditional look.

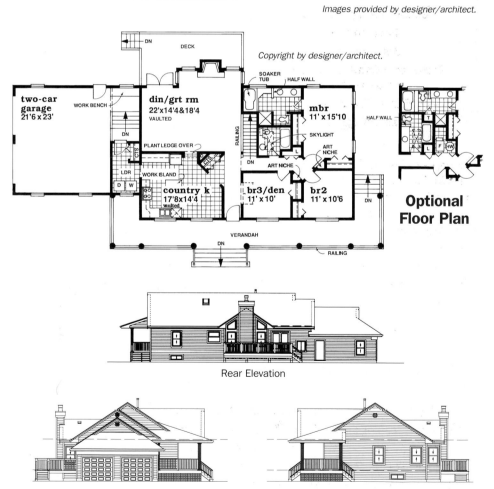

Plan #401026

Dimensions: 83' W x 40'6" D

Levels: 1

Square Footage: 1,578

Bedrooms: 3

Bathrooms: 2

Foundation: Basement

Materials List Available: Yes

Price Category: C

With a graceful pediment above and a sturdy, colonnaded veranda below, this quaint home was made for country living.

Features:

- Foyer: The veranda wraps slightly around on two sides of the facade and permits access to this central foyer with a den (or third bedroom) on the right and the country kitchen on the left.

- Kitchen: This functional kitchen features an island workspace and a plant ledge over the entry to the great room.

- Great Room: A fireplace warms this room and is flanked by windows overlooking the rear deck.

- Dining Area: This casually defined dining space has double-door access to the same deck as that off the great room.

Images provided by designer/architect.

Copyright by designer/architect.

Optional Floor Plan

Rear Elevation

Left Side Elevation

Right Side Elevation

Plan #401036

Dimensions: 42' W x 38' D
Levels: 2
Square Footage: 1,583
Main Level Sq. Ft.: 1,050
Upper Level Sq. Ft.: 533
Bedrooms: 3
Bathrooms: 2
Foundation: Basement
Materials List Available: Yes
Price Category: C

What a combination — a charming turn-of-the-century exterior with a contemporary interior! A wraparound railed porch and rear deck expand the living space to outdoor entertaining.

Features:

- **High Ceilings:** Vaulted ceilings throughout the great room and dining room add spaciousness, while a fireplace warms the area.

- **Master Suite:** Located on the first floor for privacy and convenience, this suite boasts a roomy walk-in closet and private bathroom with a whirlpool tub, separate shower, and dual vanities.

- **Bedrooms:** Two vaulted family bedrooms on the second floor share a full bathroom. Note the loft area and extra storage space.

Images provided by designer/architect.

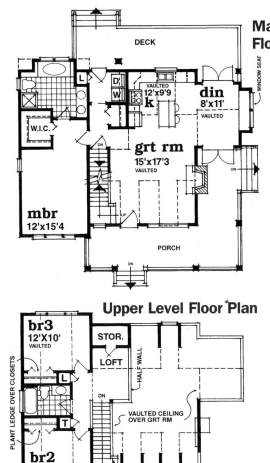

Main Level Floor Plan

DECK

din 8'x11' VAULTED

k VAULTED 12'x9'9

grt rm 15'x17'3 VAULTED

W.I.C.

mbr 12'x15'4

PORCH

Upper Level Floor Plan

br3 12'X10' VAULTED

STOR.

LOFT

HALF WALL

PLANT LEDGE OVER CLOSETS

VAULTED CEILING OVER GRT RM

br2 12'X10' VAULTED

Copyright by designer/architect.

Left Side Elevation

Rear Elevation

Right Side Elevation

Plan #181217

Dimensions: 38' W x 35' D
Levels: 2
Square Footage: 1,588
Main Level Sq. Ft.: 778
Upper Level Sq. Ft.: 810
Bedrooms: 3
Bathrooms: 1½
Foundation: Basement
Materials List Available: Yes
Price Category: C

Images provided by designer/architect.

Growing families will embrace all the charm and comfort of this Victorian-style three-bedroom home.

Features:

- **Style:** Timeless exterior styling begins with a covered front porch and beautiful windows, including a bright bay.

- **Entry:** Double windows in the closed front entrance infuse this space with cheerful natural light.

- **Kitchen:** A circular lunch counter rounds off this U-shaped kitchen, which has a nearby laundry and half bath.

- **Bathroom:** This upstairs full bath features a separate shower and tub for bathing in beauty and luxurious comfort.

Copyright by designer/architect.

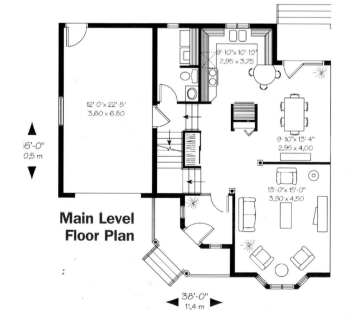

Main Level Floor Plan

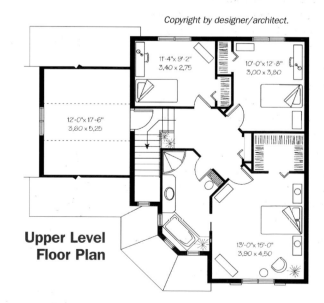

Upper Level Floor Plan

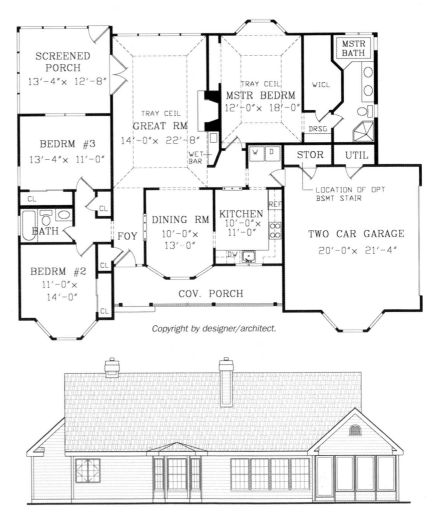

Plan #131007

Dimensions: 59'10" W x 47'8" D
Levels: 1
Square Footage: 1,595
Bedrooms: 3
Bathrooms: 2
Foundation: Crawl space, slab, basement, or walkout
Materials List Available: Yes
Price Category: D

Imagine living in this home, with its traditional country comfort and individual brand of charm.

Features:

- Exterior elements: The mixture of a front porch with a cameo front door, decorative posts, bay windows, and dormers will delight you.

- Great Room: A tray ceiling gives distinction to this large room, and a wet bar eases entertaining.

- Screened Porch: At dusk and dawn, this porch is sure to be your favorite outdoor spot.

- Kitchen: Eat any meal in this large kitchen for a touch of homey charm.

- Dining Room: Perfect for hosting a formal dinner, this bayed dining room can increase your enjoyment of simple family meals.

- Master Bedroom: For the sake of privacy, this room is somewhat secluded. Decorate to emphasize the elegant tray ceiling.

Images provided by designer/architect.

Copyright by designer/architect.

Rear Elevation

Alternate Front View

Foyer / Dining Room

Great Room

Add the Extras

Simple or plain, it's the little conveniences and miscellaneous touches that push the dining experience to perfection. Here are some extra things to think about.

- You can never have too many serving trays when you entertain outside. For carrying food or drinks from the kitchen or the grill, trays are indispensable.

- A serving cart on wheels makes a perfect movable outdoor bar and provides an additional serving surface. Look for one at yard sales or buy one new.

- Chances are you won't have a sideboard, but a few small tables to hold excess items are great substitutes for one. They're also easier to position in the different places where you need them.

- For cooler weather or even a summer's evening with a bit of nip in the air, nothing beats an outdoor fireplace for comfort. You could build one into the house, but various types of stand-alone units are sold in home centers. To add a Southwest ambiance, consider a chiminea, a clay fireplace. Try burning some piñon pine, and you'll feel as if you're in Santa Fe. Be sure to follow manufacturers' instructions when using these fireplaces. You might also have to store them during the winter.

- Pots of fragrant plants—lavender, scented geraniums, flowering tobacco, or jasmine—provide a sensual aroma. Flowers such as roses climbing up an arbor or trellis are beautiful, evoke a romantic feeling, and lend a delicate scent to the atmosphere as well.

Nothing adds romance and intrigue to an evening soiree as candlelight does. Include just a few candles for an intimate dinner. Use more for a larger gathering, placing one or more on each table. Scatter luminaries around the yard. As the beautiful evening dusk begins, light candles, a few at a time, so your eyes can adjust to the dimming light. Not only do the candles illuminate the night in a magical way but they can also keep bugs at bay.

Plan #181220

Dimensions: 38' W x 30'8" D

Levels: 2

Square Footage: 1,597

Main Level Sq. Ft.: 975

Upper Level Sq. Ft.: 622

Bedrooms: 3

Bathrooms: 1½

Foundation: Basement

Materials List Available: Yes

Price Category: C

Images provided by designer/architect.

Main Level Floor Plan

Upper Level Floor Plan

Copyright by designer/architect.

Plan #371031

Dimensions: 67'2½" W x 40'6" D

Levels: 1

Square Footage: 1,599

Bedrooms: 3

Bathrooms: 2

Foundation: Slab

Materials List Available: No

Price Category: C

Images provided by designer/architect.

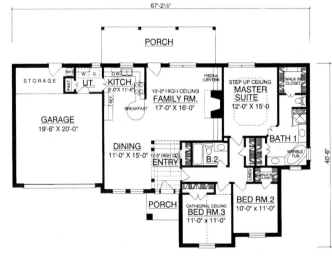

Copyright by designer/architect.

Plan #351023

Dimensions: 61'8" W x 45'8" D

Levels: 1

Square Footage: 1,600

Bedrooms: 3

Bathrooms: 2

Foundation: Crawl space, slab, or basement

Materials List Available: Yes

Price Category: C

Images provided by designer/architect.

This beautiful three-bedroom home has everything your family needs to live the comfortable life.

Features:

- Great Room: Just off the foyer is this large room. It features a cozy fireplace and access to the rear covered porch.

- Dining Room: This formal room has large windows with a view of the backyard.

- Kitchen: This kitchen has an abundance of cabinets and counter space. It is open to the dining room.

- Master Suite: This isolated suite, with its jetted tub, separate shower, large closet, and dual vanities, is a perfect retreat.

- Bedrooms: The two secondary bedrooms have large closets and share a hall bathroom.

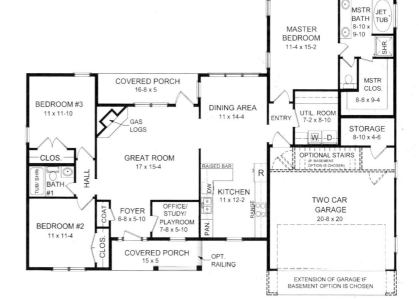

Copyright by designer/architect.

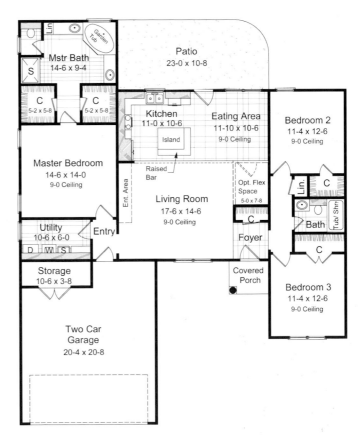

Plan #351029

Dimensions: 72'10" W x 41' D

Levels: 1

Square Footage: 1,606

Bedrooms: 3

Bathrooms: 2

Foundation: Crawl space, slab, or basement

Materials List Available: Yes

Price Category: C

Images provided by designer/architect.

This is a great family home with an excellent floor plan.

Features:

- Kitchen: This L-shaped island kitchen has a raised bar that's open to the eating area.

- Master Suite: This private area has all the amenities, like an oversized garden/jetted tub and large his and her closets.

- Flex Space: You can easily make this space into a home office, homework room, or closet for winter clothes storage.

- Bedrooms: The two secondary bedrooms have large closets.

- Garage: This large two-car garage has a storage area.

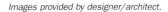

Copyright by designer/architect.

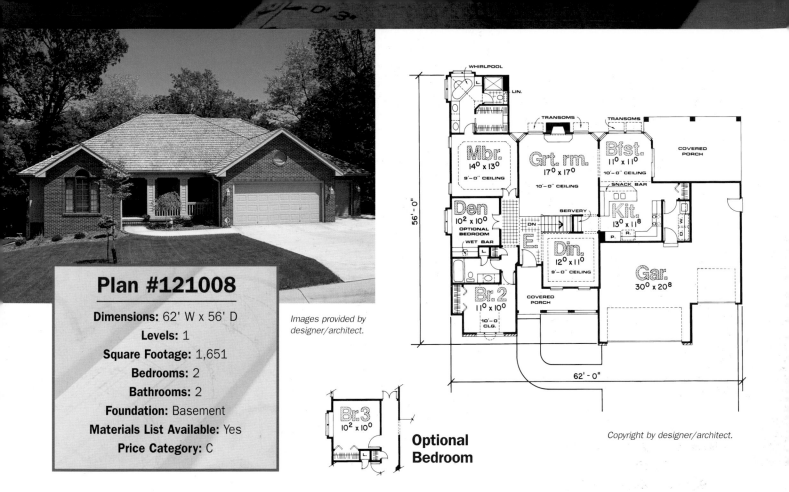

Plan #121008

Dimensions: 62' W x 56' D

Levels: 1

Square Footage: 1,651

Bedrooms: 2

Bathrooms: 2

Foundation: Basement

Materials List Available: Yes

Price Category: C

Images provided by designer/architect.

Optional Bedroom

Copyright by designer/architect.

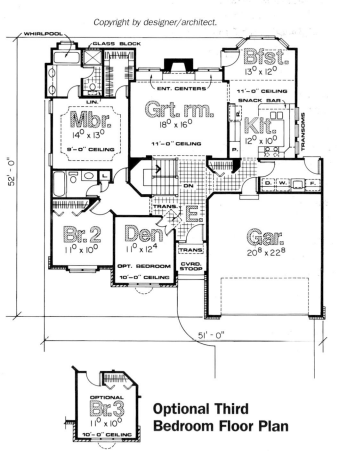

Plan #121055

Dimensions: 51' W x 52' D

Levels: 1

Square Footage: 1,622

Bedrooms: 3

Bathrooms: 2

Foundation: Basement

Materials List Available: Yes

Price Category: C

Images provided by designer/architect.

Copyright by designer/architect.

Optional Third Bedroom Floor Plan

Plan #391025

Dimensions: 54' W x 48'4" D

Levels: 1

Square Footage: 1,625

Bedrooms: 3

Bathrooms: 2

Foundation: Crawl space, slab, or basement

Materials List Available: Yes

Price Category: C

Images provided by designer/architect.

This lovely home, ideal for starters or empty nesters, conveys rustic charm while maintaining clean contemporary lines.

Features:

- Kitchen: This functional U-shaped kitchen features an adjacent utility area that can serve as a pantry and direct access to the garage for unloading groceries after a shopping trip.

- Fireplace: This cozy two-sided fireplace joins the living room and dining room, which is open to the adjacent kitchen.

- Den: The roomy den (or guest bedroom) features a beautiful Palladian window.

- Master Suite: With plenty of elbowroom, this master suite has a large walk-in closet and bathroom with double sinks, a whirlpool tub, and separate shower.

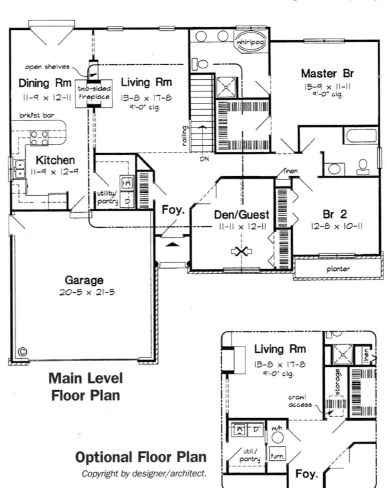

Main Level Floor Plan

Optional Floor Plan

Copyright by designer/architect.

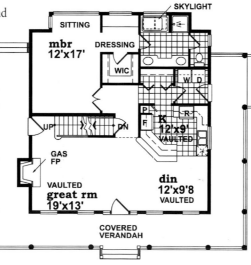

Plan #401027

Dimensions: 44'8" W x 41'4" D
Levels: 2
Square Footage: 1,634
Main Level Sq. Ft.: 1,099
Upper Level Sq. Ft.: 535
Bedrooms: 3
Bathrooms: 2
Foundation: Basement
Materials List Available: No
Price Category: C

Images provided by designer/architect.

Features:

- **Vaulted Ceilings:** Inside, the open plan includes a vaulted great room with fireplace, a vaulted dining room, and a vaulted kitchen.
- **Kitchen:** This area has a pass-through to the dining room and large pantry for the ultimate in convenience and functionality.
- **Master Suite:** Located on the first floor for privacy this retreat contains a walk-in closet with dressing room, a sitting area, and full skylighted bath.
- **Bedrooms:** Two family bedrooms are on the second floor.

This design offers several different options to make the floor plan exactly as you like it. The exterior is graced by a wrapping veranda, round columns, stone facing with cedar-shingled accents, and a trio of dormers.

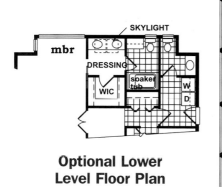

Optional Lower Level Floor Plan

Main Level Floor Plan

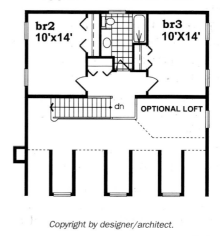

Upper Level Floor Plan

Copyright by designer/architect.

Plan #371051

Dimensions: 50'8" W x 55' D

Levels: 1

Square Footage: 1,639

Bedrooms: 3

Bathrooms: 2

Foundation: Slab

Materials List Available: No

Price Category: C

This beautiful traditional brick home says, "Welcome home".

Features:

- Living Room: Relax in front of the fireplace and media center in this large gathering room.

- Dining Room: The 9-ft.-high ceiling and large front window that brings in beautiful natural light combine to make this formal room feel airy and elegant.

- Kitchen: This large open kitchen, with its pantry, raised bar, and cozy nook, is great to bring the family together.

- Bedrooms: The two additional bedrooms share a convenient hall bathroom.

- Master Suite: This private area boasts two walk-in closets and a luxurious bathroom with his and her vanities and a marble tub.

Images provided by designer/architect.

Copyright by designer/architect.

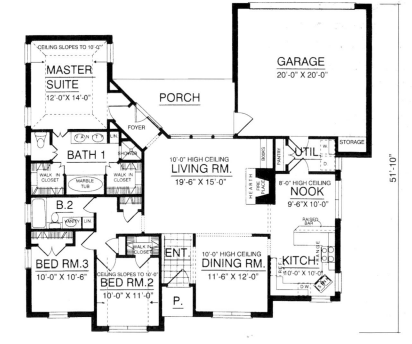

Plan #371052

Dimensions: 54'1" W x 51'10" D
Levels: 1
Square Footage: 1,640
Bedrooms: 3
Bathrooms: 2
Foundation: Slab
Materials List Available: No
Price Category: C

Images provided by designer/architect.

The beautiful windows give this traditional brick home an impressive look.

Features:

- **Living Room:** The 10-ft.-high ceiling, built-in bookcase, and cozy fireplace make this spacious gathering area someplace special.

- **Dining Room:** This large room, with its 10-ft.-high ceiling, is open to the living room, giving plenty of space for entertaining.

- **Kitchen:** This kitchen, with its raised bar, is open to a cozy nook.

- **Master Suite:** This large suite leads into a luxurious bathroom with a marble tub and his and her walk-in closets.

- **Bedrooms:** The two additional bedrooms share a convenient hall bathroom.

Copyright by designer/architect.

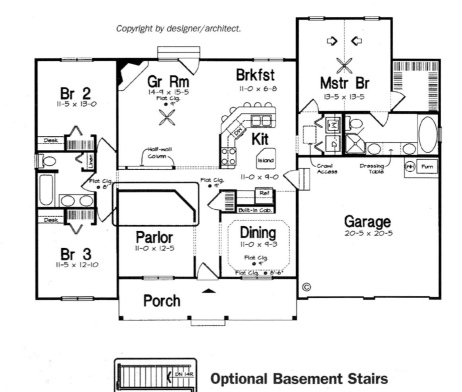

Plan #391038

Dimensions: 59' W x 44' D
Levels: 1
Square Footage: 1,642
Bedrooms: 3
Bathrooms: 2
Foundation: Crawl space, slab, or basement
Materials List Available: Yes
Price Category: C

Images provided by designer/architect.

This home features triple arches trimming a restful exterior front porch, great arched windows with shutters, and a complex classic roofline that steals the eye.

Features:

- **Dining Room:** A formal parlor sits across the hall from this spectacular room with decorative tray ceiling and built-in cabinetry.

- **Kitchen:** This kitchen is the heart of the home, with an island and peninsula counter/snack bar that opens into the great room.

- **Great Room:** This expansive room boasts a big, open layout with a corner fireplace.

- **Master Suite:** This super-private suite has a large walk-in closet and a sunny bath with a tub beneath a window.

- **Bedrooms:** These two additional bedrooms flank a full bathroom.

- **Garage:** This two-car garage makes all the difference for families with more than one automobile.

Copyright by designer/architect.

Optional Basement Stairs

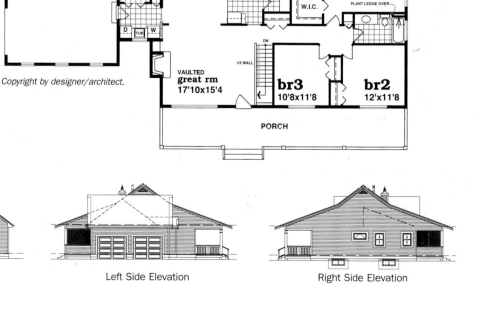

Plan #401045

Dimensions: 78'6" W x 48' D

Levels: 1

Square Footage: 1,652

Bedrooms: 3

Bathrooms: 2

Foundation: Basement

Materials List Available: Yes

Price Category: C

This long, low ranch home has outdoor living on two porches—one to the front and one to the rear.

Features:

- **High Ceilings:** Vaulted ceilings in the great room, kitchen, and master bedroom add a dimension of extra space.

- **Great Room:** A fireplace warms this room, which opens to the country kitchen.

- **Master Suite:** This fine area also has doors to the rear porch and is graced by a walk-in closet, plus a full bathroom with a garden tub and dual vanity.

- **Garage:** This two-car garage contains space for a freezer and extra storage cabinets that are built in.

Images provided by designer/architect.

two car garage 21'6x23'

FREEZER

BUILT-IN CABINETS

SCREENED PORCH

VAULTED country kitchen 12'x15'4

9'4x15'4

1/2 WALL

W.I.C.

VAULTED mbr 15'8x13'

PLANT LEDGE OVER

D TUB W

DN

1/2 WALL

VAULTED great rm 17'10x15'4

1/2 WALL

br3 10'8x11'8

br2 12'x11'8

PORCH

Copyright by designer/architect.

Rear Elevation

Left Side Elevation

Right Side Elevation

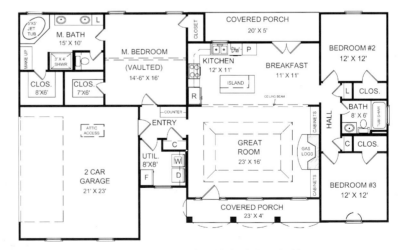

Plan #351033

Dimensions: 62'2" W x 45'8" D

Levels: 1

Square Footage: 1,654

Bedrooms: 3

Bathrooms: 2

Foundation: Crawl space, slab, or basement

Materials List Available: Yes

Price Category: C

Images provided by designer/architect.

This gorgeous three-bedroom brick home would be the perfect place to raise your family.

Features:

- Great Room: This terrific room has a gas fireplace with built-in cabinets on either side.

- Kitchen: This island kitchen with breakfast area is open to the great room.

- Master Bedroom: This private room features a vaulted ceiling and a large walk-in closet.

- Master Bath: This private area has a walk-in closet, jetted tub, and double vanities.

- Bedrooms: The two additional bedrooms share a bathroom located in the hall.

Copyright by designer/architect.

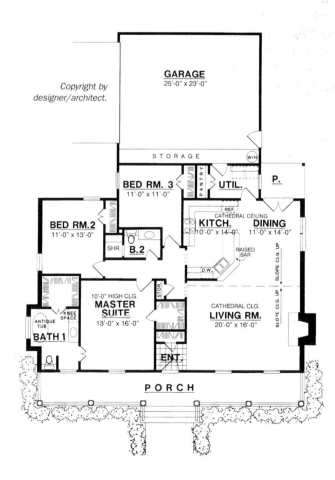

Plan #371053

Dimensions: 51'2" W x 66'7" D

Levels: 1

Square Footage: 1,654

Bedrooms: 3

Bathrooms: 2

Foundation: Slab

Materials List Available: No

Price Category: C

Images provided by designer/architect.

A cozy country porch and large inviting windows are the perfect way to say, "I'm home." This country charmer has everything you need.

Features:

- Kitchen: This large kitchen boasts a cathedral ceiling and a raised bar.

- Dining Room: This room has a cathedral ceiling and is open to the living room and kitchen.

- Living Room: The fireplace and cathedral ceiling give this room an inviting feeling.

- Master Suite: This private retreat features two walk-in closets. The old-fashioned bath with an antique tub is perfect for relaxing.

Plan #371054

Dimensions: 75'5" W x 43'7" D
Levels: 1
Square Footage: 1,656
Bedrooms: 3
Bathrooms: 2
Foundation: Slab
Materials List Available: No
Price Category: C

Images provided by designer/architect.

This traditional brick home is the essence of style. The beautiful windows and a covered porch add to the charm.

Features:

• Living Room: Just off the entry, this large room has a stepped ceiling. A bookcase and a media center flank the inviting fireplace.

• Kitchen: This fully functional kitchen opens to a formal dining room and a cozy breakfast nook.

• Master Suite: This massive hideaway boasts a high stepped ceiling and luxurious bath with two walk-in closets, a marble tub, and a separate shower.

• Bedrooms: The two large additional bedrooms share a convenient bathroom.

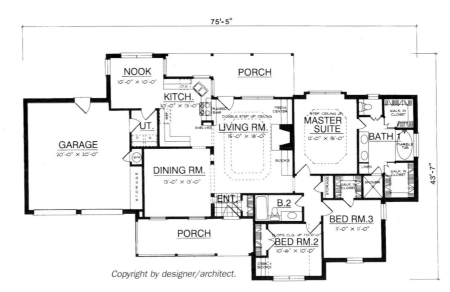

Copyright by designer/architect.

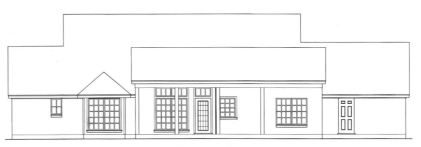

Rear Elevation

Plan #371032

Dimensions: 55'6" W x 46' D

Levels: 1

Square Footage: 1,659

Bedrooms: 3

Bathrooms: 2

Foundation: Slab

Materials List Available: No

Price Category: C

Images provided by designer/architect.

This charming country home has an impressive look that is all its own. This is the perfect home for any size family.

Features:

- Living Room: This massive room boasts a stepped ceiling, built in bookshelves and a media center.

- Kitchen: This large kitchen with walk-in pantry opens into the dining room.

- Master Suite: This area also has a high stepped ceiling and a sitting area with a view of the backyard. The large master bath has two walk-in closets and a marble tub.

- Bedrooms: The two large additional bedrooms share a convenient bath.

- Bonus Room: Located above the garage, this area can be a playroom.

Copyright by designer/architect.

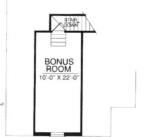

Bonus Area Floor Plan

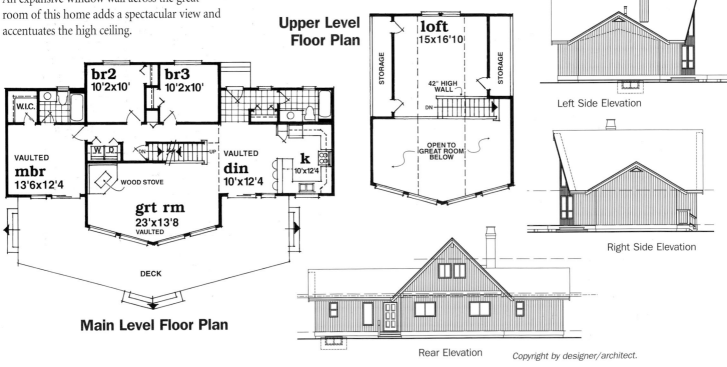

Images provided by designer/architect.

Plan #401035

Dimensions: 58' W x 32' D
Levels: 1½
Square Footage: 1,659
Main Level Sq.Ft.: 1,375
Upper Level Sq.Ft.: 284
Bedrooms: 3
Bathrooms: 2
Foundation: Basement
Materials List Available: Yes
Price Category: C

An expansive window wall across the great room of this home adds a spectacular view and accentuates the high ceiling.

Features:

- Kitchen: This open-plan workspace shares an eating bar with the dining room and features a convenient "U" shape. Sliding glass doors in the dining room lead to the deck.
- Bedrooms: Two family bedrooms sit to the back of the plan and share the use of a full bathroom.
- Master Suite: This retreat features a walk-in closet and private bathroom.
- Loft Area: Located on the upper level this loft adds living or sleeping space.

Upper Level Floor Plan

loft
15x16'10

STORAGE

STORAGE

42" HIGH WALL

DN

OPEN TO GREAT ROOM BELOW

Main Level Floor Plan

br2
10'2x10'

br3
10'2x10'

W.I.C.

VAULTED
mbr
13'6x12'4

W D

DN

UP

WOOD STOVE

VAULTED
din
10'x12'4

k
10'x12'4

grt rm
23'x13'8
VAULTED

DECK

Left Side Elevation

Right Side Elevation

Rear Elevation

Copyright by designer/architect.

Plan #121027

Dimensions: 46' W x 48' D

Levels: 2

Square Footage: 1,660

Main Level Sq. Ft.: 1,265

Upper Level Sq. Ft.: 395

Bedrooms: 3

Bathrooms: 2½

Foundation: Basement

Materials List Available: Yes

Price Category: C

Images provided by designer/architect.

Upper Level Floor Plan

Copyright by designer/architect.

Main Level Floor Plan

Plan #121004

Dimensions: 55'4" W x 48' D

Levels: 1

Square Footage: 1,666

Bedrooms: 3

Bathrooms: 2

Foundation: Basement

Materials List Available: Yes

Price Category: C

Images provided by designer/architect.

Copyright by designer/architect.

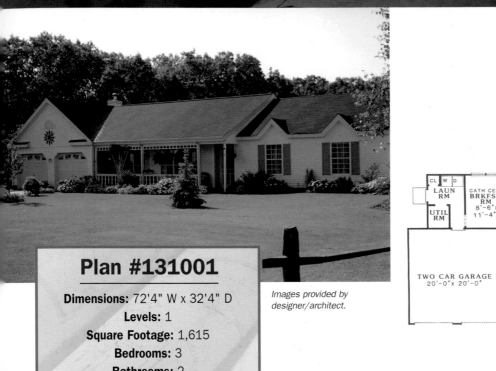

Images provided by designer/architect.

Copyright by designer/architect.

Plan #131001

Dimensions: 72'4" W x 32'4" D

Levels: 1

Square Footage: 1,615

Bedrooms: 3

Bathrooms: 2

Foundation: Crawl space, slab, basement, or walkout

Materials List Available: Yes

Price Category: D

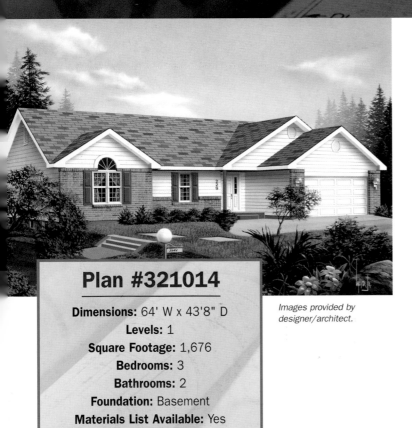

Images provided by designer/architect.

Copyright by designer/architect.

Plan #321014

Dimensions: 64' W x 43'8" D

Levels: 1

Square Footage: 1,676

Bedrooms: 3

Bathrooms: 2

Foundation: Basement

Materials List Available: Yes

Price Category: C

SMARTtip

Blending Architecture

An easy way to blend the new deck with the architecture of a house is with railings. Precut railings and caps come in many styles and sizes.

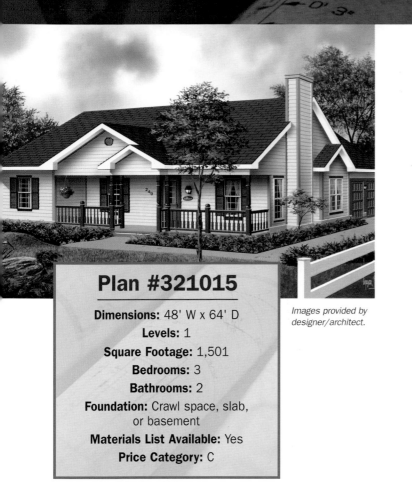

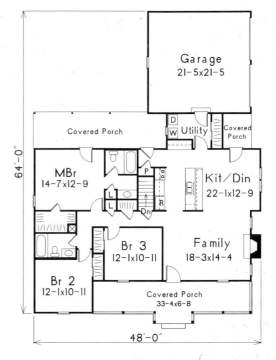

Plan #321015

Dimensions: 48' W x 64' D
Levels: 1
Square Footage: 1,501
Bedrooms: 3
Bathrooms: 2
Foundation: Crawl space, slab, or basement
Materials List Available: Yes
Price Category: C

Images provided by designer/architect.

Copyright by designer/architect.

Plan #151003

Dimensions: 51'6" W x 52'4" D
Levels: 1
Square Footage: 1,680
Bedrooms: 3
Bathrooms: 2
Foundation: Crawl space, slab, or basement
Materials List Available: No
Price Category: C

Images provided by designer/architect.

This home, as shown in the photograph, may differ from the actual blueprints. For more detailed information, please check the floor plans carefully.

Copyright by designer/architect.

Easy-Care Surfaces

Building a new home means you will be making a number of decisions on the many materials that will be visible throughout your cottage-style house. Your builder won't ask you which brand of drywall to buy, but he or she will ask what color to paint the walls, what material to use on the kitchen counters, and what type of finish you want on the faucets in the master bathroom. It is a lot to think about, but the following will help you make decisions on some of the major materials.

Countertop Materials

The market offers lots of countertop materials, all of which are worth consideration for your kitchen and bathroom surfaces. Pick the materials and designs that best suit your needs and the look of the room. You can also enhance a basic design by combining it with an eye-catching edge treatment. Another option is to combine different materials on the same surface.

Plastic Laminate. This thin, durable surface comes in hundreds of colors, textures, and patterns. The material is relatively easy to install; its smooth surface washes easily and can stand up well to everyday wear and tear. It is heat-resistant, although very hot pots can discolor or even burn it, and it will show scratches from knives and other sharp utensils; surface damage is difficult to repair.

Home centers and kitchen supply dealers sell post-formed counters. These are the types that come in 8- or 10-foot lengths that you or your builder will trim to fit. Both the laminate sheets and the post-form counters are available in a limited number of colors and patterns. Another option is to order a laminate counter from a counter fabricator—some home centers and kitchen dealers offer this service as well.

The counter will be built to your measurements, and you will get a wide variety of colors and patterns from which to choose. Most fabricators also offer a variety of edge treatments.

Ceramic Tile. Glazed tile can be magnificently decorative for counters, backsplashes, and walls, or as a display inset in another material. Tile is smooth and easy to wipe off, and it can't be burned by hot pots. In addition to the standard square tiles, ceramic tiles are available in a number of specialty shapes and sizes, allowing you to create a truly custom look. Ceramic tile costs more than laminate, but you can save money by doing the installation yourself.

When shopping, you should also consider the finish. There are two kinds: unglazed and glazed. Unglazed tiles are not sealed and always come in a matte look. They are not practical for use near water unless you apply a sealant. On the other hand, glazed tiles are coated with a material that makes them impervious to water—or spills and stains from other liquids, too. This glaze on the tile can be matte or highly polished. The upkeep of tile is fairly easy, but you must regrout and reseal periodically. White grout shows dirt easily, but a dark-color mix can camouflage stains. Still, unless it is sealed, grout will harbor bacteria. So clean the countertop regularly with a nonabrasive antibacterial cleanser. Tile that is well-maintained will last a lifetime.

Ceramic tile provides a clean, nonporous surface for countertops, opposite.

Colorful tiles make a strong design statement in the bath shown bottom left.

Solid surfacing, right, resists burns and scratches.

Plastic laminates, below, are available in a variety of colors and patterns.

Solid-Surfacing Material. Made of acrylics and composite materials, solid surfacing comes in ½ inch and ¾ inch thicknesses. This is a premium material that resists moisture, heat, stains, and cracks.

There is almost no limit to the colors and patterns of solid surfacing. It can be fabricated to resemble marble and granite, or it can be a block of solid color. Either way, the material can be carved or beveled for decorative effects just like wood. Manufacturers recommend professional installation.

The surface becomes scratched fairly easily, but the scratches are not readily appar-

ent. Because the material is a solid color, serious blemishes can be removed by sanding or buffing.

Natural Stone. Marble, slate, and granite can be formed into beautiful but expensive counters. Of the three, granite is probably the most popular because it cannot be hurt by moisture or heat, nor does it stain if finished properly. Installers polish granite to produce a high-gloss finish.

Marble scratches, cracks, and stains easily, even if waxed. Slate can be easily scratched and cracked and cannot take a high polish.

These are heavy materials that should be installed by a professional. However, you can get the look of granite and marble by installing granite or marble tiles. Cut from the natural stones, these products are available in 12 x 12-inch tiles and are installed and cut in much the same way as ceramic tiles.

Wood. Butcher block consists of hardwood laminated under pressure and sealed with oil or a polymer finish. Because it's thicker than other materials, butcher block will raise the counter level about ¾ inch above standard height. Also, wood is sub-

Natural stone, left, can be used on counters and backsplashes.

Counter fabricators can create decorative edge treatments such as the one above.

A bathroom vanity, above right, benefits from a polished quartz counter.

Strong countertop color, right, can set off neutral-color cabinets.

ject to damage by standing water or hot pans. Butcher-block tops are moderately expensive but can be installed by amateurs.

Other kinds of wood counters may be used, especially in serving areas. Any wood used near water must be resistant to moisture or well sealed to prevent water from penetrating below the surface.

Concrete. There aren't a great number of concrete counters, but the material is catching on with some in the kitchen design community. If your goal is to install a cutting-edge material that can still have a traditional look, concrete is it. Thanks to new

staining techniques, concrete can be saturated with color all the way through, and it can be preformed to any shape and finished to any texture. Set stone or ceramic tile chips into the surface for a decorative effect. Form it to drain off water at the sink. Be cautious, however, as a concrete countertop must be sealed, and it may crack. Installation is best left to a professional.

Stainless Steel. Stainless steel used for a countertop, whether it is for the entire counter or just a section of it, can look quite sophisticated, especially with a wood trim. What's practical about it is its capaci-

ty to take high heat without scorching, which makes it suitable as a landing strip for pots and pans straight from the cooktop. It is also impervious to water, so it's practical at the sink. On the negative side, stainless steel can be noisy to work on, and it will show smudges. Depending on the grade of the material, it may also be vulnerable to scrapes, stains, and corrosion. The higher the chromium and nickel content (and therefore the grade), the better. Also, look for a thick-gauge stainless steel that won't dent easily. If you prefer not to have a stainless-steel counter but like the look, consider a stainless-steel sink.

Selecting colors for walls can be intimidating. Fortunately, kitchens, above, usually have small unused wall areas so you can experiment more freely than you would in other rooms.

Wall Treatments

It's hard to beat the ease of a coat of paint for decorating a room. But there are other ways to finish off the walls, too, such as vinyl wallcovering and paneling. You can go with one, two, or all three of these options in several combinations to achieve the cottage decor that will complement your new house.

Paint. Basically, there are two kinds of paint: latex, which is a water-based formulation, and oil-based products. You can buy latex and oil paint in at least four finishes: flat, eggshell, semigloss, and gloss. In general, stay away from flat paint in the kitchen because it is difficult to keep clean. The other finishes, or sheens, resist dirt better than flat paint and are easier to clean.

Latex is a term used to describe a variety of water-based paints. They are recommended for most interior surfaces, including walls, woodwork, and cabinets. Latex paints come in a huge assortment of colors,

clean up with soap and water, and dry quickly.

Oil-based paint refers to products that use alkyd resins as the solvent. Manufacturers once used linseed or some other type of oil as the solvent and the name stuck. They provide tough, long-lasting finishes. However, the convenience of latex products, along with government regulations limiting the amount of volatile organic compounds oil-based products produce, has forced their use to decline. This kind of paint is especially good for use over bare wood and surfaces that have been

previously painted. If you plan to use it (or latex, for that matter) on new wallboard, you'll have to apply a primer first.

Wallcoverings. Vinyl wallcoverings and coordinated borders offer an easy, low-cost way to put style into your new cottage kitchen. Practical because they are nonporous, stain resistant, and washable, vinyl coatings are available in a great variety of colors, textures, and patterns. Prepasted, pretrimmed rolls are the easiest for a novice to install. Just remember to remove any old wallpaper before applying new covering to walls.

Paneling. If you're looking for a simple way to create a "cottage" feel, paneling is it. Today's paneling options include pre-finished softwood- or hardwood-veneered plywood, simulated wood grain on plywood or hardboard, pre-hung wallpaper on plywood, simulated wood grain or decorative finish panel board, tile board, or other decorative hardboard paneling, and solid pine or cedar plank paneling. For a versatile look, apply wainscoting, which is paneling that goes halfway or three-quarters of the way up the wall. Top it off with chair rail molding; paint or wallpaper the rest of the wall. Depending on how you install it, you can create horizontal, diagonal, or herringbone patterns.

Wallpaper and borders are an easy, inexpensive way to enliven a room's design, above. Pick colors and patterns to set off your cabinet finishes.

Ceramic tile is a popular choice for bathroom walls. Note how the tiles below contain decorative inlays to add sparkle to what would otherwise be a white wall.

Flooring

Floor coverings fall into two broad categories: resilient flooring, which has some resiliency, or bounce, and hard flooring, with no flex whatsoever. Resilient floors are less tiring to stand on than hard-surface floors and less likely to produce instant disaster for dropped glasses or chinaware. But the flooring you select plays more than a practical role in your kitchen.

Resilient Vinyl Tile and Sheet Flooring.

Vinyl flooring wears fairly well to very well, needs only occasional waxing or polishing (in some cases none at all), and is easy to clean. It comes in a wide variety of colors and patterns suitable to the cottage style, and is an economical alternative among flooring choices.

These products are available in individual tiles or in large sheets. (The sheets can look like individual tiles as well as a wide range of designs.) Installing vinyl tile is a

Vinyl flooring, left, comes in a variety of patterns.

Carpeting, below, adds warmth to most rooms.

popular do-it-yourself project. Installing sheet goods is a bit more complex but well within the skills of an experienced do-it-yourselfer.

Laminate. This type of flooring consists of laminate material, a tougher version of the material used on counters, bonded to fiberboard core. The decorative top layer of material can be made to look like just about anything. Currently, wood-grain patterns are the most popular, but laminates are available in many colors and patterns, including tile and natural stone designs.

Available in both plank and tile form, they are easy to install, hold up well to normal traffic, and are easy to clean.

Wood. Thanks largely to polyurethane coatings that are impervious to water, wood flooring continues to be a popular choice for just about any room of the home, except bathrooms. Wood can be finished any way you like, though much of the wood flooring available today comes prefinished in an assortment of shades.

Hardwoods like oak and maple are popular and stand up to a lot of abuse. Softwoods like pine give a more distressed, countrified look. Flooring comes in 2¼-inch strips as well as variable-width planks. Parquet flooring, another good option, consists of wood pieces glued together into

Stone flooring imparts a feeling of solidity to an area, such as the foyer above. Inlay designs such as this one are the mark of a true stone craftsman.

a geometric pattern. These prefinished squares can be installed in a way similar to that used for vinyl tiles.

Hard-Surface Flooring. Ceramic tile, stone, and slate floors are hard, durable, and easy to clean, especially when you use grout sealers. Because these floors are so inflexible, anything fragile dropped on them is likely to break. Also, they are tiring to stand on and noisy, and they conduct extremes of temperature. For those who love the look of this kind of flooring, however, the drawbacks can be mitigated with accent and area rugs that add a cushion.

Ceramic tile makes an excellent kitchen or bathroom floor when installed with proper grout and sealants. The tiles range from the earth tones of unglazed, solid-color quarry tile to the great array of colors, patterns, and finishes in surface-glazed tiles. Grout comes color-keyed, so it can be either inconspicuous or a design element. Ceramic and quarry tiles are best suited to a concrete subfloor, though you can lay them over any firm base. Cost ranges from moderate to expensive.

Stone and slate are cut into small slabs and can be laid in a regular or random pattern. Materials are inexpensive or costly, depending on quality and local availability. Even if you find these materials more expensive than other floor coverings, don't dismiss them because of price. They will never need to be replaced, making your initial investment your final one. Because stone and slate are laid in mortar and are themselves weighty materials, a concrete slab makes the ideal subfloor. In other situations, the subfloor must be able to carry a significantly heavy load. Installation is a complex job that should be left to contractors with experience in this type of stone work.

Carpeting and Rugs. The terms carpet and rug are often used interchangeably, but they're not the same. Carpeting is manufactured in rolls ranging from just over 2 feet wide to broadlooms that measure as much as 18 feet wide. Carpeting is usually laid wall-to-wall and can be installed over raw subflooring. Rugs are soft floor coverings that don't extend wall-to-wall and are used over another finished flooring surface. A mat is a small rug.

Differences in fiber composition, construction, color, texture, and cost make choosing a carpet or rug a complex job. Carpeting can be made of natural wool, synthetic fibers, or blends of wool and synthetics. Other natural fibers commonly used in area rugs, scatter rugs, and mats are cotton or plant materials known as cellulosics—hemp, jute, sisal, or grasses. Synthetic fibers are acrylics, nylon, olefin, and polyester.

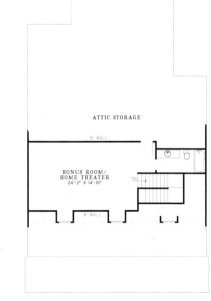

Plan #151219

Dimensions: 48' W x 74'4" D

Levels: 1.5

Square Footage: 1,712

Bedrooms: 2

Bathrooms: 2

Foundation: Crawl space or slab

Materials List Available: No

Price Category: C

Images provided by designer/architect.

Copyright by designer/architect.

This country home has a friendly open floor plan and a bonus room above.

Features:

- **Great Room:** This area has a cozy fireplace and is open into the dining area.

- **Dining Area:** With enough room for a family-sized table, this area is great for a large household and is open to the kitchen and great room.

- **Kitchen:** This U-shaped kitchen has a breakfast bar and is close to the garage.

- **Master Suite:** This large retreat has a private bathroom with a large walk-in closet.

48'-0"

© 1994 NELSON DESIGN GROUP, LLC

GARAGE
22'-2" X 26'-2"

LAU.
9'-6" X 11'-0"

KITCHEN
13'-6" X 14'-4"

GLASS SHWR

M.B.
7'-8"X 20'-10"

WHP TUB

MASTER SUITE
17'-6" X 15'-6"

GRILLING PORCH
8'-0" X 22'-0"

DW   REF

DINING
13'-6" X 9'-4"

OPTIONAL BASEMENT STAIRS

BATH
6'-0" X 13'-6"

GREAT ROOM
21'-6" X 15'-6"

BEDROOM 2
17'-6" X 11'-4"

COVERED PORCH
40'-0" X 8'-0"

Main Level Floor Plan

ATTIC STORAGE

8' WALL

BONUS ROOM/
HOME THEATER
24'-2" X 14'-10"

8' WALL

Upper Level Floor Plan

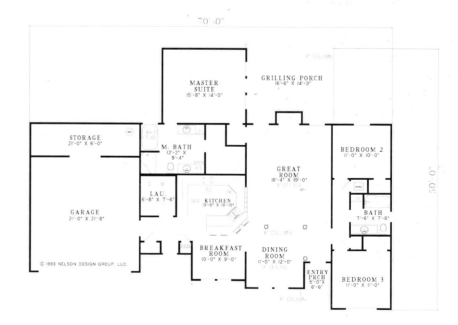

Plan #151210

Dimensions: 70' W x 50' D
Levels: 1
Square Footage: 1,716
Bedrooms: 3
Bathrooms: 2
Foundation: Crawl space or slab
Materials List Available: No
Price Category: C

This traditional three-bedroom brick home will be the envy of the neighborhood.

Features:

- **Great Room:** This large gathering room, with a cozy fireplace, has access to the rear porch.

- **Dining Room:** This room with a view of the front yard is located just of the entry.

- **Kitchen:** This kitchen boasts an abundant amount of cabinets, and counter space is open to the breakfast area and the great room.

- **Master Suite:** This suite features a private bathroom with double vanities and a whirlpool tub.

- **Bedrooms:** Two secondary bedrooms have large closets and share a hall bathroom.

Plan #371012

Dimensions: 56'4" W x 52'10" D

Levels: 1

Square Footage: 1,720

Bedrooms: 3

Bathrooms: 2

Foundation: Slab

Materials List Available: No

Price Category: C

Images provided by designer/architect.

The beautifully designed front of this traditional brick home makes it special from the start.

Features:

- Living Room: 10-ft.-high ceilings and a cozy fireplace make this large gathering area special.

- Dining Room: Truly grand, this formal room has 10-ft.-high ceilings.

- Kitchen: This kitchen has a raised bar and a breakfast nook that is open to the porch.

- Master Suite: This private area boasts a luxurious bathroom with a marble tub, a glass shower, and two walk-in closets.

- Bedrooms: The two secondary bedrooms share a private bathroom with a powder room.

Copyright by designer/architect.

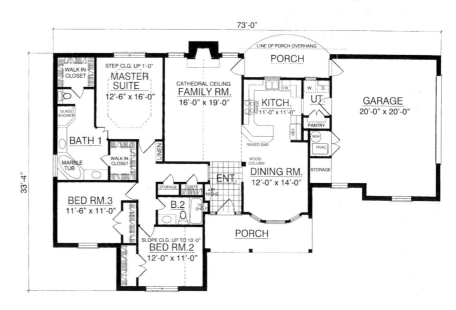

Images provided by designer/architect.

Plan #371033

Dimensions: 73' W x 33' 4" D

Levels: 1

Square Footage: 1,724

Bedrooms: 3

Bathrooms: 2

Foundation: Slab

Materials List Available: No

Price Category: C

This beautiful brick-and-stone country home will be the envy of the neighborhood.

Features:

• Front Porch: This charming yet functional porch welcomes you home.

• Family Room: This large room, with its cathedral ceiling and cozy fireplace, is ideal for entertaining.

• Kitchen: This gourmet kitchen has all the necessities you will ever need, including a raised bar area.

• Master Suite: This cozy area features a stepped ceiling. The luxurious bath boasts a marble tub and two walk-in closets.

Copyright by designer/architect.

Plan #371071

Dimensions: 73' W x 47'4" D
Levels: 1
Square Footage: 1,729
Bedrooms: 3
Bathrooms: 2
Foundation: Crawl space, slab
Materials List Available: No
Price Category: C

Images provided by designer/architect.

This beautiful brick-and-stone country home will be the envy of the neighborhood.

Features:

- Front Porch: This charming yet functional porch welcomes you home.

- Family Room: This large room, with its cathedral ceiling and cozy fireplace, is ideal for entertaining.

- Kitchen: This gourmet kitchen has all the necessities you will ever need, including a raised bar area.

- Master Suite: This master bedroom features a stepped ceiling. The luxurious bath boasts a marble tub and two walk-in closets.

Copyright by designer/architect.

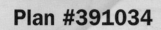

Plan #391034

Dimensions: 72'4" W x 43' D
Levels: 1
Square Footage: 1,737
Bedrooms: 3
Bathrooms: 2
Foundation: Crawl space, slab, or basement
Materials List Available: Yes
Price Category: C

This lovely home brings together traditional single-level architectural elements, current features, and just the right amount of living space.

Features:

• Entry: A demure covered porch and well-mannered foyer deliver all the important rooms.

• Dining Room: This formal room features exquisite vaulted ceilings.

• Kitchen: This close-knit kitchen with pantry embraces a cheerful breakfast nook with sliding doors to the deck.

• Master Suite: This suite is a visual treat, with its own vaulted ceiling as well as a skylight over the master bathtub and shower area.

Images provided by designer/architect.

• Bedrooms: The two secondary bedrooms are pampered with good closeting, proximity to a shared bath with double sink vanities, and wonderful windows that enhance the spacious atmosphere.

Rear Elevation

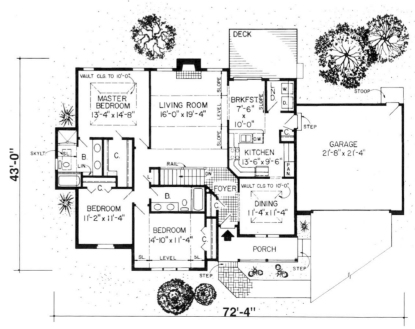

Copyright by designer/architect.

Plan #181225

Dimensions: 31' W x 31' D

Levels: 2

Square Footage: 1,746

Main Level Sq. Ft.: 873

Upper Level Sq. Ft.: 873

Bedrooms: 3

Bathrooms: 1½

Foundation: Basement

Materials List Available: Yes

Price Category: C

A quaint wraparound country porch and a covered terrace invite families to enjoy the outdoors.

Features:

- **Entry:** This formal entrance flows to a bright home office or through French doors to the family room.
- **Kitchen:** A super-sized lunch counter is central to this spacious corner kitchen.
- **Dining Room:** This dining area, with private porch entrance, shares an open floor plan with the kitchen.
- **Relax:** A reading nook on the mezzanine basks under cathedral ceilings in the hallway.
- **Bedrooms:** The master bedroom has his and her walk-in closets, while two secondary bedrooms enjoy wall-length closets.

Main Level Floor Plan

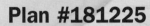

10'-4" X 10'-4"
3,10 X 3,10

13'-0" X 11'-0"
3,90 X 3,30

11'-0" X 10'-0"
3,30 X 3,00

12'-0" X 15'-0"
3,60 X 4,50

31'-0"
9,3 m

31'-0"
9,3 m

Upper Level Floor Plan

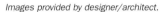
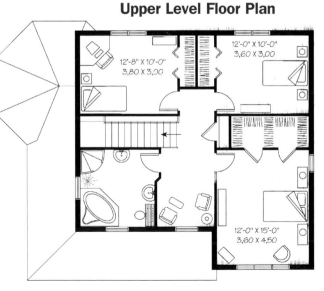

12'-0" X 10'-0"
3,60 X 3,00

12'-8" X 10'-0"
3,80 X 3,00

12'-0" X 15'-0"
3,60 X 4,50

Copyright by designer/architect.

Plan #391004

Dimensions: 66' W x 52' D

Levels: 1

Square Footage: 1,750

Bedrooms: 2

Bathrooms: 2

Foundation: Crawl space, slab, or basement

Materials List Available: Yes

Price Category: C

Images provided by designer/architect.

This creatively compact ranch is made especially for effortless everyday living.

Features:

- Kitchen: This centralized U-shaped kitchen and look-alike breakfast nook with professional pantry have a wonderful view of the porch.

- Laundry Room: Laundry facilities are cleverly placed within reach while neatly out of the way.

- Great Room: Step into this lavish-looking sunken great room for fire-side gatherings, and move easily into the nearby formal dining area where a screened porch allows you to entertain guests after dinner.

- Master Suite: Flanking one side of the house, this master suite is serenely private and amenity-filled. Its features include full bath, a wall of walk-in closets and a dressing area.

- Bedroom: This second spacious bedroom enjoys great closeting, (with double-doors), a full bath and a close-at-hand den (or bedroom #3).

- Garage: This three-car garage goes beyond vehicle protection, providing plenty of storage and work space.

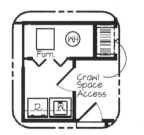

Crawl Space/Slab Option

Copyright by designer/architect.

Rear View

Plan #371034

Dimensions: 49'2" W x 53'2" D

Levels: 1

Square Footage: 1,753

Bedrooms: 3

Bathrooms: 2

Foundation: Slab

Materials List Available: No

Price Category: C

This spectacular brick-and-stucco traditional home conceals a stylish floor plan.

Features:

- **Living Room:** This entertaining area boasts a 10-ft.-high ceiling, a media center, and a fireplace.

- **Kitchen:** The raised bar in this functional kitchen gives it and the adjoining dining area an open feel.

- **Master Suite:** This private retreat has a step-up ceiling and a luxurious bathroom with his and her vanities and two walk-in closets.

- **Bedrooms:** There are two additional bed rooms, with an optional third bedroom or office that allows for plenty of growing space.

Images provided by designer/architect.

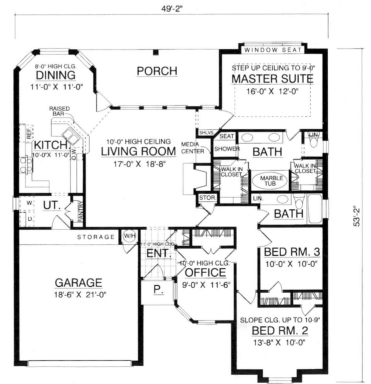

Copyright by designer/architect.

Plan #371035

Dimensions: 59'2" W x 48'8" D

Levels: 1

Square Footage: 1,758

Bedrooms: 3

Bathrooms: 2

Foundation: Slab

Materials List Available: No

Price Category: C

Images provided by designer/architect.

This classic traditional brick residence will welcome you home.

Features:

- **Living Room:** This large room with a double-stepped-up ceiling and cozy fireplace, is great for entertaining.

- **Dining Room:** A cathedral ceiling and wooden columns adorn this formal room.

- **Kitchen:** This kitchen has a pass-through window and opens into a cozy breakfast nook.

- **Bedrooms:** The two additional bedrooms share a convenient hall bathroom.

- **Master Suite:** This large area boasts a luxurious bathroom with a relaxing marble tub and two walk-in closets.

Copyright by designer/architect.

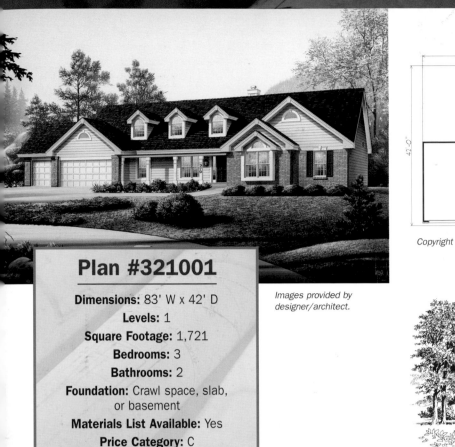

Copyright by designer/architect.

Rear View

Plan #321001

Dimensions: 83' W x 42' D

Levels: 1

Square Footage: 1,721

Bedrooms: 3

Bathrooms: 2

Foundation: Crawl space, slab, or basement

Materials List Available: Yes

Price Category: C

Images provided by designer/architect.

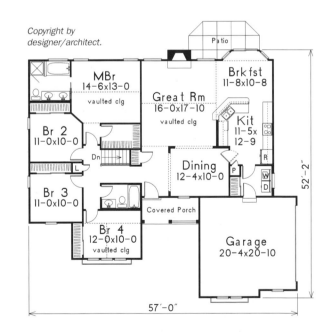

Copyright by designer/architect.

Plan #321008

Dimensions: 57' W x 52'2" D

Levels: 1

Square Footage: 1,761

Bedrooms: 4

Bathrooms: 2

Foundation: Basement

Materials List Available: Yes

Price Category: C

Images provided by designer/architect.

SMARTtip

Hanging Wallpaper

Use liner paper to smooth out a damaged wall and to provide uniform support for expensive paper.

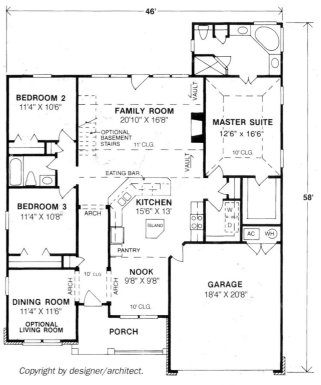

Images provided by designer/architect.

Plan #121006

Dimensions: 46' W x 58' D

Levels: 1

Square Footage: 1,762

Bedrooms: 3

Bathrooms: 2

Foundation: Slab

Materials List Available: Yes

Price Category: C

Copyright by designer/architect.

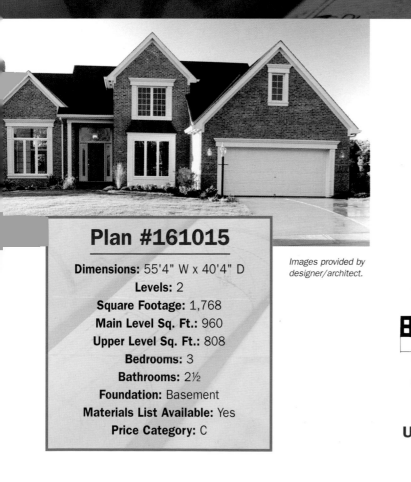

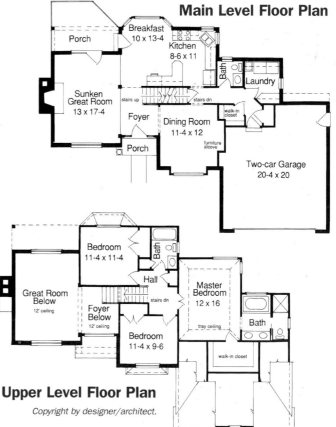

Images provided by designer/architect.

Main Level Floor Plan

Upper Level Floor Plan

Copyright by designer/architect.

Plan #161015

Dimensions: 55'4" W x 40'4" D

Levels: 2

Square Footage: 1,768

Main Level Sq. Ft.: 960

Upper Level Sq. Ft.: 808

Bedrooms: 3

Bathrooms: 2½

Foundation: Basement

Materials List Available: Yes

Price Category: C

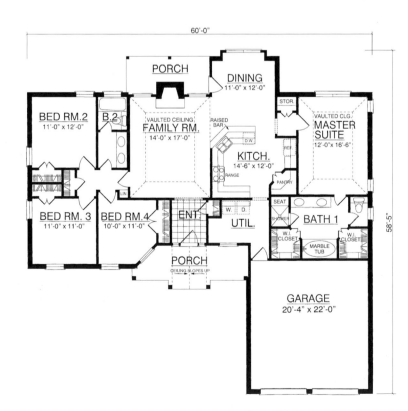

N. Ibarra

Plan #371036

Dimensions: 60' W x 58'5" D

Levels: 1

Square Footage: 1,764

Bedrooms: 4

Bathrooms: 2

Foundation: Slab

Materials List Available: No

Price Category: C

Images provided by designer/architect.

This quaint traditional brick house is the perfect place to call home.

Features:

- Family Room: This large room boasts a vaulted ceiling and cozy fireplace.

- Dining Room: This area has access to the rear porch and is open to the kitchen.

- Kitchen: This spacious kitchen has a raised bar and views into the family room.

- Master Suite: This private area also has a vaulted ceiling. The luxurious master bath boasts his and her vanities, a marble tub, a large shower area, and two walk-in closets.

- Bedrooms: The three additional bedrooms are on the opposite side of the house from the master suite and share a convenient second bath.

60'-0"

PORCH

DINING
11'-0" x 12'-0"

STOR.

BED RM.2
11'-0" x 12'-0"

B. 2

VAULTED CEILING
FAMILY RM.
14'-0" x 17'-0"

RAISED
BAR

D.W.

VAULTED CLG.
MASTER
SUITE
12'-0" x 16'-6"

KITCH.
14'-6" x 12'-0"

REF.

RANGE

PANTRY

LIN.

SEAT

BED RM. 3
11'-0" x 11'-0"

BED RM.4
10'-0" x 11'-0"

ENT.

W. D.

UTIL.

SHOWER

BATH 1

W.I.
CLOSET

MARBLE
TUB

W.I.
CLOSET

PORCH
CEILING SLOPES UP

58'-5"

GARAGE
20'-4" x 22'-0"

Copyright by designer/architect.

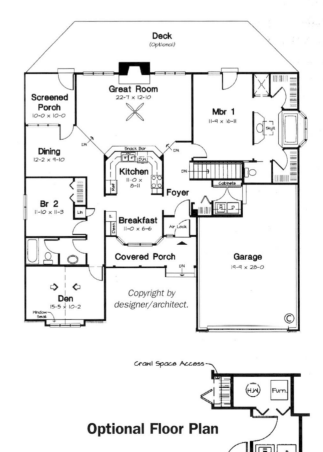

Plan #391028

Dimensions: 54' W x 50' D
Levels: 1
Square Footage: 1,771
Bedrooms: 2
Bathrooms: 2
Foundation: Crawl space, slab
Materials List Available: Yes
Price Category: C

Images provided by designer/architect.

Here's a "real-life" rancher, where there's plenty of room for stretching out and growing your family in contemporary comfort.

Features:

- **Dining Area:** This dining area, a demure space for formal affairs, owns an entrance to the back deck and flows easily into the great room.

- **Kitchen:** This creative U-shaped kitchen serves up a snack bar that reaches into the enormous sunken great room with fireplace.

- **Master Suite:** This expansive suite with dual walk-in closets and private entrance to the deck lives luxuriously on the other side of this home. The master bath flaunts a platform tub set beneath a grand geometric window.

- **Bedroom:** A stylish secondary bedroom, with nearby full bathroom, and cheerful den with a window seat are arranged on one side of the house.

Plan #371072

Dimensions: 75'10" W x 38'8" D

Levels: 1

Square Footage: 1,772

Bedrooms: 3

Bathrooms: 2

Foundation: Crawl space, slab

Materials List Available: No

Price Category: C

Images provided by designer/architect.

This home, with its enclosed covered porch, defines country charm.

Features:

- **Living Room:** This large room has a 10-foot-high ceiling and large windows looking out onto a covered back porch. The cozy fireplace and built-in media center will be great for relaxing.

- **Kitchen:** This large country kitchen with breakfast nook features a raised bar.

- **Dining Room:** This beautiful room has large windows located in a boxed-out extension.

- **Master Suite:** This secluded suite has a large walk-in closet and a luxurious master bath.

Copyright by designer/architect.

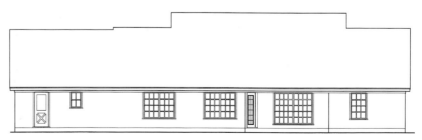

Rear Elevation

Plan #371037

Dimensions: 48'8" W x 53'10" D

Levels: 1

Square Footage: 1,774

Bedrooms: 4

Bathrooms: 2

Foundation: Slab

Materials List Available: No

Price Category: C

Images provided by designer/architect.

This beautiful traditional design, with growing room for years to come, will make you feel right at home.

Features:

- **Living Room:** This large room boasts a 10-ft.-high ceiling, a media center, and a cozy fireplace.

- **Kitchen:** The raised bar in this kitchen brings the dining space, kitchen, and living room together as one large area.

- **Master Suite:** This retreat, with its stepped-up ceiling, includes a luxurious bathroom with his and her vanities, a marble tub, and two walk-in closets in its list of amenities.

- **Bedrooms:** The three additional bedrooms share a convenient hall bathroom.

Copyright by designer/architect.

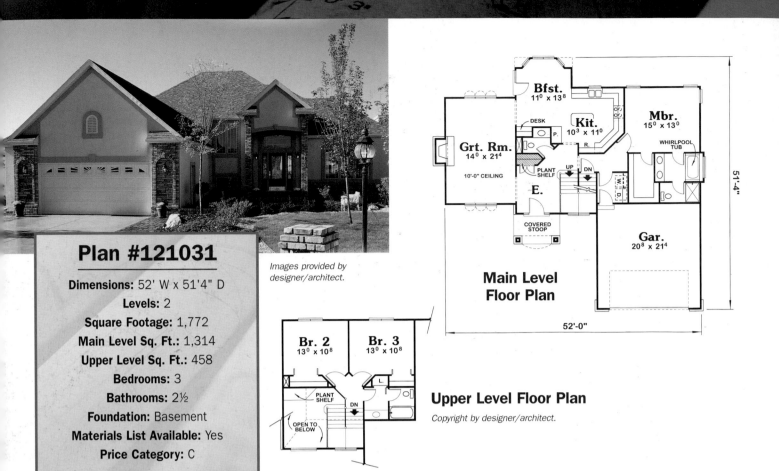

Plan #121031

Dimensions: 52' W x 51'4" D

Levels: 2

Square Footage: 1,772

Main Level Sq. Ft.: 1,314

Upper Level Sq. Ft.: 458

Bedrooms: 3

Bathrooms: 2½

Foundation: Basement

Materials List Available: Yes

Price Category: C

Images provided by designer/architect.

Main Level Floor Plan

Upper Level Floor Plan

Copyright by designer/architect.

Plan #151016

Dimensions: 60'2" W x 39'10" D

Levels: 2

Square Footage: 1,783; 2,107 with bonus

Main Level Sq. Ft.: 1,124

Upper Level Sq. Ft.: 659

Bonus Room Sq. Ft.: 324

Bedrooms: 3

Bathrooms: 2½

Foundation: Crawl space, slab, or basement

Materials List Available: No

Price Category: C

Images provided by designer/architect.

Main Level Floor Plan

Bonus Room Above Garage

Upper Level Floor Plan

Copyright by designer/architect.

Plan #131047

Dimensions: 69'10" W x 51'8" D
Levels: 1
Square Footage: 1,793
Bedrooms: 3
Bathrooms: 2
Foundation: Crawl space, slab, or basement
Materials List Available: Yes
Price Category: C

Images provided by designer/architect.

The country charm of this well-designed home is mixed with the convenience and luxury normally reserved for more contemporary plans.

Features:

• Great Room: The spaciousness of this great room is enhanced by the 11-ft. stepped ceiling. A fireplace makes it cozy on cool evenings or on chilly winter days, and two sets of French sliding glass doors open to the back porch.

• Kitchen: In addition to the convenient layout of this design, you'll also love its bright, airy position. It includes an old-fashioned pantry,

a sink under a window, and a sunny breakfast area that opens to the wraparound porch.

• Master Suite: You'll find 11-ft. ceilings in both the master bedroom and the bayed sitting area that the suite includes. In the bath, the circular spa tub is surrounded by a glass-block wall.

• Bonus Space: A permanent staircase leads to an unfinished bonus space on the upper level.

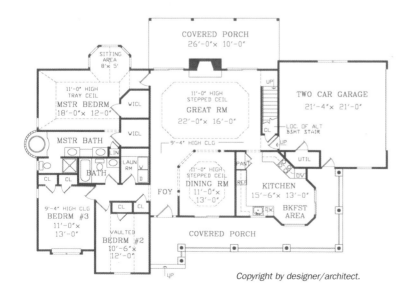

Copyright by designer/architect.

Rear Elevation

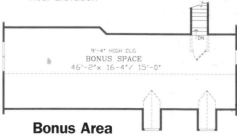

Bonus Area

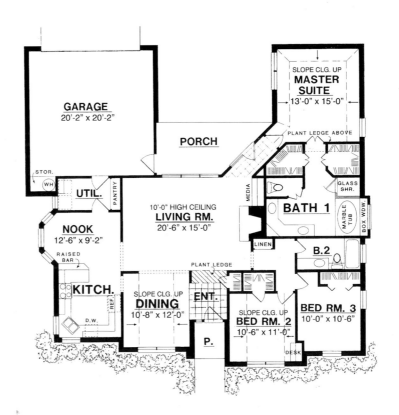

Plan #371073

Dimensions: 54'6" W x 52' D
Levels: 1
Square Footage: 1,783
Bedrooms: 3
Bathrooms: 2
Foundation: Slab
Materials List Available: No
Price Category: C

Images provided by designer/architect.

The tall arched windows make this home stand out.

Features:

- Living Room: This large gathering area has a lovely fireplace, a built-in media center, and a view onto the rear porch.

- Dining Room: A sloped ceiling makes this formal eating area feel much larger than it is.

- Kitchen: This efficient U-shaped kitchen looks into the adjoining breakfast nook, which has a bay window.

- Master Suite: Secluded and luxurious, this area features a sloped ceiling and a huge master bathroom with his and her walk-in closets.

- Bedrooms: The two secondary bedrooms have large closets and share a common bathroom.

Copyright by designer/architect.

Plan #391016

Dimensions: 45'8" W x 35'8" D
Levels: 2
Square Footage: 1,785
Main Level Sq. Ft.: 891
Upper Level Sq. Ft.: 894
Bedrooms: 3
Bathrooms: 2½
Foundation: Crawl space, slab, or basement
Materials List Available: Yes
Price Category: C

Images provided by designer/architect.

The entire family can be proud to come home to this beautiful design, with its Palladian window under a trio of peaked roofs.

Features:

- **Entry:** A covered entry makes way for a warm welcome as the open-style hall leads to the great room and homey hearth.

- **Dining Room:** This room is wedded to the kitchen, where an enormous prep counter doubles as a breakfast bar.

- **Utility Areas:** Past the pantry, find additional storage. Laundry facilities and a windowed half-bath in the backroom support other necessities.

- **Great Room:** From over the half-walled balcony, you can look into this great room, wish good day or night, and slip into the tranquility of the master suite.

- **Master Suite:** The private shower room is merely steps from the deep walk-in closet in this suite.

- **Bedrooms:** A second bath with window and corner tub is nestled between two secondary bedrooms at the rear of the house.

Main Level Floor Plan

Copyright by designer/architect.

Upper Level Floor Plan

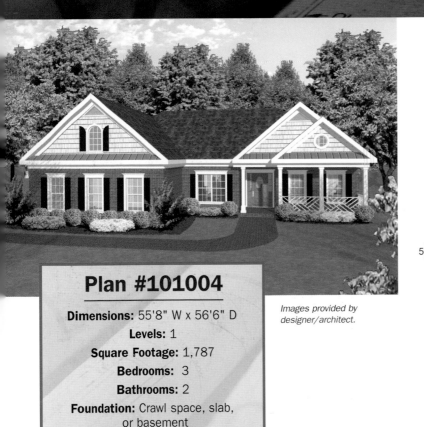

Plan #371013

Dimensions: 58'4" W x 49'6" D

Levels: 1

Square Footage: 1,791

Bedrooms: 3

Bathrooms: 2

Foundation: Slab

Materials List Available: No

Price Category: C

Images provided by designer/architect.

58'-4"

49'-6"

STEP UP CEILING

MASTER SUITE 16'-0" x 12'-0"

NOOK 9'-10" X 11'-0"

PORCH

BED RM.2 11'-0" x 12'-0"

BATH 1

SHR

WALK IN CLOSET

MARBLE TUB

WALK IN CLOSET

REF.

D.W.

RANGE

PANT.

RAISED BAR

KITCH. 10'-8" x 11'-0"

10'-0" HIGH CEILING

LIVING RM. 17'-10" x 16'-3"

STOR.

LIN.

B.2

W/H

STORAGE

GARAGE 18'-9" x 20'-0"

W. D.

UTIL.

SLOPE CLG. UP

DINING RM. 11'-0" x 13'-0"

SLOPE CLG. UP

ENT.

P.

SLOPE CLG. UP TO 10'-0"

BED RM.3 11'-6" x 11'-0"

Copyright by designer/architect.

Plan #101004

Dimensions: 55'8" W x 56'6" D

Levels: 1

Square Footage: 1,787

Bedrooms: 3

Bathrooms: 2

Foundation: Crawl space, slab, or basement

Materials List Available: Yes

Price Category: C

Images provided by designer/architect.

SITTING

TRAY CEILING

DECK

MASTER BDRM 21'-4" x 15'-0"

SCREEN PORCH

SKYLIGHT SKYLIGHT

BEDROOM 3 13'-0" x 12'-0"

HERS HIS

LINEN

FAMILY ROOM 18'-0" x 16'-2"

LINEN

11' HIGH CEILING

SERVING BAR

56'-6"

BRKFST 9'-4" x 10'-0"

BRKFST BAR

DW

KITCHEN 12'-4" x 11'-0"

DESK

K/S

STAIRS TO BASEMENT

STAIRS TO BONUS ROOM

UP

35'-0"

COAT

PANTRY

BONUS ROOM 12'-2" x 20'-4"

DINING 11'-0" x 12'-0"

ENTRY 11' HIGH CEILING

BEDROOM 2 13'-0" x 12'-0"

GARAGE 21'-4" x 20'-4"

55'-8"

PORCH

Copyright by designer/architect.

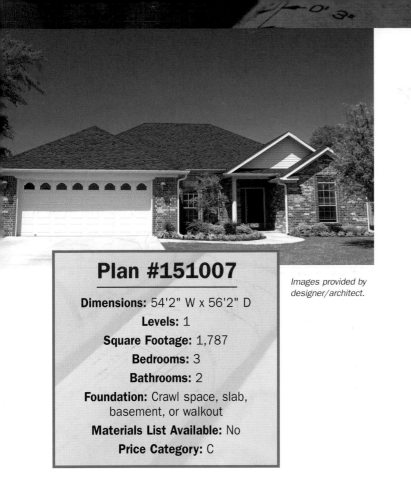

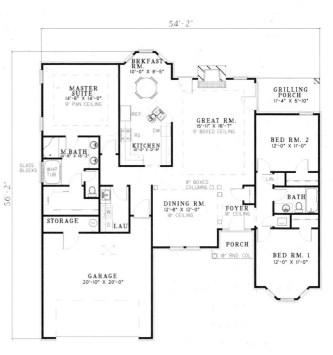

Plan #151007

Dimensions: 54'2" W x 56'2" D

Levels: 1

Square Footage: 1,787

Bedrooms: 3

Bathrooms: 2

Foundation: Crawl space, slab, basement, or walkout

Materials List Available: No

Price Category: C

Images provided by designer/architect.

Copyright by designer/architect.

Plan #321003

Dimensions: 67'4" W x 48' D

Levels: 1

Square Footage: 1,791

Bedrooms: 4

Bathrooms: 2

Foundation: Basement

Materials List Available: Yes

Price Category: C

Images provided by designer/architect.

Copyright by designer/architect.

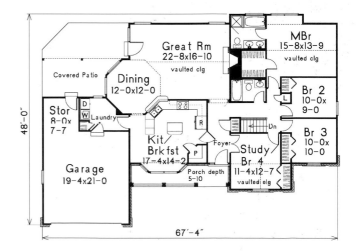

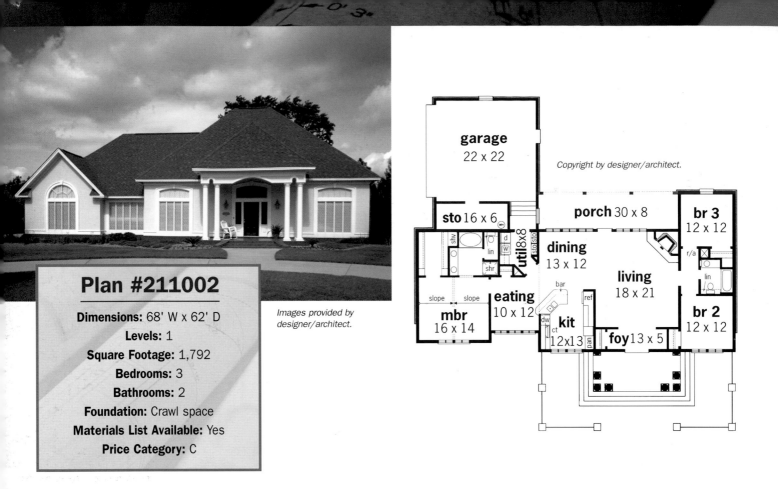

Plan #211002

Dimensions: 68' W x 62' D

Levels: 1

Square Footage: 1,792

Bedrooms: 3

Bathrooms: 2

Foundation: Crawl space

Materials List Available: Yes

Price Category: C

Images provided by designer/architect.

Copyright by designer/architect.

garage 22 x 22

sto 16 x 6

porch 30 x 8

br 3 12 x 12

util 8 x 8

dining 13 x 12

living 18 x 21

br 2 12 x 12

eating 10 x 12

mbr 16 x 14

kit 12x13

foy 13 x 5

bar

Plan #271077

Dimensions: 69'6" W x 53' D

Levels: 1

Square Footage: 1,786

Bedrooms: 1

Bathrooms: 1½

Foundation: Basement or daylight basement

Materials List Available: No

Price Category: C

Images provided by designer/architect.

PORCH 13' X 10'

DINING 15' X 11'

GREAT RM 16' X 14'

OWNER'S SUITE 16' X 13'

LAUN

MUD

KITCHEN 14' X 14'

STUDY 11' X 13'

ENTRY

BATH

WI CL

GARAGE 32' X 24'

PORCH

Optional Basement Level Floor Plan

BED RM 12' X 12'

BED RM 14' X 15'

FAMILY RM 23' X 19'

BATH

BED RM 15' X 12'

HALL

MECH 17' X 13'

MUSIC 9' X 13'

Copyright by designer/architect.

Plan #391019

Dimensions: 56' W x 32' D
Levels: 1
Square Footage: 1,792
Bedrooms: 3
Bathrooms: 1¾
Foundation: Basement
Materials List Available: Yes
Price Category: C

Images provided by designer/architect.

This southern-style cottage with sociable porch fits in almost anywhere, from a leafy lane to hillside or curbside and renders a lot of living space and hospitality.

Features:

- Family Room: This room features a central stone fireplace, plus two walls of windows to usher in the light. Sloping ceilings and decorative beams boost its rustic charm. An enormously generous space, it opens wide to the corner kitchen.

- Dining Room: This room has its own level of sophistication, including entry outside to the deck.

- Utility Areas: The family-sized pantry and laundry area are set off by themselves to avoid interference with everyday living.

- Master Suite: A leisurely hall leads to the master bedroom and private full bath, wide walk-in closets, and a trio of windows.

- Bedrooms: Across the hall the two secondary bedrooms share a roomy bath and a view of the front porch.

Side/Rear View

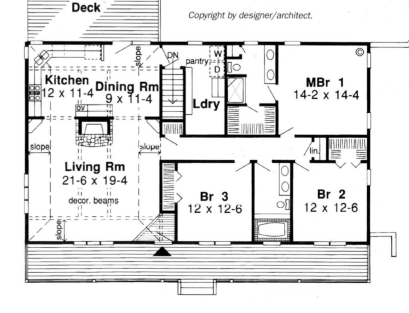

Copyright by designer/architect.

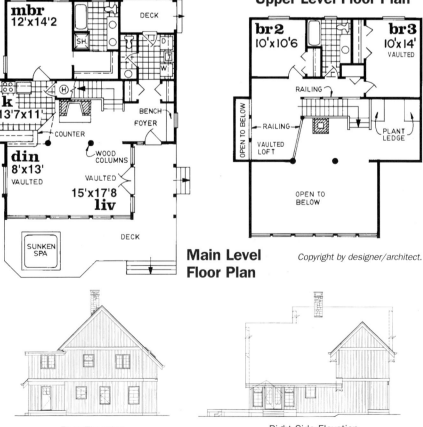

Images provided by designer/architect.

Plan #401030

Dimensions: 36' W x 40' D
Levels: 1½
Square Footage: 1,795
Main Level Sq. Ft.: 1,157
Upper Level Sq. Ft.: 638
Bedrooms: 3
Bathrooms: 2½
Foundation: Crawl space
Materials List Available: Yes
Price Category: C

A sun deck is what makes this design so popular, but it is enhanced by views through an expansive wall of glass in the living and dining rooms.

Features:

- **Living Room:** Both this room and the dining room are warmed by a woodstove and enjoy vaulted ceilings.

- **Kitchen:** This area has a vaulted ceiling and a food-preparation island and breakfast bar. Behind the kitchen is a laundry room with side access.

- **Master Bedroom:** This master bedroom and its walk-in closet and private bath are conveniently located on the first floor.

- **Bedrooms:** Two bedrooms and a full bath room are found on the second floor.

Upper Level Floor Plan

br2 10'x10'6
br3 10'x14' VAULTED
RAILING
RAILING
OPEN TO BELOW
VAULTED LOFT
PLANT LEDGE
OPEN TO BELOW

Main Level Floor Plan

Copyright by designer/architect.

mbr 12'x14'2
DECK
SH.
D
W
k 13'7"x11'
H
BENCH FOYER
COUNTER
WOOD COLUMNS
din 8'x13' VAULTED
VAULTED
15'x17'8 liv
SUNKEN SPA
DECK

Left Side Elevation

Rear Elevation

Right Side Elevation

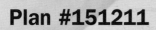

Images provided by designer/architect.

Plan #151211

Dimensions: 58' W x 71'8" D

Levels: 1

Square Footage: 1,797

Bedrooms: 3

Bathrooms: 2

Foundation: Crawl space or slab (basement for fee)

Materials List Available: No

Price Category: C

This three-bedroom brick home was designed with the family in mind.

Features:

- Great Room: This large space, with a fireplace, will provide the perfect setting for movie night.

- Kitchen: Enjoy meals in your breakfast or dining room—or quick snacks at the bar in this kitchen.

- Master Suite: Retiring to this suite is truly a luxury in itself. A 10-ft. boxed ceiling enhances the generous bedroom, while the bathroom includes a glass shower and whirlpool tub.

- Bedrooms: These two additional bedrooms, which share a full bathroom, round out the lovely design.

Copyright by designer/architect.

Plan #351036

Dimensions: 78' W x 46' D
Levels: 1
Square Footage: 1,799
Bedrooms: 3
Bathrooms: 2½
Foundation: Crawl space or slab
Materials List Available: Yes
Price Category: D

This beautifully styled home has everything your family needs.

Features:

- Great Room: There is cozy fireplace in the corner of this room, plus a view out to the grilling porch.

- Kitchen: This country kitchen with island and raised bar will keep family and friends close but out of the work triangle.

- Master Suite: This suite is well appointed with a jetted tub, dual vanities, a separate walk-in shower, and large closets.

- Bonus Room: This optional bonus room over the garage may serve as a fourth bedroom, game room, or office.

Images provided by designer/architect.

Optional Bonus Area Floor Plan

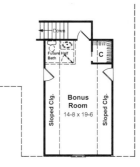

Copyright by designer/architect.

Rear View

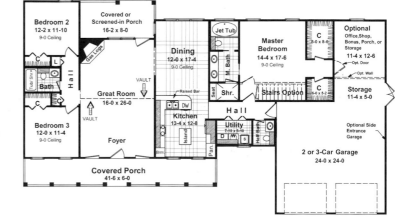

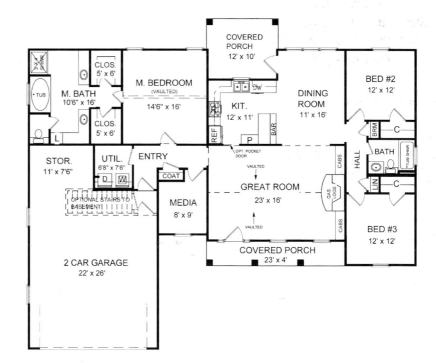

Plan #351038

Dimensions: 65' W x 50' D
Levels: 1
Square Footage: 1,800
Bedrooms: 3
Bathrooms: 2
Foundation: Crawl space, slab, or basement
Materials List Available: Yes
Price Category: D

Images provided by designer/architect.

This elegant brick home has an excellent floor plan.

Features:

• **Great Room:** This entertainment area, with a vaulted ceiling, has a gas fireplace flanked by built-in cabinets.

• **Media Room:** This all-purpose room may be used for home schooling or as a computer center, nursery, or hobbies area.

• **Master Suite:** This impressive area features a vaulted ceiling, his and her closets, a jetted tub, a walk-in shower, and a makeup area.

• **Bedrooms:** Two secondary bedrooms, located on the opposite side of the home from the master suite, share a common bathroom.

• **Garage:** This large garage is great storage for four-wheeler ATVs, bikes, lawn mowers, and perhaps a golf cart.

Copyright by designer/architect.

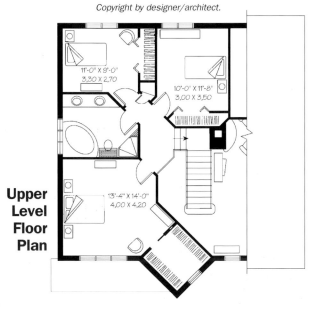

Plan #181222

Dimensions: 34'8" W x 39'4" D
Levels: 2
Square Footage: 1,670
Main Level Sq. Ft.: 935
Upper Level Sq. Ft.: 735
Bedrooms: 3
Bathrooms: 1½
Foundation: Basement
Materials List Available: Yes
Price Category: C

Images provided by designer/architect.

Contemporary chic starts here, with a shed roof and geometric exterior detailing.

Features:

• Entry: This unusual entry, with its sidelight windows, introduces an open L-shaped layout for new-age living.

• Family Room: This elongated gathering area, with a fireplace, is a highly versatile space for entertaining.

• Dining Room: This central dining area makes entertaining easy, with smooth access to both the living room and the kitchen.

• Closets: The master bedroom features a massive walk-in closet, and the two secondary bedrooms have wall-length closets.

Copyright by designer/architect.

Main Level Floor Plan

12'-4" X 12'-8"
3,70 X 3,80

12'-0" X 12'-8"
3,60 X 3,80

13'-0" X 22'-8"
3,90 X 6,80

12'-0" X 20'-0"
3,60 X 6,00

Upper Level Floor Plan

11'-0" X 9'-0"
3,30 X 2,70

10'-0" X 11'-8"
3,00 X 3,50

13'-4" X 14'-0"
4,00 X 4,20

order direct: 1-800-523-6789

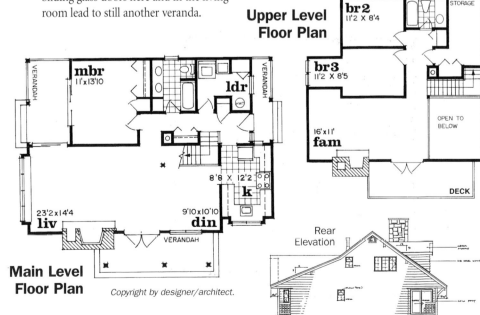

Plan #401006

Dimensions: 43' W x 35'4" D
Levels: 1½
Square Footage: 1,670
Main Level Sq.Ft.: 1,094
Upper Level Sq.Ft.: 576
Bedrooms: 3
Bathrooms: 2
Foundation: Crawl space
Materials List Available: Yes
Price Category: C

Images provided by designer/architect.

This vacation cottage's covered veranda (with a covered patio above) leads to French doors, which open to the living/dining area.

Features:

- **Living/Dining Area:** A masonry fireplace with a wood storage bin warms these rooms.
- **Kitchen:** This modified U-shaped kitchen serves the dining room; a laundry is just across the hall with access to a side veranda.
- **Master Bedroom:** Located on the first floor, this main bedroom has the use of a full bath. Sliding glass doors here and in the living room lead to still another veranda.
- **Family Room:** Located upstairs, this room has a fireplace, double doors to a deck, and a balcony overlooking the living and dining rooms. A large storage area on this level adds convenience.
- **Bedrooms:** The second floor also has two family bedrooms and a full bath.

Right Side Elevation

Left Side Elevation

Main Level Floor Plan

Copyright by designer/architect.

Upper Level Floor Plan

Rear Elevation

Plan #371011

Dimensions: 55'4" W x 49'10" D

Levels: 1

Square Footage: 1,681

Bedrooms: 3

Bathrooms: 2½

Foundation: Slab

Materials List Available: No

Price Category: C

Images provided by designer/architect.

Copyright by designer/architect.

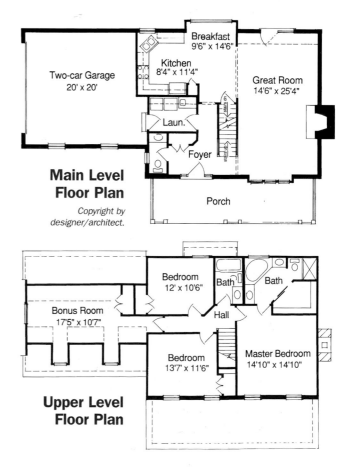

Plan #161024

Dimensions: 54'4" W x 26'8" D

Levels: 2

Square Footage: 1,698

Main Level Sq. Ft.: 868

Upper Level Sq. Ft.: 830

Bonus Space Sq. Ft.: 269

Bedrooms: 3

Bathrooms: 2½

Foundation: Basement

Materials List Available: No

Price Category: C

Images provided by designer/architect.

This home, as shown in the photograph, may differ from the actual blueprints. For more detailed information, please check the floor plans carefully.

Main Level Floor Plan

Copyright by designer/architect.

Upper Level Floor Plan

Plan #351035

Dimensions: 65' W x 41' D

Levels: 1

Square Footage: 1,701

Bedrooms: 3

Bathrooms: 2

Foundation: Crawl space or slab

Materials List Available: Yes

Price Category: C

Images provided by designer/architect.

Copyright by designer/architect.

Plan #131002

Dimensions: 70'1" W x 60'7" D

Levels: 1

Square Footage: 1,709

Bedrooms: 3

Bathrooms: 2½

Foundation: Crawl space, slab, or basement

Materials List Available: Yes

Price Category: D

Images provided by designer/architect.

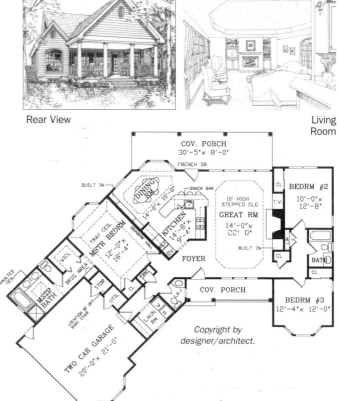

Rear View

Living Room

Copyright by designer/architect.

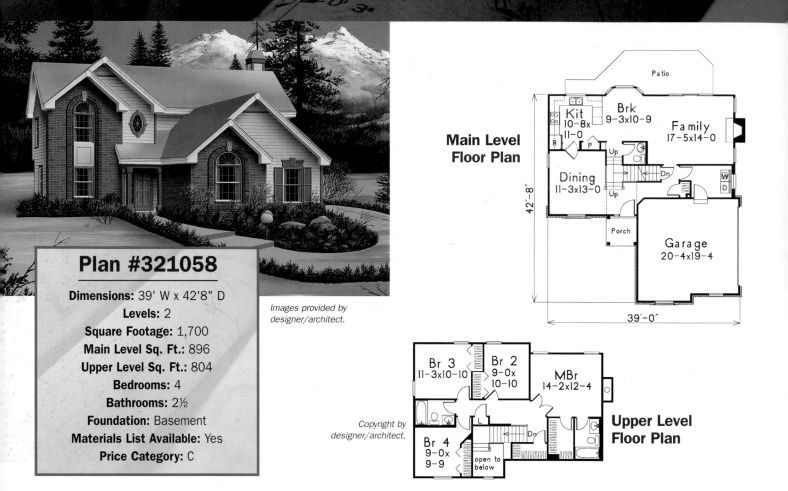

Main Level Floor Plan

Patio

Brk
9–3x10–9

Kit
10–8x
11–0

Family
17–5x14–0

Dining
11–3x13–0

Up
Dn
Up

W D

Porch

Garage
20–4x19–4

42'–8"

39'–0"

Images provided by designer/architect.

Br 3
11–3x10–10

Br 2
9–0x
10–10

MBr
14–2x12–4

Copyright by designer/architect.

Br 4
9–0x
9–9

open to below

Dn

Upper Level Floor Plan

Plan #321058

Dimensions: 39' W x 42'8" D
Levels: 2
Square Footage: 1,700
Main Level Sq. Ft.: 896
Upper Level Sq. Ft.: 804
Bedrooms: 4
Bathrooms: 2½
Foundation: Basement
Materials List Available: Yes
Price Category: C

Images provided by designer/architect.

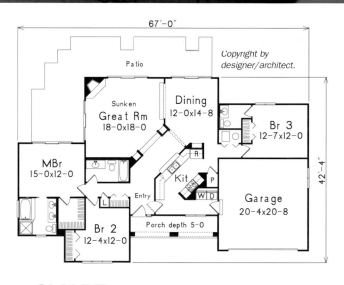

67'–0"

Copyright by designer/architect.

Patio

Sunken
Great Rm
18–0x18–0

Dining
12–0x14–8

Br 3
12–7x12–0

MBr
15–0x12–0

Kit

R

Entry

W D

Garage
20–4x20–8

Br 2
12–4x12–0

Porch depth 5–0

L

42'–4"

Plan #321026

Dimensions: 67' W x 42'4" D
Levels: 1
Square Footage: 1,712
Bedrooms: 3
Bathrooms: 2½
Foundation: Crawl space
Materials List Available: Yes
Price Category: C

SMARTtip

Deck Design with Computers

Consider using a computer-aided design (CAD) program to plan your deck. Some programs let you see three-dimensional views of your design complete with railings, stairs, planters, hot tubs, and the surrounding landscaping.

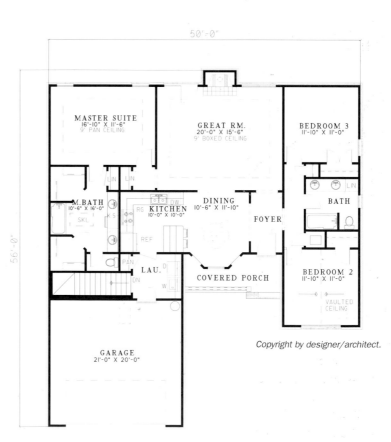

Plan #151037

Dimensions: 50' W x 56' D
Levels: 1
Square Footage: 1,538
Bedrooms: 3
Bathrooms: 2
Foundation: Crawl space, slab, or basement
Materials List Available: No
Price Category: C

Images provided by designer/architect.

You'll love this traditional-looking home, with its covered porch and interesting front windows.

Features:

- Ceiling Height: 8 ft.

- Great Room: This large room has a boxed window that emphasizes its dimensions and a fireplace where everyone will gather on chilly evenings. A door opens to the backyard.

- Dining Room: A bay window overlooking the front porch makes this room easy to decorate.

- Kitchen: This well-planned kitchen features ample counter space, a full pantry, and an eating bar that it shares with the dining room.

- Master Suite: A pan ceiling in this lovely room gives an elegant touch. The huge private bath includes two walk-in closets, a whirlpool tub, a dual-sink vanity, and a skylight in the ceiling.

- Additional Bedrooms: On the opposite side of the house, these bedrooms share a large bath, and both feature excellent closet space.

Copyright by designer/architect.

Outdoor Living

Many homeowners treat their decks and patios as another room of the house. To gain the fullest use of these areas, homeowners often add cooking areas, outdoor lighting centers, and other features to their outdoor living areas.

Cooking Centers

As the trend toward outdoor entertaining gains popularity, many people are setting up complete, permanent outdoor cooking centers, which often become the focus of their decks. Others content themselves with a simple grill. In either case, practical planning makes outdoor cooking efficient and more enjoyable, whether it is for everyday family meals or for a host of guests.

Decide exactly what features you want in the outdoor kitchen area. If you prefer to keep it simple with just a grill, you'll still have some decisions to make. Do you want a charcoal, gas, or electric unit? A charcoal grill is the least expensive option; a natural gas grill will cost you the most because it must be professionally installed. (Check with your local building department beforehand. Some localities will require a permit or may not allow this installation.) Extra features and accessories, such as rotisseries, woks, burners, smoke ovens, and warming racks increase the cost, too. Just remember: if you intend to locate the grill in a wooden enclosure, choose a model designed for this application.

In addition to a grill, do you want an elaborate setup with a sink, countertop, or a refrigerator? If so, these amenities will need protection from the elements. However, some refrigerators designed specifically for outdoor use can withstand harsh weather conditions. These high-end units are vented from the front and can be built-in or freestanding on casters.

Typically, outdoor refrigerators are countertop height (often the same size as standard wine chilling units that mount underneath a kitchen countertop) and have shelving for food trays or drinks and indoor storage for condiments. Outdoor refrigerators intended strictly for cold beer storage come with a tap and can accommodate a half-keg.

More Entertainment Options

Do you entertain frequently? Think about including a custom-designed wet bar and countertop in your plans. Besides a sink, the unit can offer enclosed storage for beverages, ice, and glasses, and the countertop will be handy for serving or buffets. But if you can't handle the expense, consider a prefabricated open-air wet bar. It can be portable or built-in. Some portable wet-bars feature: a sink that you can hook up to the house plumbing or a garden hose (with a filter), ice bins with sliding lids, sectioned compartments for garnishes, a speed rail for bottles, and a beverage-chilling well. Deluxe models may come with extra shelves and side-mounted food warmers.

Practical Advantages

Integrating a cooking center with your deck provides easy access to the kitchen indoors. Remember, elaborate outdoor kitchens require gas, electricity, and plumbing; it is easier and less expensive to run those lines when the cooking area isn't at the other end of the yard. However, you'll have to carefully plan the cooktop so that it isn't too close to the house and so that the heat and smoke are directed away from seating areas.

In general, when arranging any outdoor cooking area, be sure that all accouterments—including serving platters, insulated mitts, basting brushes, spatulas, forks and knives, and long-handled tongs—are

readily at hand for the cook. And don't forget to plan enough surface room for setting down a tray of spices, condiments, sauces, and marinade or swiftly unloading a plate of hot grilled meats or vegetables. Because you'll have to juggle both uncooked and cooked foods, a roll-around cart may suffice. For safety's sake, always keep the pathway from the kitchen to the outdoor cooking area clear, and as a precaution, keep a fire extinguisher nearby.

Countertop Options

Any outdoor countertop should be able to withstand varying weather conditions. Rain, snow, and bright sunlight will pit and rot some materials, so choose carefully. Tile, concrete, or natural stone (such as slate) are the best options. Concrete can be tinted and inlaid for decorative effect but, like stone, it is porous and must be sealed. Avoid a surface laminate unless it's for use in a well-protected area because exposure to the weather causes the layers to separate. Solid-surfacing material is more durable, but it's better left to a sheltered location.

Think twice about using teak or other decay-resistant woods for a countertop. Although these woods weather handsomely, they are not sealed against bacteria, so you can't expose them directly to food. If you do select a wooden countertop, insert a tray or plate under any uncooked meats and vegetables. Decay-resistant woods such as redwood, cedar, teak, or mahogany are, however, good choices for outdoor cabinetry. Other types of wood will have to be sealed and stained or painted. Another option is oriented-strand board (OSB) that is weatherproof.

Side burners, opposite, help you prepare an entire meal at the grill.

Small, outdoor refrigerators, far right, save steps when entertaining outdoors.

What to Look for in a Grill

A grill cover should fit snugly. Some covers have adjustable lids, which allow airflow so that food cooks slowly and evenly.

Adjustable controls allow you to control the heat level of burners.

Side burners let you sauté toppings, simmer sauces, or fry side dishes. A side burner can come with a protective cover that also doubles as an extra landing surface for utensils.

A towel hook is a useful detail on a grill. Check for other extras, such as utility hooks for utensils, condiment compartments on side shelves, or warming racks.

Casters make the grill portable so that it is easy to reposition at your convenience. Keep in mind that a large stainless-steel grill can be as heavy as 230 pounds.

Grill Checklist

Look for these important features:

■ **An electronic push-button ignition.** It starts better because it emits a continuous spark; knob igniters emit two to three sparks per turn.

■ **Insulated handles.** These are convenient because they don't get hot. Otherwise you'll need a grilling mitt to protect yourself from burns when using the controls.

■ **Easy access to the propane tank.** Some gas grills feature tilt-out bins, which make connecting and changing the tank a snap.

Large grills, left, offer multiple, individually controlled burners, warming trays, and storage.

Outdoor Lighting

In terms of lighting and electricity, a deck can be as fully functional as any room inside your house. And if you add outdoor lighting, you will find that you get much more use out of your deck, patio, or outdoor living area. In addition to natural light, a pleasing combination of even, diffused general (also called "ambient") light, as well as accent and task lighting from artificial sources, can illuminate your deck for use after the sun goes down.

Developing an outdoor lighting plans differs from developing an interior lighting scheme. The basics are the same, but exterior lighting relies heavily on low-voltage systems. These operate on 12 volts as opposed to the 120 volts of a standard line system. A good outdoor plan will combine both types of lighting.

Developing a Lighting Planning

First decide how much light you need and where it should go. Besides general overall illumination, locate fixtures near activity zones: the food preparation and cooking area, the wet bar, or wherever you plan to set up drinks, snacks, or a buffet when you entertain. Be sure that there is adequate light near the dining table, conversation areas, and recreational spots, such as the hot tub, if you plan to use them in the evening. You may want separate switches for each one, and you might consider dimmers; you don't need or want the same intensity of light required for barbecuing as you do for relaxing in the hot tub.

What type of fixtures should you choose? That partly depends on the location. Near a wall or under a permanent roof, sconces and ceiling fixtures will provide light while staying out of the way. For uncovered areas, try post or railing lamps.

Lighting the Way

Walkways and staircases need lighting for safety. There are a number of practical options: path lights (if the walkway is ground level), brick lights that can be inserted into your walls near the steps, and railing fixtures that can be tucked under

Selecting a Grill

It's not the size of the grill that counts; it's whether you have the space on the deck to accommodate it. Measure the intended cooking area before shopping, and take those measurements with you to the store or home center. Depending upon your budget, you may also want to consider one of the high-end units that luxury kitchen appliance manufacturers have introduced into the marketplace. They have lots of features and are built to last, but they are expensive and must be professionally installed. Serious cooks like them.

Think about the grill's location in relationship to the traffic, dining, and lounging zones. How far away will the grill be from the house? If your space is limited or if you expect a lot of activity—large crowds or kids underfoot—you may have to relegate the cooking area to someplace close, but not on the deck itself. Also consider how many people you typically cook for. Check out the grill's number of separate heating zones (there should be at least two) before buying it. If you have a large family or entertain frequently, you'll need a grill that can accommodate large quantities or different types of food at the same time.

Grill Features

Because you'll probably be using your new grill more often and with a greater variety of foods, buy one that has some important basic options. Are there any special features that you'd like with your grill? Extra burners, a rotisserie, a warming rack, or a smoker? What do you like to cook? Today, you can prepare more than hamburgers and barbecued chicken on your grill. In fact, tasty, healthy grilled food is popular year-round, and so you may be cooking outdoors from spring through late fall.

Many models now come with two burners, but larger ones have more. The burners should have adjustable temperature controls that will allow you to set the heat at high, medium, or low. Ideally, a unit should sustain an even cooking temperature and provide at least 33,000 Btu (British thermal units, the measurement for heat output) when burners are set on high. Generally, the larger the grill the higher the Btu output. A slow-roasting setting is optional on some models. Another good option is gauge that records the temperature when the lid is closed. If you enjoy sauces, make sure your grill comes with adjustable side burners, which can accommodate pots.

deck railings or steps. Less-functional but more-decorative lighting such as post lamps can provide illumination for high traffic areas; sconces can be effective on stair landings or near doors. Walk lights also provide a needed measure of safety.

Don't forget about areas that may call for motion-sensitive floodlights, such as entrances into the house and garage, underneath a raised deck, and deep yards are all excellent locations for floodlights. Keep these fixtures on separate switches so that they don't interfere with the atmosphere you want to create while you are using the deck.

Railing- and bench-mounted lights, above, provide a subtle lighting option. They illuminate small areas without casting glare into the eyes of those on the deck.

Step lights, right, are a must for stairs leading down into the yard. Use these lights sparingly as shown. A little outdoor light goes a long way.

Provide a lighted backdrop to your outdoor living area by installing yard and garden lighting, above. Use lights to line walks, accent flower beds, or highlight a fountain or pond.

Adding Accent Light

Are there any noteworthy plantings or objects in your garden that you can highlight? By using in-ground accent lighting or spotlights, you can create dramatic nighttime effects or a focal point. Artful lighting can enhance the ambience of your deck by drawing attention to the shape of a handsome tree, a garden statue, a fountain or pond, or an outdoor pool.

Choosing the Right Fixture

If your home is formal, traditional fixtures in brass or an antique finish will complement the overall scheme nicely. For a modern setting, choose streamlined fixtures with matte or brushed-metal finishes. Landscape lighting is often utilitarian, but it is intended to blend unobtrusively into the landscape; the light, not the fixture, is noticeable. Path and post lighting, however, can be decorative and comes in a variety of styles and finishes, from highly polished metals to antique and matte looks.

Depending on the lighting system you buy, you may be able to install the fixtures yourself. But working with electricity does pose technical, code, and safety concerns. It's probably best to hire a qualified professional for the installation. For complex projects, you may also want to consult a landscape lighting professional. Home centers sometimes provide this type of expertise. If you decide to plot a design yourself, remember not to overlight the deck.

Other Considerations

As you plan to install deck lighting, think about the space's other electrical or wiring needs. If there is an outdoor kitchen, a grill area, or a bar, you may want outlets for a refrigerator or small appliances. You might include additional outlets for a stereo or speakers, or even a TV. Don't overlook a phone jack for the modem on your laptop computer. Some decking systems come prewired and are ready to be hooked up. So with forethought, you can incorporate everything you need into your outdoor living plans.

Water Features

There is nothing like the sight and sound of water to add a refreshing quality to your deck or patio. In fact, water can be a dynamic element in both the deck's design and its function. It can be in the form of one of the ultimate outdoor luxuries—a pool, spa, or hot tub—or in a water feature such as a fountain, waterfall, or pond. In any case, because of the relaxing qualities of water, you should consider integrating some form of it into your plans.

Planning a deck or patio near a pool requires taking the size and shape of the pool into consideration. In most cases, the pool will be a focal point in a landscape, so the design of the surrounding deck, including the flooring patterns, materials, and other details, can either enhance or detract from its appeal. Aside from looks, think about how a pool deck will function.

Adding a Spa. Another way to enjoy water with your deck is with a soothing spa. Requiring less space than a pool, a spa uses hydrojets to move heated water. One type, a hot tub, is a barrel-like enclosure filled with water. It may or may not have jets and usually features an adjustable but simple bench. It offers a deeper soak—as much as 4 feet—than other types of spas, and many homeowners like the look of an aboveground hot tub's wood exterior. The tub comes with a vinyl or plastic liner.

A built-in spa is set into a deck or the ground (in-ground). It can be acrylic, or it can be constructed of poured concrete, gunite, or shotcrete. A spa can stand alone or be integrated with a large pool.

A portable spa is a completely self-contained unit that features an acrylic shell, a wooden surround, and all of the equipment needed to heat and move the water. A small portable spa costs less than an in-ground unit, and it runs on a standard 120-volt circuit. You can locate a portable spa on a concrete slab. But you can also install one on the deck. Just make sure there is proper structural support underneath the deck to sustain the additional weight of the unit, the water, and bathers.

Small, portable spas, opposite, are self-contained units that run on standard line-voltage electricity. Check weight restrictions if installing a spa on a deck.

Spas complete an outdoor living area, above. This sunken spa is a natural complement to the nearby pool and to the large multilevel deck.

Plan #151245

Dimensions: 35' W x 80'6" D
Levels: 1
Square Footage: 1,923
Bedrooms: 3
Bathrooms: 2
Foundation: Crawl space or slab
Materials List Available: No
Price Category: D

This brick home, with a stone-and-wood-sided front elevation, has great styling and offers three bedrooms.

Features:

- Entry: You enter the home though an arched covered entry foyer. On the left, French doors open to bedroom 3. Across the hall is bedroom 2, with a large walk-in closet.

- Great Room: This large gathering area, with a 10-ft. boxed ceiling, features a fireplace and access to the grilling porch.

- Kitchen: This kitchen boasts a snack bar and walk-in pantry and is open to the dining room.

- Master Suite: This private area has a 10-ft. boxed ceiling and ample closet storage. The master bath features a corner whirlpool tub with glass blocks, split vanities, and a corner shower.

Copyright by designer/architect.

Main Level Floor Plan

Deck

Dining 10x11

Kitchen

Brkfst 8x11

Family 15x11-6

Pantry

DN

M W D

Living 13-10x14-6

UP

3 Car Garage 30-4x21

Images provided by designer/architect.

Upper Level Floor Plan

Br 4 10-4x10

Br 3 11x10

DN

Mas. Suite 14x15-6 11-6 vaulted clg

open to below

Br 2 12-8x10

High Glass above

Plan #271038

Dimensions: 60' W x 35'4" D
Levels: 2
Square Footage: 1,820
Main Level Sq. Ft.: 987
Upper Level Sq. Ft.: 833
Bedrooms: 4
Bathrooms: 2½
Foundation: Basement
Materials List Available: No
Price Category: D

Plan #301005

Dimensions: 71' W x 42' D
Levels: 1
Square Footage: 1,930
Bedrooms: 3
Bathrooms: 2
Foundation: Crawl space, slab
Materials List Available: Yes
Price Category: D

Images provided by designer/architect.

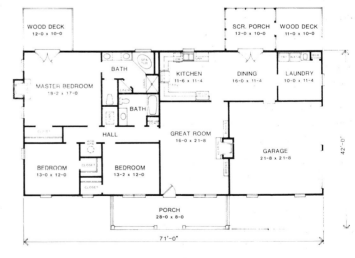

WOOD DECK 12-0 x 10-0

SCR. PORCH 12-0 x 10-0

WOOD DECK 11-0 x 10-0

BATH

KITCHEN 11-6 x 11-4

DINING 16-0 x 11-4

LAUNDRY 10-0 x 11-4

MASTER BEDROOM 18-2 x 17-0

BATH

GREAT ROOM 16-0 x 21-8

GARAGE 21-8 x 21-8

HALL

BEDROOM 13-0 x 12-0

BEDROOM 13-2 x 12-0

PORCH 28-0 x 8-0

71'-0"

42'-0"

Copyright by designer/architect.

Plan #351001

Dimensions: 78'8" W x 51' D

Levels: 1

Square Footage: 1,855

Bedrooms: 3

Bathrooms: 2½

Foundation: Crawl space, slab, or basement

Materials List Available: Yes

Price Category: D

From the lovely arched windows on the front to the front and back covered porches, this home is as comfortable as it is beautiful.

Features:

- **Great Room:** Come into this room with 12-ft. ceilings, and you're sure to admire the corner gas fireplace and three windows overlooking the porch.

- **Dining Room:** Set off from the open design, this room is designed to be used formally or not.

- **Kitchen:** You'll love the practical walk-in pantry, broom closet, and angled snack bar here.

- **Breakfast Room:** Brightly lit and leading to the covered porch, this room will be a favorite spot.

- **Bonus Room:** Develop a playroom or study in this area.

- **Master Suite:** The large bedroom is complemented by the private bath with garden tub, separate shower, double vanity, and spacious walk-in closet.

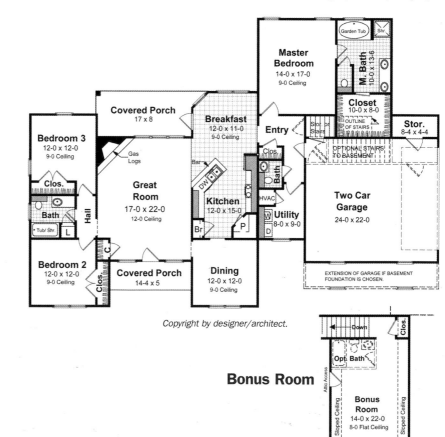

Bonus Room

Great Room

Kitchen/Great Room

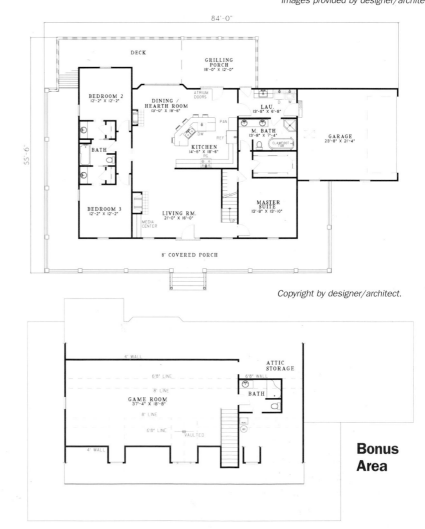

Plan #151089

Dimensions: 84' W x 55'6" D
Levels: 1
Square Footage: 1,921
Bedrooms: 3
Bathrooms: 3
Foundation: Crawl space, slab, or basement
Materials List Available: No
Price Category: D

Images provided by designer/architect.

Copyright by designer/architect.

Bonus Area

If your family loves to combine indoor and outdoor living, this home's fabulous porches and deck space make it perfect.

Features:

- Porches: A huge wraparound front porch, sizable rear porch, and deck that joins them give you space for entertaining or simply lounging.

- Living Room: A fireplace and built-in media center could be the focal points in this large room.

- Hearth Room: Open to both the living room and kitchen, this hearth room also features a fireplace.

- Kitchen: This step-saving kitchen includes ample storage and work space, as well as an angled bar it shares with the hearth room. Atrium doors lead to the rear porch.

- Bonus Upper Level: A large game room and a full bath make this area a favorite with the children.

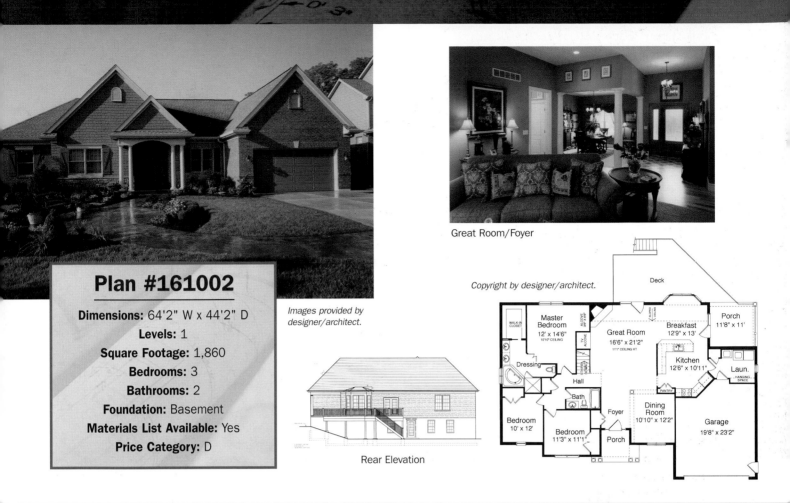

Great Room/Foyer

Images provided by designer/architect.

Copyright by designer/architect.

Rear Elevation

Plan #161002

Dimensions: 64'2" W x 44'2" D
Levels: 1
Square Footage: 1,860
Bedrooms: 3
Bathrooms: 2
Foundation: Basement
Materials List Available: Yes
Price Category: D

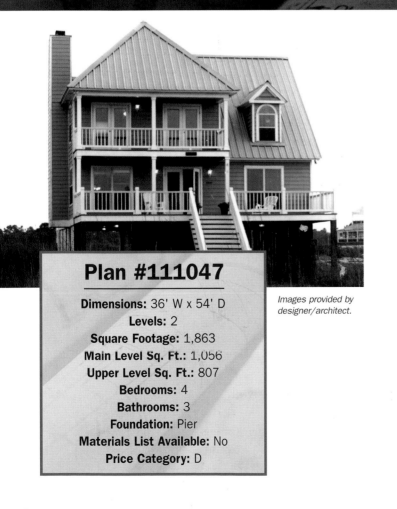

Images provided by designer/architect.

Plan #111047

Dimensions: 36' W x 54' D
Levels: 2
Square Footage: 1,863
Main Level Sq. Ft.: 1,056
Upper Level Sq. Ft.: 807
Bedrooms: 4
Bathrooms: 3
Foundation: Pier
Materials List Available: No
Price Category: D

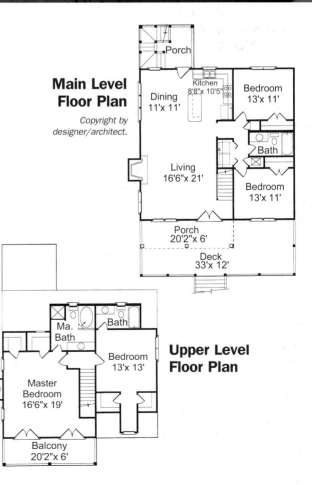

Main Level Floor Plan

Copyright by designer/architect.

Upper Level Floor Plan

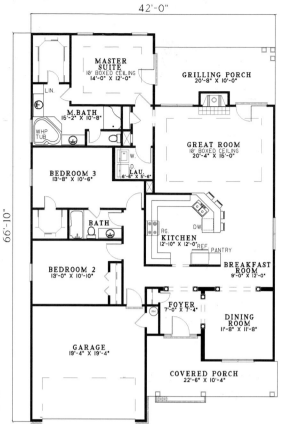

Plan #151008

Dimensions: 42' W x 66'10" D

Levels: 1

Square Footage: 1,892

Bedrooms: 3

Bathrooms: 2

Foundation: Crawl space, slab, basement, or daylight basement

Materials List Available: No

Price Category: D

Images provided by designer/architect.

This home, as shown in the photograph, may differ from the actual blueprints. For more detailed information, please check the floor plans carefully.

Copyright by designer/architect.

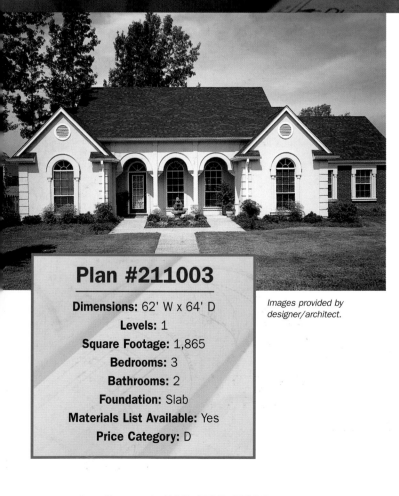

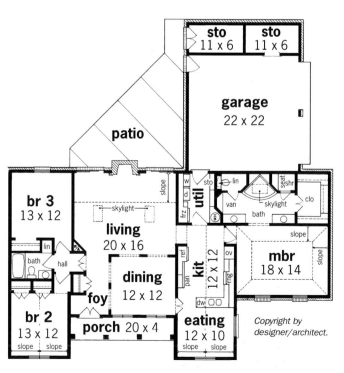

Plan #211003

Dimensions: 62' W x 64' D

Levels: 1

Square Footage: 1,865

Bedrooms: 3

Bathrooms: 2

Foundation: Slab

Materials List Available: Yes

Price Category: D

Images provided by designer/architect.

Copyright by designer/architect.

Plan #321012

Dimensions: 58'8" W x 51'2" D

Levels: 1

Square Footage: 1,882

Bedrooms: 3

Bathrooms: 2

Foundation: Basement

Materials List Available: Yes

Price Category: D

Images provided by designer/architect.

Copyright by designer/architect.

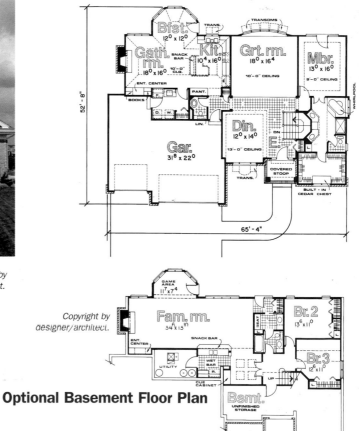

Plan #121092

Dimensions: 65'4" W x 52'8" D

Levels: 1

Square Footage: 1,887

Bedrooms: 3

Bathrooms: 2½

Foundation: Basement

Materials List Available: Yes

Price Category: D

Images provided by designer/architect.

Copyright by designer/architect.

Optional Basement Floor Plan

Plan #121051

Dimensions: 64' W x 44' D
Levels: 1
Square Footage: 1,808
Bedrooms: 3
Bathrooms: 2½
Foundation: Basement
Materials List Available: Yes
Price Category: D

Images provided by designer/architect.

Copyright by designer/architect.

Plan #121064

Dimensions: 44' W x 40' D
Levels: 2
Square Footage: 1,846
Main Level Sq. Ft.: 919
Upper Level Sq. Ft.: 927
Bedrooms: 4
Bathrooms: 2½
Foundation: Basement
Materials List Available: Yes
Price Category: D

Images provided by designer/architect.

Main Level Floor Plan

Upper Level Floor Plan

Copyright by designer/architect.

Plan #391013

Dimensions: 52' W x 41'4" D
Levels: 2
Square Footage: 1,894
Main Level Sq. Ft.: 1,108
Upper Level Sq. Ft.: 786
Bedrooms: 3
Bathrooms: 2½
Foundation: Crawl space, slab, or basement
Materials List Available: Yes
Price Category: D

This home hints at Tudor lineage, with its rising half-timber-effects and peaked roofline. Inside, it's a different, more contemporary story.

Features:

• Living Room. The foyer opens to this room, which basks in the light of a two-story arched window. Even the open dining room enjoys the brightness.

• Family Room: This room warms up with a fireplace, plus a built-in desk, wet bar, and entry to an outdoor deck.

Rear View

Images provided by designer/architect.

• Kitchen: The angular plan of this room, with a convenient pass-through to the dining area, features a picture window with built-in seat for taking time to meditate. Excellent shelving, storage, half-bath, and hall coat closet offer behind-the-scenes support.

• Bedrooms: Bedroom 2 looks over the front yard and shares a bath with bedroom 3, which oversees the backyard.

Main Level Floor Plan

• Master Bedroom: The second level master bedroom overlooks the living room from a beautiful balcony. Double windows along one wall fill the area with natural light, and a windowed corner illuminates the master bath.

Copyright by designer/architect.

Upper Level Floor Plan

Optional Crawl Space/Slab Floor Plan

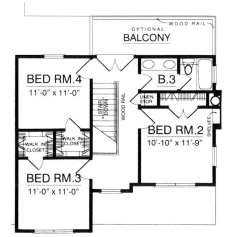

Images provided by designer/architect.

Plan #371038

Dimensions: 52'8" W x 44' D

Levels: 2

Square Footage: 1,896

Main Level Sq. Ft.: 1,253

Upper Level Sq. Ft.: 661

Bedrooms: 4

Bathrooms: 2½

Foundation: Crawl space or slab

Materials List Available: No

Price Category: D

This beautiful two-story country home has everything you need. You'll find attention to detail both inside and out.

Features:

• Living Room: This large gathering area boasts a cozy fireplace and a convenient media center for quiet family time.

• Kitchen: This spacious kitchen opens to the formal dining room at one end and a large breakfast nook at the other.

• Master Suite: This secluded area boasts a stepped-up ceiling and luxurious master bathroom with two walk-in closets and a marble tub.

• Bedrooms: Upstairs you will find three additional large bedrooms, which share a convenient hall bathroom.

Main Level Floor Plan

Copyright by designer/architect.

Upper Level Floor Plan

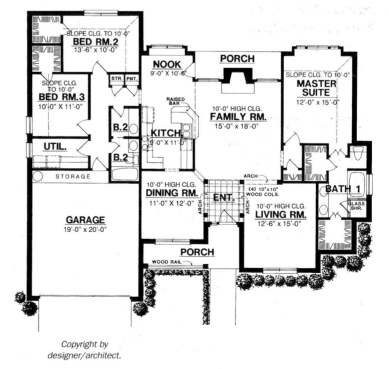

Plan #371039

Dimensions: 60'4" W x 51'4" D

Levels: 1

Square Footage: 1,898

Bedrooms: 3

Bathrooms: 2

Foundation: Slab

Materials List Available: No

Price Category: D

Images provided by designer/architect.

This charming traditional home has everything you need, from the beautifully styled windows to the spacious rooms inside.

Features:

- Living Room: This formal entertaining area, with a 12-ft.-high ceiling and wooden columns, opens into the family room.

- Family Room: A large casual room with a 10-ft.-high ceiling, this room has a cozy fireplace that makes it perfect for entertaining.

- Dining Room: This elegant room has a 10-ft.-high ceiling and wooden columns.

- Kitchen: The breakfast nook opens to this large, fully equipped kitchen, which has a raised bar that brings the nook and the family room together.

- Master Suite: This secluded suite boasts a luxurious bathroom with his and her vanities and two walk in closets.

- Bedrooms: The two secondary bedrooms with sloped ceilings and walk-in closets share a convenient bathroom with a separate dressing room.

Copyright by designer/architect.

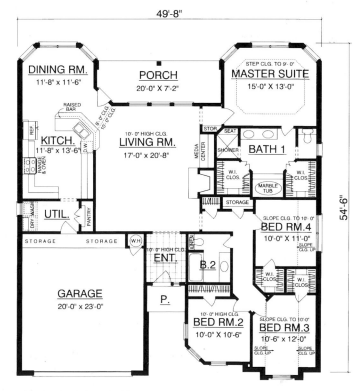

Plan #371075

Dimensions: 49'8" W x 54'6" D

Levels: 1

Square Footage: 1,904

Bedrooms: 4

Bathrooms: 2

Foundation: Crawl space or slab

Materials List Available: No

Price Category: E

This beautiful traditional brick home will make you feel right at home.

Features:

- **Living Room:** With high ceilings spelling luxury, this large entertaining area also has a media center, fireplace, and large window overlooking the back porch.

- **Kitchen:** This large gourmet kitchen has a raised bar that brings the dining area and living room together.

- **Master Suite:** With a stepped-up ceiling, this large, relaxing area boasts a luxurious master bathroom with his and her vanities, a marble tub, and two walk-in closets.

- **Bedrooms:** The additional three bedrooms, with walk-in closets, share a convenient hall bathroom.

Images provided by designer/architect.

Copyright by designer/architect.

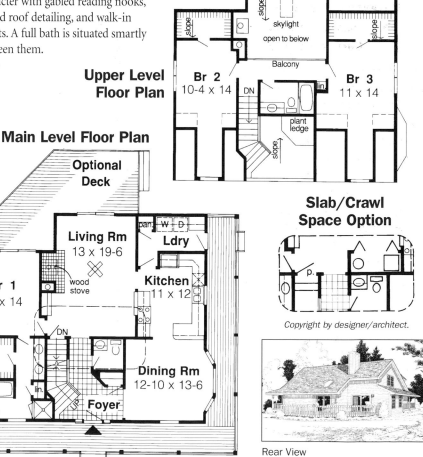

Plan #391003

Dimensions: 47' W x 39' D
Levels: 2
Square Footage: 1,907
Main Street Sq. Ft.: 1,269
Upper Street Sq. Ft.: 638
Bedrooms: 3
Bathrooms: 2½
Foundation: Crawl space, slab, or basement
Materials List Available: Yes
Price Category: D

A family-loving wraparound porch and the quaint clapboard exterior open to an interior that boasts current styling.

Features:

• Foyer: This light-filled two-story room evokes a special aura, with a high-perching ledge for growing plants or showcasing treasures.

• Living Room: The woodstove basks in light from the soaring sky-lit ceiling. Sliding doors go out to the deck or backyard.

• Kitchen: This room features a spacious back-room laundry area and a curved counter that also serves the dining room.

• Dining Room: A beautiful bay window illuminates this room.

• Master Suite: This main-floor suite enjoys sliders to the deck, plus generous windows even in the private bath.

• Bedrooms: Two secondary bedrooms embrace their own unique storybook character with gabled reading nooks, sloped roof detailing, and walk-in closets. A full bath is situated smartly between them.

Images provided by designer/architect.

Upper Level Floor Plan

slope
slope
slope
skylight
open to below
slope
Balcony
Br 2
10-4 x 14
DN
lin
Br 3
11 x 14
plant ledge
slope

Main Level Floor Plan

Optional Deck
Living Rm
13 x 19-6
Ldry
pan. W D
Kitchen
11 x 12
MBr 1
13-6 x 14
wood stove
DN
Dining Rm
12-10 x 13-6
lin
Foyer

Slab/Crawl Space Option

p.

Copyright by designer/architect.

Rear View

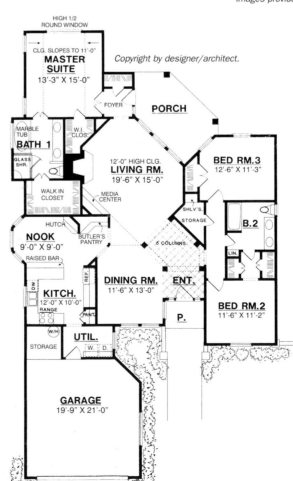

Plan #371014

Dimensions: 46' W x 70'10" D

Levels: 1

Square Footage: 1,908

Bedrooms: 3

Bathrooms: 2

Foundation: Slab

Materials List Available: No

Price Category: D

Images provided by designer/architect.

This elegant French-style stucco home will show off your good taste.

Features:

- **Living Room:** This large area has a 12-ft.-high ceiling with a media center and fireplace, which makes it great for entertaining.

- **Dining Room:** Elegant columns separate this formal room from the living room.

- **Kitchen:** This kitchen has a raised bar and a breakfast nook with a built-in hutch and butler's pantry.

- **Master Suite:** You'll find a luxurious bath room with a marble tub, a glass shower, a his-and-her vanity, and large walk in closets in this suite.

- **Bedrooms:** The two secondary bedrooms share a private bathroom.

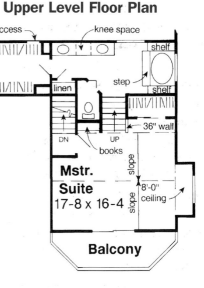

Plan #391022

Dimensions: 39' W x 48' D
Levels: 2
Square Footage: 1,908
Main Level Sq. Ft.: 1,316
Upper Level Sq. Ft.: 592
Bedrooms: 3
Bathrooms: 2
Foundation: Crawl space, slab, or basement
Materials List Available: Yes
Price Category: D

This home is made for today's environment-minded homeowners. Sun-loving walls of windows and effortless sliding doors to the outdoor deck seem to commune with nature while interior spaces seem to flow with each other.

Features:

• Kitchen: The dining room and this kitchen, a well-matched pair, open generously to the living room, with its sloped ceiling and far-reaching fireplace.

• Stairs: An abbreviated staircase tucks in two secondary bedrooms and a conveniently located laundry room. Ascend a second short set of steps for the master suite, which rivals most others.

• Master Suite: An entirely private level is devoted to this master retreat. A sloped ceiling, restful balcony, plus a spa-style step-up bathtub in the master bath showcase beauty and innovation.

Images provided by designer/architect.

• Storage: Excellent closeting and attic access are among many hardworking components of the home.

Rear View

Upper Level Floor Plan

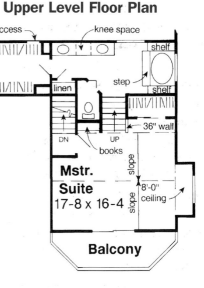

Copyright by designer/architect.

Main Level Floor Plan

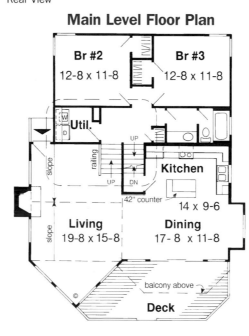

Pier/Crawl Space Option

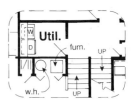

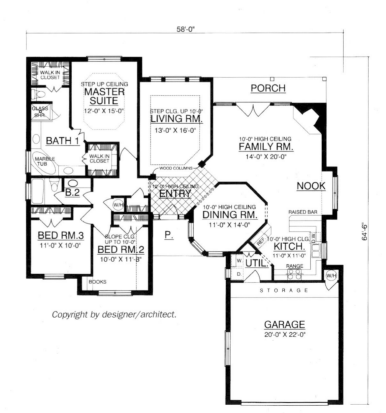

Plan #371040

Dimensions: 58' W x 64'6" D

Levels: 1

Square Footage: 1,913

Bedrooms: 3

Bathrooms: 2

Foundation: Slab

Materials List Available: No

Price Category: D

The beautiful front windows of this traditional brick home make it something special.

Features:

- Living Room: This formal room has a 10-ft.-high ceiling and wooden columns.

- Family Room: A 10-ft.-high ceiling and a cozy corner fireplace grace this large gathering a area.

- Dining Room: This formal dining room has a 10-ft.-high ceiling and easy access to the kitchen.

- Kitchen: This large kitchen has a raised bar and is open to the breakfast nook and family room.

- Master Suite: A large, restful oasis with a stepped-up ceiling, this suite boasts a luxurious master bathroom with a marble tub and two walk-in closets.

- Bedrooms: Two secondary bedrooms share a convenient hall bathroom.

Plan #121001

Dimensions: 56' W x 58' D

Levels: 1

Square Footage: 1,911

Bedrooms: 3

Bathrooms: 2

Foundation: Basement

Materials List Available: Yes

Price Category: D

Images provided by designer/architect.

Copyright by designer/architect.

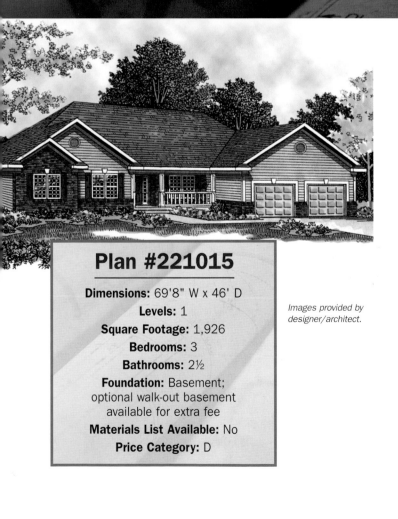

Rear Elevation

Plan #221015

Dimensions: 69'8" W x 46' D

Levels: 1

Square Footage: 1,926

Bedrooms: 3

Bathrooms: 2½

Foundation: Basement; optional walk-out basement available for extra fee

Materials List Available: No

Price Category: D

Images provided by designer/architect.

Copyright by designer/architect.

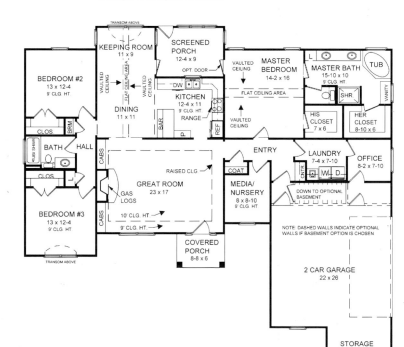

Images provided by designer/architect.

Plan #351045

Dimensions: 66' W x 60' D

Levels: 1

Square Footage: 2,000

Bedrooms: 3

Bathrooms: 2

Foundation: Crawl space, slab, or basement

Materials List Available: Yes

Price Category: E

This fine home offers a functional split-floor-plan layout with a variety of innovative features that serve to make this house a great value.

Features:

• **Great Room:** This large gathering area, with a raised ceiling, has a cozy gas fireplace with built-in cabinets on each side.

• **Casual Entertaining:** The keeping room and the oversized dining room are for those wonderful family get-togethers.

• **Office:** Tucked away off the laundry room is this quiet space, which you've always needed.

• **Master Suite:** This private area, with a vaulted ceiling, boasts plenty of closet space. The large master bathroom features a separate shower and a jetted tub.

Copyright by designer/architect.

Plan #151244

Dimensions: 35' W x 80'6" D

Levels: 1

Square Footage: 1,923

Bedrooms: 3

Bathrooms: 2

Foundation: Crawl space or slab

Materials List Available: No

Price Category: D

Images provided by designer/architect.

This brick home, with stone accents on the front elevation, has great styling and offers three bedrooms.

Features:

- **Entry:** You enter the home though an arched covered entry foyer. On the left, French doors open to bedroom 3. Across the hall is bedroom 2, with a large walk-in closet.

- **Great Room:** This large gathering area, with a 10-ft. boxed ceiling, features a fireplace and access to the grilling porch.

- **Kitchen:** This kitchen boasts a snack bar and walk-in pantry and is open to the dining room.

- **Master Suite:** This private area has a 10-ft. boxed ceiling and ample closet storage. The master bath features a corner whirlpool tub with glass blocks, split vanities, and a corner shower.

Copyright by designer/architect.

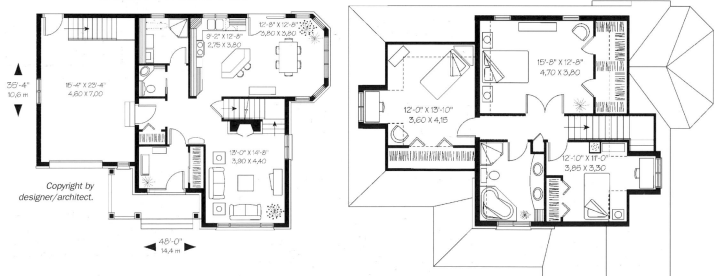

Plan #181242

Dimensions: 48' W x 35'4" D

Levels: 2

Square Footage: 1,826

Main Level Sq. Ft.: 918

Upper Level Sq. Ft.: 908

Bedrooms: 3

Bathrooms: 2

Foundation: Basement

Materials List Available: Yes

Price Category: D

Images provided by designer/architect.

This charming home has room for everyone.

Features:

- Foyer: This closed entry space will work as an "air-lock" to help keep heating and cooling costs down.

- Kitchen: L-shaped, with an eat-in design, this kitchen has a lunch counter for added seating space.

- Family Room: This relaxing area has a cozy fireplace and a large window looking onto the front yard.

- Master Bedroom: A his-and-her walk-in closet graces this large bedroom.

- Bedrooms: The two secondary bedrooms have large closets, and each has a unique nook.

Main Level Floor Plan

Upper Level Floor Plan

Images provided by designer/architect.

Plan #401037

Dimensions: 53' W x 44' D
Levels: 2
Square Footage: 1,924
Main Level Sq. Ft.: 1,007
Upper Level Sq. Ft.: 917
Bedrooms: 3
Bathrooms: 2½
Foundation: Basement
Materials List Available: Yes
Price Category: D

- Master Suite: Located on the second floor, this area boasts a vaulted ceiling, a walk-in closet, and a tiled bath.

- Bedrooms: Upstairs, two family bedrooms share a full bath and a gallery hall with a balcony overlook to the foyer.

This charming country exterior conceals an elegant interior, starting with formal living and dining rooms, each with a bay window. Decorative columns help define an elegant dining room.

Features:

- Kitchen: This gourmet kitchen features a work island and a breakfast area with its own bay window.

- Family Room: A fireplace warms this room, which opens to the rear porch through French doors.

Left Side Elevation

Main Level Floor Plan

(din 12'X13'8; k 10'4X13'8; brk; fam 17'4X13'8; WORK ISLAND; GAS F.P.; PORCH; DN; liv 12'X15'; UP DN; DN; COATS SHELVES; W D; two-car garage 20'8X22'10; PORCH; DN)

Right Side Elevation

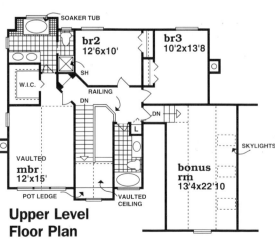
Upper Level Floor Plan

(SOAKER TUB; br2 12'6X10'; br3 10'2X13'8; W.I.C.; SH; RAILING; DN; VAULTED; mbr 12'X15'; POT LEDGE; VAULTED CEILING; DN; L; bonus rm 13'4X22'10; SKYLIGHTS)

Rear Elevation

Copyright by designer/architect.

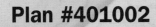

Plan #401002

Dimensions: 47' W x 42' D

Levels: 2

Square Footage: 1,938

Main Level Sq. Ft.: 936

Upper Level Sq. Ft.: 1002

Bedrooms: 4

Bathrooms: 2½

Foundation: Basement

Materials List Available: Yes

Price Category: D

A covered, railed veranda and decorative woodwork adorn this family home.

Features:

- **Foyer:** Dormer windows brighten this vaulted foyer, which opens on the right to the formal living areas.

- **Kitchen:** This centralized kitchen holds a cooking island and bayed breakfast nook.

- **Family Room:** A fireplace and sliding glass doors that lead to the rear yard enhance this room.

- **Master Suite:** This area features a huge walk-in closet and a private bath.

Images provided by designer/architect.

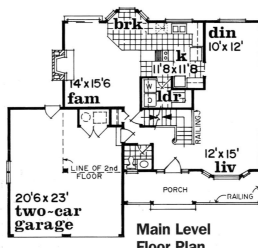

Main Level Floor Plan

Upper Level Floor Plan

Rear Elevation

Left Side Elevation

Right Side Elevation

Copyright by designer/architect.

Main Level Floor Plan

35'-8"
10,7 m

13'-0" x 10'-4"
4,15 x 3,10

11'-0" x 11'-0"
3,30 x 3,30

11'-8" x 21'-0"
3,50 x 6,30

14'-8" x 21'-0"
4,40 x 6,30

32'-4"
9,7 m

Upper Level Floor Plan

11'-0" x 9'-10"
3,30 x 2,95

11'-0" x 9'-10"
3,30 x 2,95

12'-0" x 15'-8"
3,60 x 4,70

11'-0" x 11'-8"
3,30 x 3,50

Plan #181230

Dimensions: 32'4" W x 35'8" D
Levels: 2
Square Footage: 1,943
Main Level Sq. Ft.: 836
Upper Level Sq. Ft.: 1,107
Bedrooms: 3
Bathrooms: 2½
Foundation: Basement
Materials List Available: Yes
Price Category: D

Images provided by designer/architect.

Copyright by designer/architect.

Copyright by designer/architect.

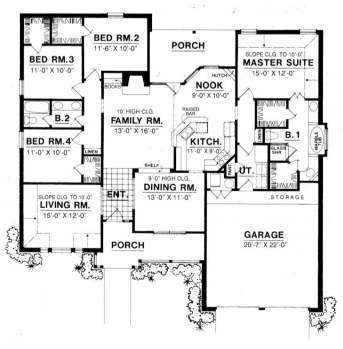

BED RM.2
11'-6" X 10'-0"

PORCH

SLOPE CLG. TO 10'-0"
MASTER SUITE
15'-0" X 12'-0"

BED RM.3
11'-0" X 10'-0"

BOOKS

NOOK
9'-0" X 10'-0"

HUTCH

B.2

10' HIGH CLG.
FAMILY RM.
13'-0" X 16'-0"

RAISED BAR

LINEN

B.1

BED RM.4
11'-0" X 10'-0"

LINEN

KITCH.
11'-0" X 9'-0"

GLASS SHR.

MARBLE TUB

SHELF

PANT.

UT.

STORAGE

SLOPE CLG. TO 10'-0"
LIVING RM.
15'-0" X 12'-0"

ENT.

9'-0" HIGH CLG.
DINING RM.
13'-0" X 11'-0"

GARAGE
20'-7" X 22'-0"

PORCH

Plan #371041

Dimensions: 57' W x 56' D
Levels: 1
Square Footage: 1,950
Bedrooms: 4
Bathrooms: 2
Foundation: Slab
Materials List Available: No
Price Category: D

Images provided by designer/architect.

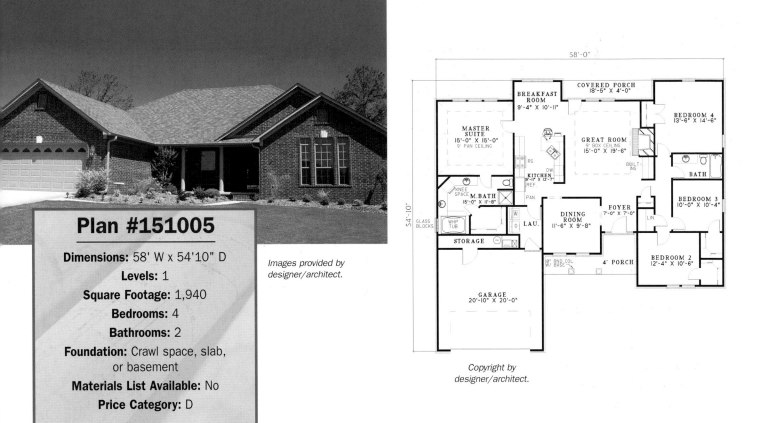

Images provided by designer/architect.

Copyright by designer/architect.

Plan #151005

Dimensions: 58' W x 54'10" D

Levels: 1

Square Footage: 1,940

Bedrooms: 4

Bathrooms: 2

Foundation: Crawl space, slab, or basement

Materials List Available: No

Price Category: D

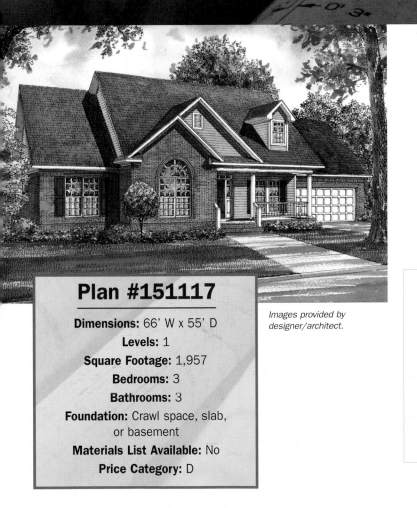

Images provided by designer/architect.

Bonus Area

Plan #151117

Dimensions: 66' W x 55' D

Levels: 1

Square Footage: 1,957

Bedrooms: 3

Bathrooms: 3

Foundation: Crawl space, slab, or basement

Materials List Available: No

Price Category: D

Plan #151205

Dimensions: 65' W x 56' D

Levels: 1

Square Footage: 1,969

Bedrooms: 3

Bathrooms: 2

Foundation: Crawl space or slab

Materials List Available: No

Price Category: C

Images provided by designer/architect.

Copyright by designer/architect.

Plan #121089

Dimensions: 54' W x 51'8" D

Levels: 2

Square Footage: 1,976

Main Level Sq. Ft.: 1,413

Upper Level Sq. Ft.: 563

Bedrooms: 4

Bathrooms: 2½

Foundation: Basement

Materials List Available: Yes

Price Category: D

Images provided by designer/architect.

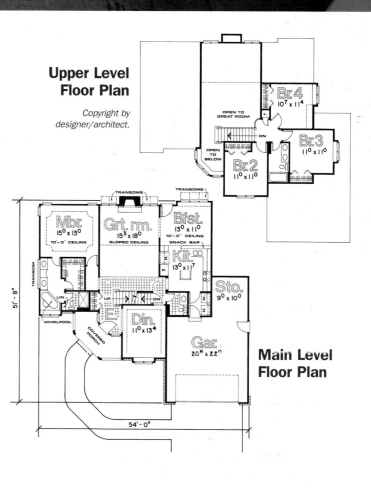

Upper Level Floor Plan

Copyright by designer/architect.

Main Level Floor Plan

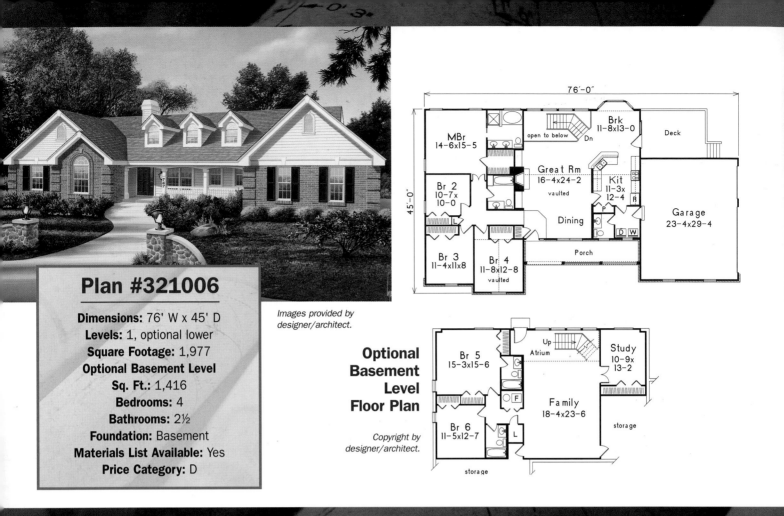

Plan #321006

Dimensions: 76' W x 45' D
Levels: 1, optional lower
Square Footage: 1,977
Optional Basement Level
Sq. Ft.: 1,416
Bedrooms: 4
Bathrooms: 2½
Foundation: Basement
Materials List Available: Yes
Price Category: D

Images provided by designer/architect.

Optional Basement Level Floor Plan

Copyright by designer/architect.

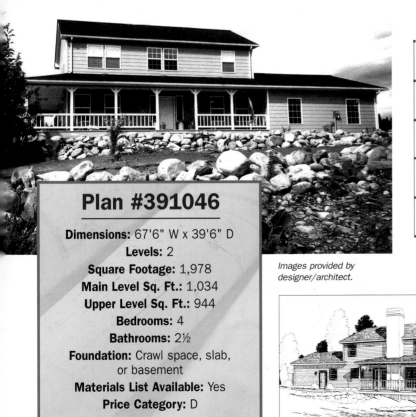

Plan #391046

Dimensions: 67'6" W x 39'6" D
Levels: 2
Square Footage: 1,978
Main Level Sq. Ft.: 1,034
Upper Level Sq. Ft.: 944
Bedrooms: 4
Bathrooms: 2½
Foundation: Crawl space, slab, or basement
Materials List Available: Yes
Price Category: D

Images provided by designer/architect.

Main Level Floor Plan

Copyright by designer/architect.

Rear View

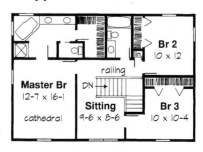

Upper Level Floor Plan

Images provided by designer/architect.

Copyright by designer/architect.

Plan #101006

Dimensions: 63' W x 58' D
Levels: 1
Square Footage: 1,982
Bedrooms: 3
Bathrooms: 2½
Foundation: Crawl space, slab basement, or walkout
Materials List Available: Yes
Price Category: D

SMARTtip

Art in Pools

The tiled walls and floor of a pool make great canvases for art, so incorporate a serious or whimsical design. Also, make the stairs wide and shallow to form a wading area for kids.

Plan #321053

Dimensions: 35' W x 56' D
Levels: 2
Square Footage: 1,985
Main Level Sq. Ft.: 1,114
Upper Level Sq. Ft.: 871
Bedrooms: 4
Bathrooms: 3½
Foundation: Basement
Materials List Available: Yes
Price Category: D

Images provided by designer/architect.

Main Level Floor Plan

Copyright by designer/architect.

Upper Level Floor Plan

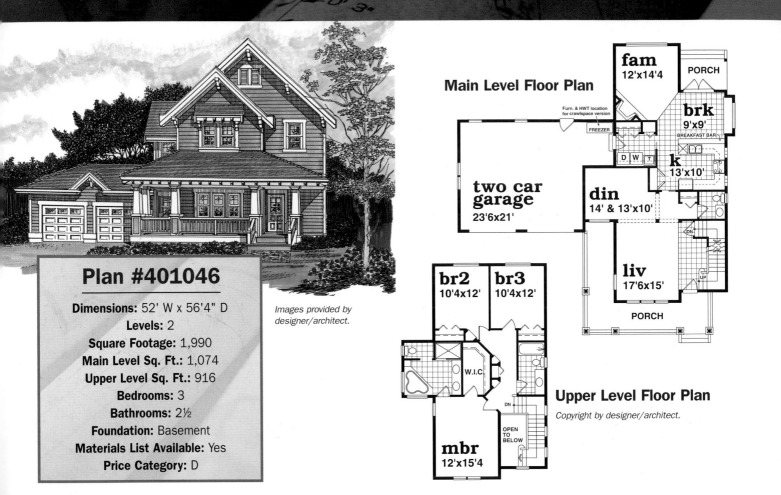

Main Level Floor Plan

fam 12'x14'4
PORCH

brk 9'x9'
BREAKFAST BAR

k 13'x10'

Furn. & HWT location for crawlspace version
FREEZER
D W T

two car garage 23'6x21'

din 14' & 13'x10'

liv 17'6x15'

PORCH

UP
DN

br2 10'4x12'

br3 10'4x12'

W.I.C

DN

OPEN TO BELOW

mbr 12'x15'4

Upper Level Floor Plan

Copyright by designer/architect.

Plan #401046

Dimensions: 52' W x 56'4" D

Levels: 2

Square Footage: 1,990

Main Level Sq. Ft.: 1,074

Upper Level Sq. Ft.: 916

Bedrooms: 3

Bathrooms: 2½

Foundation: Basement

Materials List Available: Yes

Price Category: D

Images provided by designer/architect.

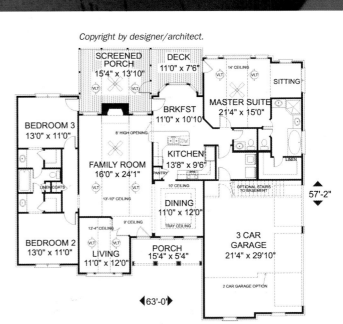

Copyright by designer/architect.

SCREENED PORCH 15'4" x 13'10"
VLT

DECK 11'0" x 7'6"
14' CEILING VLT VLT

SITTING

MASTER SUITE 21'4" x 15'0"

BEDROOM 3 13'0" x 11'0"

BRKFST 11'0" x 10'10"

LINEN

8' HIGH OPENING

KITCHEN 13'8" x 9'6"
PANTRY

LINEN COATS

FAMILY ROOM 16'0" x 24'1"
VLT VLT
13'-10" CEILING

10' CEILING

OPTIONAL STAIRS TO BASEMENT

57'-2"

BEDROOM 2 13'0" x 11'0"

DINING 11'0" x 12'0"
TRAY CEILING

13'-4" CEILING 9' CEILING

3 CAR GARAGE 21'4" x 29'10"

VLT VLT
LIVING 11'0" x 12'0"

PORCH 15'4" x 5'4"

2 CAR GARAGE OPTION

63'-0"

Plan #101005

Dimensions: 63' W x 57'2" D

Levels: 1

Square Footage: 1,992

Bedrooms: 3

Bathrooms: 2½

Foundation: Slab, crawl space, or basement

Materials List Available: Yes

Price Category: D

Images provided by designer/architect.

Rear View

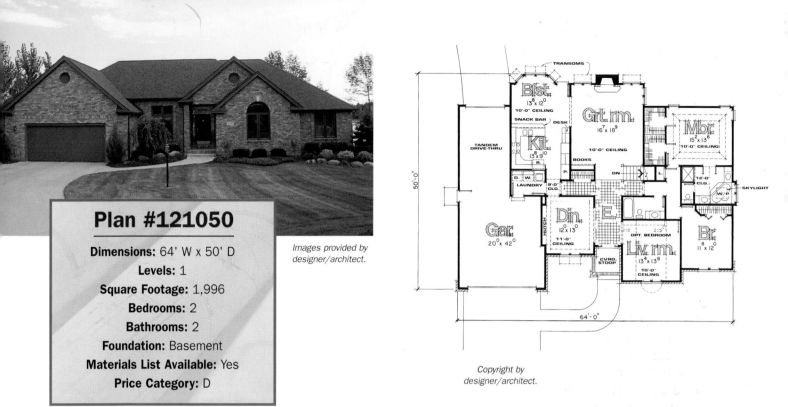

Plan #121050

Dimensions: 64' W x 50' D

Levels: 1

Square Footage: 1,996

Bedrooms: 2

Bathrooms: 2

Foundation: Basement

Materials List Available: Yes

Price Category: D

Images provided by designer/architect.

Copyright by designer/architect.

Plan #121086

Dimensions: 55'4" W x 37'8" D

Levels: 2

Square Footage: 1,998

Main Level Sq. Ft.: 1,093

Upper Level Sq. Ft.: 905

Bedrooms: 3

Bathrooms: 2½

Foundation: Basement

Materials List Available: Yes

Price Category: D

Images provided by designer/architect.

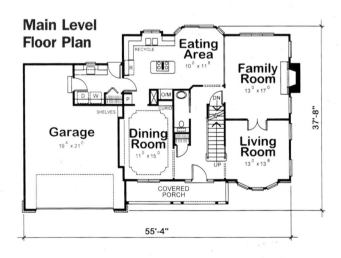

Main Level Floor Plan

Upper Level Floor Plan

Copyright by designer/architect.

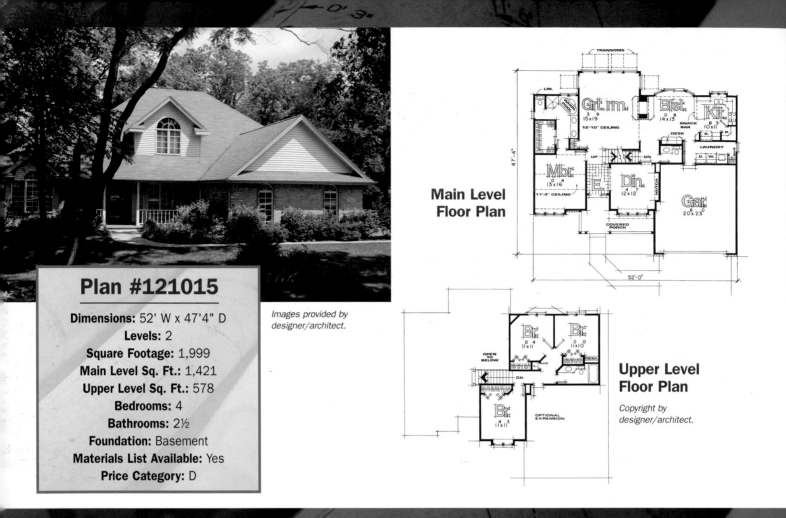

**Main Level
Floor Plan**

*Images provided by
designer/architect.*

**Upper Level
Floor Plan**

*Copyright by
designer/architect.*

Plan #121015

Dimensions: 52' W x 47'4" D

Levels: 2

Square Footage: 1,999

Main Level Sq. Ft.: 1,421

Upper Level Sq. Ft.: 578

Bedrooms: 4

Bathrooms: 2½

Foundation: Basement

Materials List Available: Yes

Price Category: D

Copyright by designer/architect.

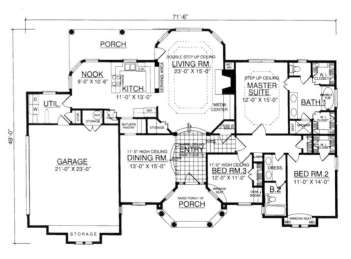

Plan #371042

Dimensions: 71'6" W x 49' D

Levels: 1

Square Footage: 1,999

Bedrooms: 3

Bathrooms: 2

Foundation: Slab

Materials List Available: No

Price Category: D

*Images provided by
designer/architect.*

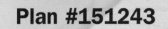

Plan #151243

Dimensions: 35' W x 80'6" D

Levels: 1

Square Footage: 1,923

Bedrooms: 3

Bathrooms: 2

Foundation: Crawl space or slab

Materials List Available: No

Price Category: D

This brick home has great styling and offers three bedrooms.

Features:

- Entry: You enter the home though an arched covered entry foyer. On the left, French doors open to bedroom 3. Across the hall is bedroom 2, with a large walk-in closet.

- Great Room: This large gathering area, with a 10-ft. boxed ceiling, features a fireplace and access to the grilling porch.

- Kitchen: This kitchen boasts a snack bar and walk-in pantry and is open to the dining room.

- Master Suite: This private area has a 10-ft. boxed ceiling and ample closet storage. The master bath features a corner whirlpool tub with glass blocks, split vanities, and a corner shower.

Images provided by designer/architect.

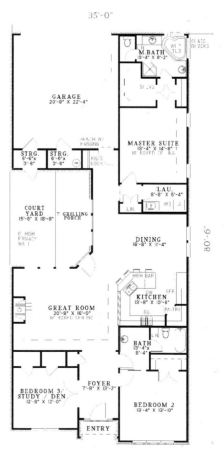

Copyright by designer/architect.

Plans and Ideas for Your Landscape

Landscapes change over the years. As plants grow, the overall look evolves from sparse to lush. Trees cast cool shade where the sun used to shine. Shrubs and hedges grow tall and dense enough to provide privacy. Perennials and ground covers spread to form colorful patches of foliage and flowers. Meanwhile, paths, arbors, fences, and other structures gain the patina of age.

Constant change over the years—sometimes rapid and dramatic, sometimes slow and subtle—is one of the joys of landscaping. It is also one of the challenges. Anticipating how fast plants will grow and how big they will eventually get is difficult, even for professional designers, and was a major concern in formulating the designs for this book.

To illustrate the kinds of changes to expect in a planting, these pages show a landscape design at three different "ages." Even though a new planting may look sparse at first, it will soon fill in. And because of careful spacing, the planting will look as good in 10 to 15 years as it does after 3 to 5. It will, of course, look different, but that's part of the fun.

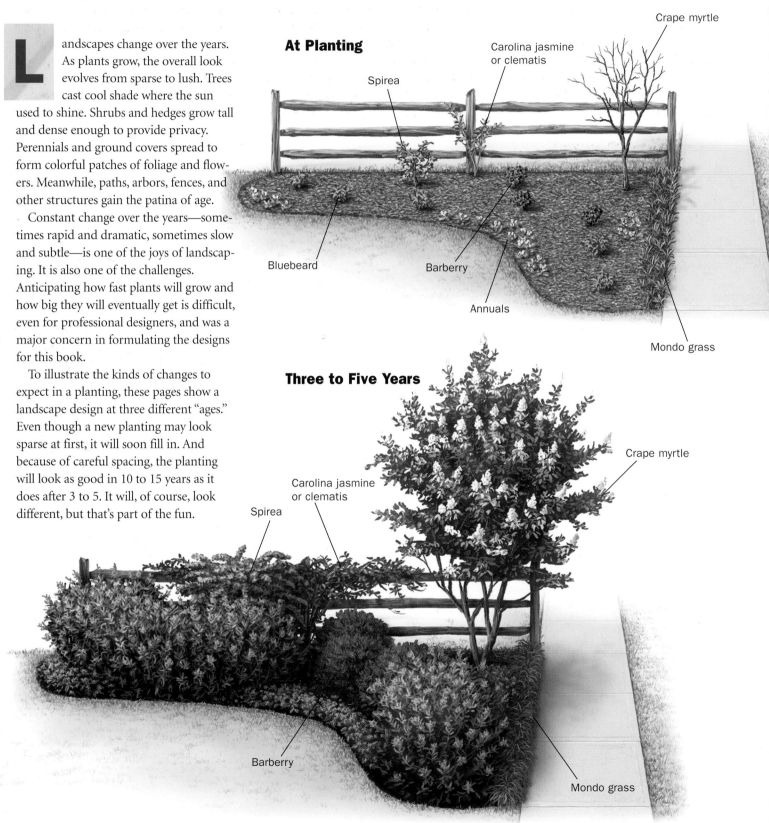

At Planting

Crape myrtle

Carolina jasmine or clematis

Spirea

Bluebeard

Barberry

Annuals

Mondo grass

Three to Five Years

Carolina jasmine or clematis

Crape myrtle

Spirea

Barberry

Mondo grass

At Planting—Here's how a corner planting might appear in spring immediately after planting. The fence and mulch look conspicuously fresh, new, and unweathered. The crape myrtle is only 4 to 5 ft. tall, with trunks no thicker than broomsticks. It hasn't leafed out yet. The spirea and barberries are 12 to 18 in. tall and wide, and the Carolina jasmine (or clematis) just reaches the bottom rail of the fence. Evenly spaced tufts of mondo grass edge the sidewalk. The bluebeards are stubby now but will grow 2 to 3 ft. tall by late summer, when they bloom. Annuals such as vinca and ageratum start flowering right away and soon form solid patches of color. The first year after planting, be sure to water during dry spells and to pull or spray any weeds that pop through the mulch.

Three to Five Years—Shown in summer now, the planting has begun to mature. The mondo grass has spread to make a continuous, weed-proof patch. The Carolina jasmine (or clematis) reaches partway along the fence. The spirea and barberries have grown into bushy, rounded specimens. From now on, they'll get wider but not much taller. The crape myrtle will keep growing about 1 ft. taller every year, and its crown will broaden. As you continue replacing the annuals twice a year, keep adding compost or organic matter to the soil and spreading fresh mulch on top.

Ten to Fifteen Years—As shown here in late summer, the crape myrtle is now a fine specimen, about 15 ft. tall, with a handsome silhouette, beautiful flowers, and colorful bark on its trunks. The bluebeards recover from an annual spring pruning to form bushy mounds covered with blooms. The Carolina jasmine, (or clematis) spirea, and barberry have reached their mature size. Keep them neat and healthy by pruning out old, weak, or dead stems every spring. If you get tired of replanting annuals, substitute low-growing perennials or shrubs in those positions.

Ten to Fifteen Years

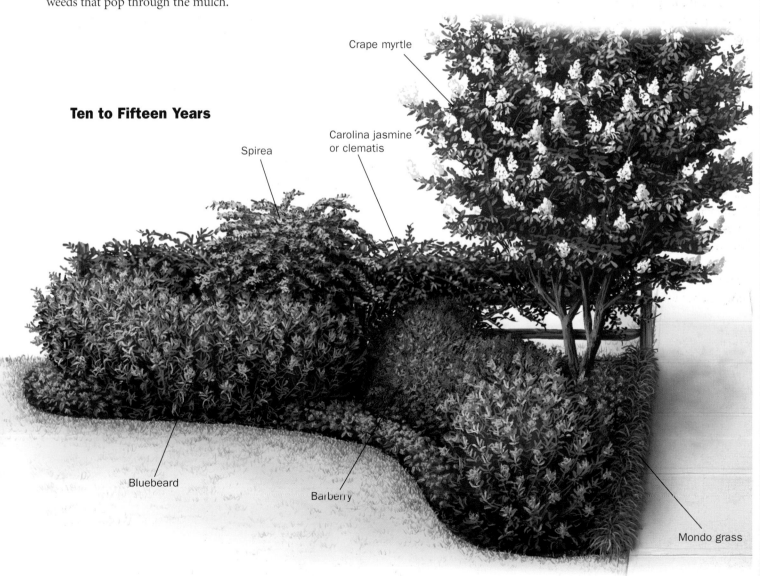

Crape myrtle

Carolina jasmine or clematis

Spirea

Bluebeard

Barberry

Mondo grass

"Around Back"

Dress Up the Area

When people think of landscaping the entrance to their home, the public entry at the front of the house comes immediately to mind. It's easy to forget that the back door often gets more use. If you make the journey between back door and driveway or garage many times each day, why not make it as pleasant a trip as possible? For many properties, a simple planting can transform the space bounded by the house, garage, and driveway, making it at once more inviting and more functional.

In a high-traffic area frequented by ball-bouncing, bicycle-riding children as well as busy adults, delicate, fussy plants have no place. The design shown here employs a few types of tough low-care plants, all of which look good year-round. The low yew hedge links the house and the garage and separates the more private backyard from the busy driveway. The star magnolia is just the right size for its spot. Its early-spring flowers will be a delight whether viewed coming up the driveway or from a window overlooking the backyard. The wide walk makes passage to and from the car easy—even with your arms full of groceries.

Note: All plants are appropriate for USDA Hardiness Zones 5, 6, and 7

A Star magnolia

See site plan for **F**

B 'Hicksii' hybrid yew

C 'Steeds' Japanese holly

D 'Hidcote' hypericum

E 'Big Blue' lilyturf

Walkway **G**

'Big Blue' lilyturf **E**

Site: Sunny
Season: Summer
Concept: A planting to raise spirits weighed down by shopping bags and to separate activities in the backyard from the driveway.

Plants & Projects

The watchword in this planting is evergreen. Except for the magnolia, all the plants here are fully evergreen or are nearly so. Spring and summer see lovely flowers from the magnolia and hypericum, and the carpet of lilyturf turns a handsome blue in August. For a bigger splash in spring, underplant the lily-turf with daffodils. Choose a single variety for uniform color, or select several varieties for a mix of colors and bloom times. Other than shearing the hedge, the only maintenance required is cutting back the lilyturf and hypericum in late winter.

A Star magnolia *Magnolia stellata* (use 1 plant)
Lovely white flowers cover this small deciduous tree

before the leaves appear. Starlike blooms, slightly fragrant and sometimes tinged with pink, appear in early spring and last up to two weeks. In summer, the dense leafy crown of dark green leaves helps provide privacy in the backyard. A multi-trunked specimen will fill the space better and display more of the interesting winter bark.

B 'Hicksii' hybrid yew *Taxus x media* (use 9)
A fast-growing evergreen shrub that is ideal for this 3-ft.-tall, neatly sheared hedge. Needles are glossy dark green and soft, not prickly. Eight plants form the L-shaped portion, while a single sheared plant extends the hedge on the other side of the walk connecting it to the house. (If the hedge needs to play a part in confining a family pet, you could easily set posts either side of the walk and add a gate.)

C 'Steeds' Japanese holly *Ilex crenata* (use 3 or more)

Several of these dense, upright evergreen shrubs can be grouped at the corner as specimen plants or to tie into an existing foundation planting. You could also extend them along the house to create a foundation planting, as shown here. The small dark green leaves are thick and leathery and have tiny spines. Plants attain a pleasing form when left to their own devices. Resist the urge to shear them; just prune to control size if necessary.

D 'Hidcote' hypericum *Hypericum* (use 1)
All summer long, clusters of large golden flowers cover the arching stems of this tidy semievergreen shrub, brightening the entrance to the backyard.

E 'Big Blue' lilyturf *Liriope muscari* (use 40 or more)
Grasslike evergreen clumps of this perennial ground cover grow together to carpet the ground flanking the driveway and walk. (Extend

the planting as far down the drive as you like.) Slim spires of tiny blue flowers rise above the dark green leaves in June. Lilyturf doesn't stand up to repeated tromping. If the drive is also a basketball court, substitute periwinkle (Vinca minor, p. 197), a tough ground cover with late-spring lilac flowers.

F Stinking hellebore *Helleborus foetidus* (use 5 or more)
This clump-forming perennial is ideal for filling the space between the walk and house on the backyard side of the hedge. (You might also consider extending the planting along the L-shaped side of the hedge.) Its pale green flowers are among the first to bloom in the spring and continue for many weeks; dark green leaves are attractive year-round.

G Walkway
Precast concrete pavers, 2 ft. by 2 ft., replace an existing walk or form a new one.

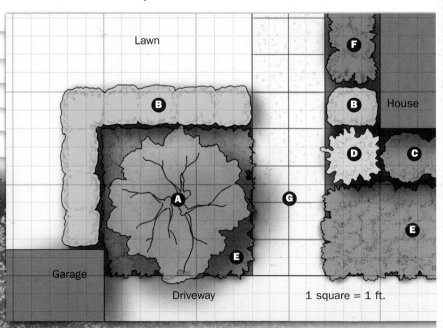

Beautify Your Garden Shed

Just as you enhance your living room by hanging paintings on the walls, you can decorate blank walls in your outdoor "living rooms." The design shown here transforms a nondescript shed wall into a living fresco, showcasing lovely plants in a framework of roses and flowering vines. Instead of a view of peeling paint, imagine gazing at this scene from a nearby patio, deck, or kitchen window.

This symmetrical composition frames two crape myrtles between arched latticework trellises. Handsome multitrunked shrubs, the crape myrtles perform year-round, providing sumptuous pink flowers in summer, orange-red foliage in fall, and attractive bark in winter. On either side of the crape myrtles, roses and clematis scramble over the trellis in a profusion of yellow and purple flowers.

A tidy low boxwood hedge sets off a shallow border of shrubs and perennials at the bottom of the "frame." Cheerful long-blooming daylilies and asters, airy Russian sage, and elegant daphne make sure that the ground-level attractions hold their own with the aerial performers covering the wall above. The flowers hew to a color scheme of yellows, pinks, blues, and purples.

Wider or narrower walls can be accommodated by expanding the design to include additional "panels," or by reducing it to one central panel. To set off the plants, consider painting or staining the wall and trellises in an off-white, an earth tone, or a light gray color.

Plants and Projects

These plants will all do well in the hot, dry conditions often found near a wall with a sunny exposure. Other than training and pruning the vines, roses, and hedge, maintenance involves little more than fall and spring cleanup. The trellises, supported by 4x4 posts and attached to the garage, are well within the reach of average do-it-yourselfers.

A **'Hopi' crape myrtle** *Lagerstroemia indica* (use 2 plants)
Large multitrunked deciduous shrubs produce papery pink flowers for weeks in summer. They also contribute colorful fall foliage and attractive flaky bark for winter interest.

B **'Golden Showers' rose** *Rosa* (use 3)
Tied to each trellis, the long canes of these climbers display large, fragrant, double yellow flowers in abundance all summer long.

C **Golden clematis** *Clematis tangutica* (use 1)
Twining up through the rose canes, this deciduous vine adds masses of small yellow flowers to the larger, more elaborate roses all summer. Feathery silver seed heads in fall.

D **Jackman clematis** *Clematis x jackmanii* (use 2)
These deciduous vines clamber among the rose canes at the corners of the wall. The combination of their large but simple purple flowers and the double yellow roses is spectacular.

E **'Green Beauty' littleleaf boxwood** *Buxus microphylla* (use 15)
Small evergreen leaves make this an ideal shrub for this neat hedge. The leaves stay bright green all winter. Trim it about 12 to 18 in. high so it won't obscure the plants behind.

F **Carol Mackie' daphne** *Daphne x burkwoodii* (use 2)
This small rounded shrub marks the far end of the bed with year-round green-and-cream variegated foliage. In spring, pale pink flowers fill the yard with their perfume.

G **Russian sage** *Perovskia atriplicifolia* (use 7)
Silver-green foliage and tiers of tiny blue flowers create a light airy effect in the center of the design from midsummer until fall. Cut stems back partway in early summer to control the size and spread of this tall perennial.

H **'Happy Returns' daylily** *Hemerocallis* (use 6)
These compact grassy-leaved perennials provide yellow trumpet-shaped flowers from early June to frost. A striking combination of color and texture with the Russian sage behind.

I **'Monch' aster** *Aster x frikartii* (use 4)
Pale purple daisylike flowers bloom gaily from June until frost on these knee-high perennials. Cut stems partway back in midsummer if they start to flop over the hedge.

J **Trellis**
Simple panels of wooden lattice frame the crape myrtles while supporting the roses and clematis.

K **Steppingstones**
Rectangular flagstone slabs provide a place to stand while pruning and tying nearby shrubs and vines.

Jackman clematis **D**

'Golden Showers' rose **B**

'Carol Mackie' daphne **F**

'Happy Returns' daylily **H**

'Green Beauty' littleleaf boxwood **E**

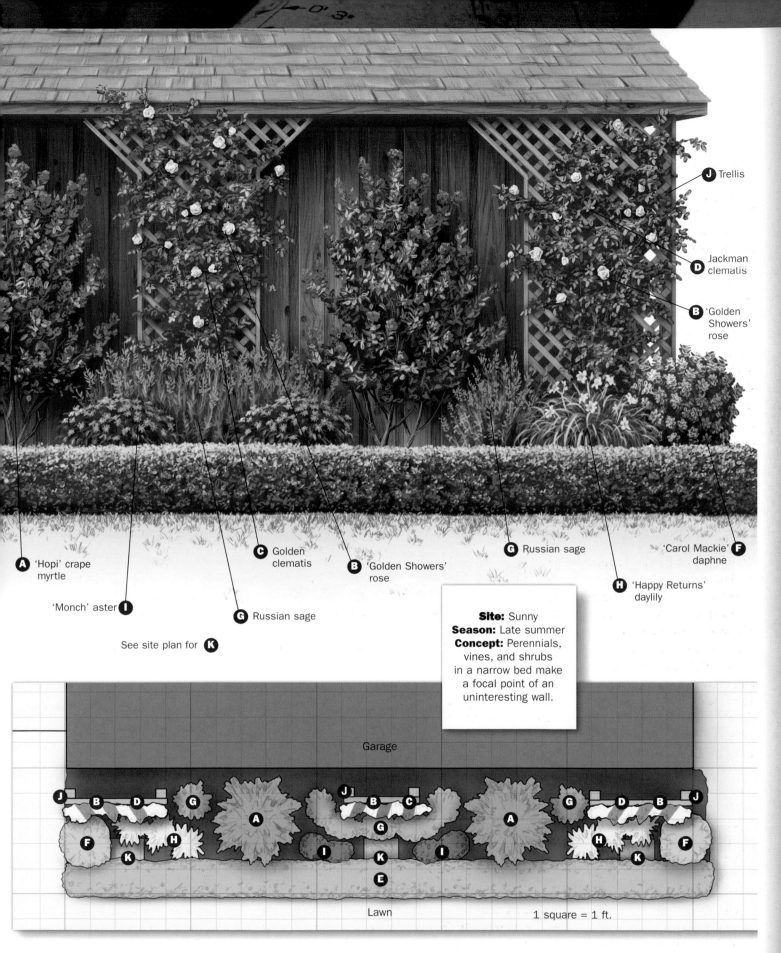

J Trellis

D Jackman clematis

B 'Golden Showers' rose

F 'Carol Mackie' daphne

G Russian sage

C Golden clematis

B 'Golden Showers' rose

H 'Happy Returns' daylily

A 'Hopi' crape myrtle

'Monch' aster **I**

G Russian sage

See site plan for **K**

Site: Sunny
Season: Late summer
Concept: Perennials, vines, and shrubs in a narrow bed make a focal point of an uninteresting wall.

Garage

Lawn

1 square = 1 ft.

Note: All plants are appropriate for USDA Hardiness Zones 5, 6, and 7

Pleasing Passage

Entrances are an important part of any landscape. They can welcome visitors onto your property; highlight a special feature, such as a rose garden; or mark passage between two areas with different character or function. The design shown here can serve in any of these situations. A picket fence and perennial plantings create a friendly, attractive barrier, just enough to signal the confines of the front yard or contain the family dog. The vine-covered arbor provides welcoming access.

The design combines uncomplicated elements imaginatively, creating interesting details to catch the eye and a slightly formal but comfortable overall effect. Picketed enclosures and compact evergreen shrubs broaden the arbor, giving it greater presence. The wide flagstone apron, flanked by neat deciduous shrubs, reinforces this effect and frames the entrance. Massed perennial plantings lend substance to the fence, which serves as a backdrop to their handsome foliage and colorful flowers.

J Arbor

A White clematis

A White clematis

B 'Green Beauty' littleleaf boxwood

C Pale yellow daylily

Pale yellow daylily

C

'Green Beauty' littleleaf boxwood B

G Evergreen candytuft

I White bugleweed

L Walkway

G Evergreen candytuft

F 'Autumn Joy' sedum

D 'Longwood Blue' bluebeard

See site plan for H

Note: All plants are appropriate for USDA Hardiness Zones 5, 6, and 7

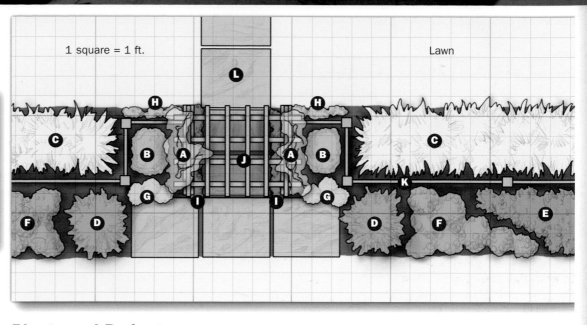

1 square = 1 ft.

Lawn

Site: Sunny
Season: Late summer
Concept: Perennials, and flowering vines accent traditional fence entry and arbor.

K Picket fence

E 'Wargrave Pink' geranium

F 'Autumn Joy' sedum

D 'Longwood Blue' bluebeard

Plants and Projects

For many people, a picket fence and vine-covered arbor represent old-fashioned "Cottage" style. The plantings here further encourage this feeling.

Pretty white flowers cover the arbor for much of the summer. Massed plantings of daylilies, geraniums, and sedums along the fence produce wide swaths of flowers and attractive foliage from early summer to fall. Plant drifts of snowdrops in these beds; their late-winter flowers are a welcome sign that spring will soon come.

The structures and plantings are easy to build, install, and care for. You can extend the fence and plantings as needed. To use an existing concrete walk, just pour pads either side to create the wide apron in front of the arbor.

A White clematis *Clematis* (use 4 plants)
Four of these deciduous climbing vines, one at each post, will cover the arbor in a few years. For large white flowers, try the cultivar 'Henryi', which blooms in early and late summer.

B 'Green Beauty' littleleaf boxwood *Buxus microphylla* (use 2)
This evergreen shrub forms a neat ball of small bright green leaves without shearing. It is colorful in winter when the rest of the plants are dormant.

C Pale yellow daylily *Hemerocallis* (use 24)
A durable perennial whose cheerful trumpet-shaped flowers nod above clumps of arching foliage. Choose from the many yellow-flowered cultivars (some fragrant); mix several to extend the season of bloom.

D 'Longwood Blue' bluebeard *Caryopteris x clandonensis* (use 2)
A pair of these small deciduous shrubs with soft gray foliage frame the entry. Sky blue late-summer flowers cover the plants for weeks.

E 'Wargrave Pink' geranium *Geranium endressii* (use 9)
This perennial produces a mass of bright green leaves and a profusion of pink flowers in early summer. Cut it back in July and it will bloom intermittently until frost.

F 'Autumn Joy' sedum *Sedum* (use 13)
This perennial forms a clump of upright stems with distinctive fleshy foliage. Pale flower buds that appear during summer are followed by pink flowers during fall and rusty seed heads that stand up in winter.

G Evergreen candytuft *Iberis sempervirens* (use 12)
A perennial ground cover that spreads to form a small welcome mat at the foot of the boxwoods. White flowers stand out against glossy evergreen leaves in spring.

H Lamb's ears *Stachys byzantina* (use 6)
Favorites of children, the long woolly gray leaves of this perennial form a soft carpet. In early summer, thick stalks carry scattered purple flowers.

I White bugleweed *Ajuga reptans 'Alba'* (use 20)
Edging the walk under the arbor, this perennial ground cover has pretty green leaves and, in late spring, short spikes of white flowers.

J Arbor Thick posts give this simple structure a sturdy visual presence. Paint or stain it, or make it of cedar and let it weather as shown here.

K Picket fence Low picket fence adds character to the planting; materials and finish should match the arbor.

L Walkway Flagstone walk can be large pavers, as shown here, or made up of smaller rectangular flags.

Streetwise and Stylish

Give Your Curbside Strip a New Look

Homeowners seldom think much about the area that runs between the sidewalk and street. At best this is a tidy patch of lawn; at worst, a weed-choked eyesore. Yet this is one of the most public parts of many properties. Planting this strip with attractive perennials, shrubs, and trees can give pleasure to passersby and visitors who park next to the curb, as well as enhancing the streetscape you view from the house. (This strip is usually city-owned, so check local ordinances for restrictions before you start a remake.)

It might help to think of this curbside strip as an island bed between two defined boundaries: the street and the sidewalk. These beds are divided further by a wide pedestrian walkway, providing ample room for visitors to get in and out of front and rear car doors. A pair of handsome evergreen trees form a gateway. The diagonal skew of this design keeps the symmetry of the plantings either side from appearing staid. You can expand the beds to fill a longer strip, or plant lawn next to the beds.

This can be a difficult site. Summer drought and heat, pedestrian and car traffic, and errant dogs are the usual conditions found along the street. Plants have to be tough to perform well here, but they need not look tough. These combine colorful foliage and flowers for a dramatic impact from spring until fall. Evergreen foliage and clumps of tawny grass look good through the winter. The plantings beneath the trees won't grow tall enough to block your view of the street as you pull out of the driveway.

Japanese **A** ligustrum

'Little Princess' **B** spirea

Note: All plants are appropriate for USDA Hardiness Zones 6, 7, and 8.

'Crimson Pygmy' **C** Japanese barberry

E Dwarf fountain grass

'Stella d'Oro' **F** daylily

D 'Blue Pacific' shore juniper

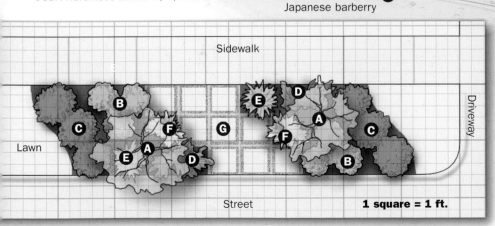

Sidewalk

Driveway

Lawn

Street

1 square = 1 ft.

Site: Sunny

Season: Summer

Concept: Small but varied planting transforms an often neglected area and treats visitors and passersby to a colorful display.

Plants and Projects

Tough as they are, these plants will benefit from a generous bark mulch, which conserves moisture, helps control weeds, and makes the bed look neat in this highly visible location. In addition to seasonal cleanup, you'll need to prune the shrubs occasionally to keep them tidy and healthy. Divide the clumps of daylilies when they get crowded.

A **Japanese ligustrum** *Ligustrum japonicum* (use 2 plants)
The dark green, waxy leaves of this small broad-leaved evergreen tree are a perfect background for the fragrant white flowers it bears in early summer. Dark blue berries follow in fall and winter. Grows quickly; prune lower branches as necessary to accommodate visitors using the walk.

B **'Little Princess' spirea** *Spiraea japonica* (use 6)
The small fine leaves and rosy pink flowers of this dainty deciduous shrub belie its tough nature. It will bloom happily for weeks in conditions next to the street in early summer.

C **'Crimson Pygmy' Japanese barberry** *Berberis thunbergii* (use 6)
The dark maroon leaves of this deciduous shrub turn crimson in late fall. Naturally forms a broad tidy mound.

D **'Blue Pacific' shore juniper** *Juniperus conferta* (use 2)
This low, trailing evergreen ground cover has handsome blue-green foliage that can stand up to street life. Makes a subtle carpet beneath the trees.

E **Dwarf fountain grass** *Pennisetum alopecuroides* 'Hameln' (use 2)
This perennial grass is a year-round presence. Fluffy flower spikes rise above neat clumps of arching green leaves in midsummer. Flowers and foliage turn shades of gold and tan in autumn and last through the winter.

F **'Stella d'Oro' daylily** *Hemerocallis* (use 8)
This very popular perennial produces golden yellow flowers from late spring until frost; quite a feat considering that each flower lasts only a day. The grassy foliage is attractive, too.

G **Walk**
This design provides interest underfoot. Set the framework of pressure-treated 2x4s on a sand-and-gravel base; position the square precast concrete pavers in the center of each cell; and fill between paver and frame with crushed rock, tamped firm.

A Japanese ligustrum

Dwarf E fountain grass

F 'Stella d'Oro' daylily

G Walk

B 'Little Princess' spirea

C 'Crimson Pygmy' Japanese barberry

Landscaping a Low Wall

A Colorful Low-Tier Garden Replaces a Bland Slope

For some, walls are nothing more than a barrier or obstruction; for others (especially in cities) they merely represent a "canvas" for their artwork. For plants, walls offer warmth for an early start in spring and good drainage for roots. Gardeners appreciate the rich visual potential for composing a garden on two levels, as well as the practical advantage of working on two relatively flat surfaces instead of a single sloping one. If you have a wall, or have a place to put one, grasp the opportunity for some handsome landscaping.

This design places two complementary perennial borders above and below a wall bounded at one end by a set of stairs. While each bed is relatively narrow, when viewed from the lower level the two combine to form a border almost 10 ft. deep, with plants rising to eye level or more. The planting can be extended with the same or similar plants.

Building the wall that makes this impressive sight possible doesn't require the time or skill it once did. Nor is it necessary to scour the countryside for tons of fieldstone or to hire an expensive contractor. Thanks to precast retaining-wall systems, a knee-high do-it-yourself wall can be installed in as little as a weekend. More experienced or ambitious wall builders may want to tackle a natural stone wall, but anyone with a healthy back (or access to energetic teenagers) can succeed with a prefabricated system.

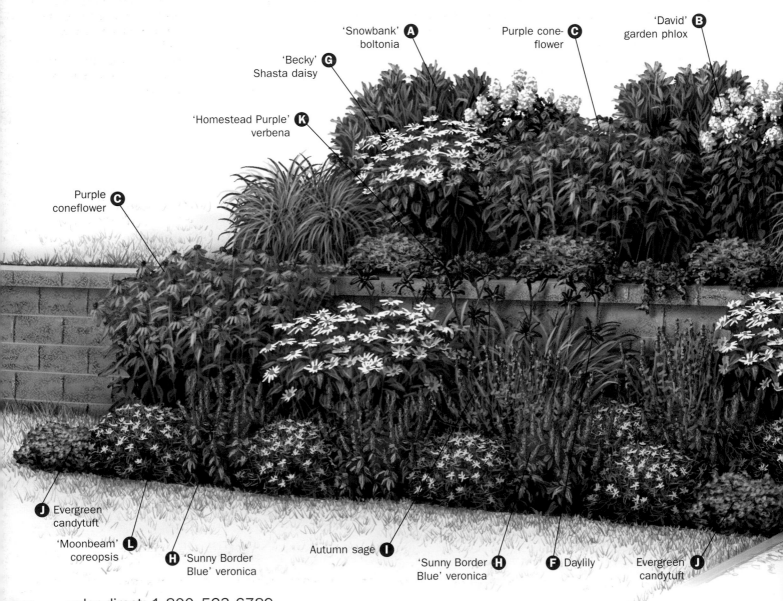

'Becky' **G** Shasta daisy

'Snowbank' **A** boltonia

Purple cone- **C** flower

'David' **B** garden phlox

'Homestead Purple' **K** verbena

Purple **C** coneflower

J Evergreen candytuft

'Moonbeam' **L** coreopsis

H 'Sunny Border Blue' veronica

Autumn sage **I**

'Sunny Border **H** Blue' veronica

F Daylily

Evergreen **J** candytuft

Plants and Projects

Drifts of blues, whites, yellows, and pinks, a dash of cherry red, and the flash of butterfly wings keep the garden popping with color from summer through fall. For more color in spring, plant small bulbs like crocus or grape hyacinth throughout the beds. Care is basic: spring and fall cleanup, snipping spent flowers, and dividing a plant now and then.

A **'Snowbank' boltonia** *Boltonia asteroides* (use 2 plants)
White daisylike flowers cover this tough perennial for three to five weeks in fall. An upright plant with fine blue-green leaves, it never needs staking.

B **'David' garden phlox** *Phlox paniculata* (use 3)
A sturdy perennial topped with clusters of clear white, fragrant flowers in late summer. It forms a patch of upright stems clothed in healthy green leaves, a pleasing backdrop for the plants in front of it.

C **Purple coneflower** *Echinacea purpurea* (use 9)
Thick flower stalks rise above this perennial's clump of dark green foliage in midsummer, displaying large daisylike blossoms. Each flower has dark pink petals surrounding a dark central cone. Leave some seed heads for winter interest and the finches they attract.

D **'Caesar's Brother' Siberian iris** *Iris sibirica* (use 4)
The erect grassy leaves of this perennial provide an interesting spiky look along the wall, and the graceful flowers add deep purple color in late spring.

E **Gold moneywort** *Lysimachia nummularia* 'Aurea' (use 4)
Planted at the feet of the irises, the bright yellow coin-shaped leaves of this creeping perennial spill over the wall. Yellow flowers in summer complement the coreopsis in the lower bed.

F **Daylily** *Hemerocallis* (use 5)
Grassy foliage and colorful trumpet-shaped flowers, fresh every day, make this perennial a lovely centerpiece for the lower bed. Choose a cultivar with maroon flowers to blend with the pink coneflowers, or mix several kinds to give a longer blooming period.

G **'Becky' Shasta daisy** *Chrysanthemum × superbum* (use 9)
This popular perennial's big white daisies bloom all summer on sturdy stalks that never need staking. The shiny foliage looks good through the winter.

H **'Sunny Border Blue' veronica** *Veronica* (use 6)
Lustrous green crinkled leaves topped with bright blue flower spikes make this perennial a cheerful recurring presence in the garden. It will bloom from early summer to frost if you clip off the spent flowers.

I **Autumn sage** *Salvia greggii* (use 2)
A bushy low-growing perennial with loose clusters of bright red flowers that keep coming through summer and fall.

J **Evergreen candytuft** *Iberis sempervirens* (use 6)
An excellent evergreen perennial for a wall, with a low, rounded form that falls loosely over the edge. It's topped with clusters of white flowers in early spring.

K **'Homestead Purple' verbena** *Verbena canadensis*, (use 2)
This perennial also trails over the edge of the wall and bears purple flowers from spring to frost if you clip off the spent blossoms.

L **'Moonbeam' coreopsis** *Coreopsis verticillata* (use 6)
Edging the lower bed, this perennial's tidy mound of fine foliage sparkles with small yellow flowers for months.

M **Retaining wall and steps**
This 2-ft.-tall wall and the steps are built from a precast concrete block system. Select a color that complements your house.

N **Path**
Gravel is an attractive, informal surface, easy to install and to maintain.

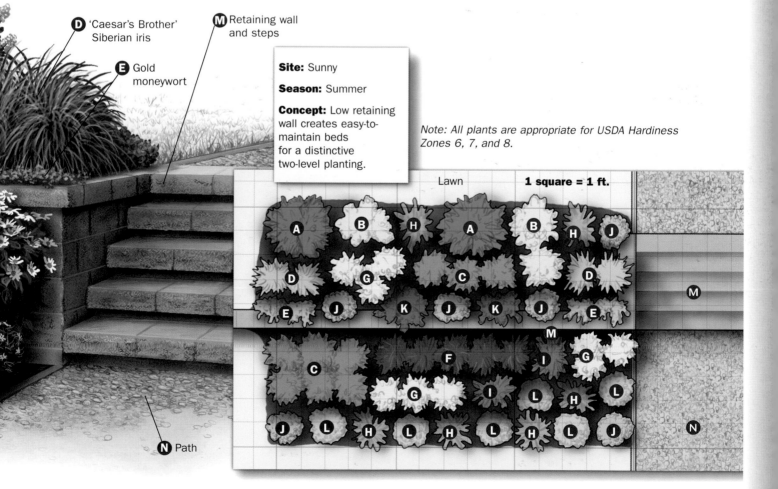

D 'Caesar's Brother' Siberian iris

E Gold moneywort

M Retaining wall and steps

Site: Sunny

Season: Summer

Concept: Low retaining wall creates easy-to-maintain beds for a distinctive two-level planting.

Note: All plants are appropriate for USDA Hardiness Zones 6, 7, and 8.

Lawn   1 square = 1 ft.

N Path

Plan #351065

Dimensions: 65'2" W x 71' D
Levels: 1
Square Footage: 2,005
Bedrooms: 3
Bathrooms: 2½
Foundation: Crawl space or slab
Materials List Available: Yes
Price Category: D

Are you looking for a home that is designed for the way your family actually lives? Well, look no further.

Features:

- Foyer: This tiled entry opens up the home and flows into the dining room, the great room, and the "flex space" room.

- Great Room: This large meeting area, with a tray ceiling, features a beautiful gas fireplace with side windows that look out onto the rear covered porch.

- Kitchen: This well-equipped kitchen has a built-in pantry and a raised bar that's open to the breakfast area.

- Flex Space: This oversized flex space provides a secluded spot for that home office, media center, or the small guest room that you've always wanted.

- Master Suite: This private area, located on the opposite side of the home from the secondary bedrooms, features a large walk-in closet and a private bathroom.

- Garage: This oversized three-car garage has plenty of storage space.

Images provided by designer/architect.

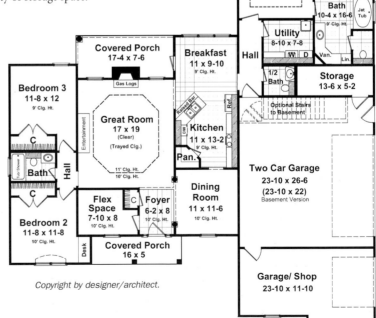

Copyright by designer/architect.

Plan #391033

Dimensions: 48' W x 48' D
Levels: 2
Square Footage: 2,007
Main Level Sq. Ft.: 1,345
Upper Level Sq. Ft.: 662
Bedrooms: 3
Bathrooms: 2½
Foundation: Crawl space, slab, or basement
Materials List Available: Yes
Price Category: D

This home, as shown in the photograph, may differ from the actual blueprints. For more detailed information, please check the floor plans carefully.

Images provided by designer/architect.

Make the most of daily life with this stylish yet practical plan.

Features:

• Living Room: A joy in either summer or winter, this spacious living room has a fireplace and broad views of the deck and backyard.

• Kitchen: This kitchen contains a breakfast area large enough for most informal meals and provides easy access the dining and living rooms, as well as the deck.

• Master Suite: The prominent feature of this secluded area is the large private bathroom with a walk-in closet.

• Bedrooms: The two secondary bedrooms are located upstairs and share a hall bathroom.

Upper Level Floor Plan

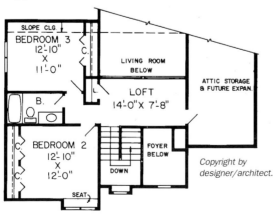

Copyright by designer/architect.

Main Level Floor Plan

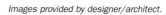

Plan #371043

Dimensions: 40' W x 56'6" D

Levels: 2

Square Footage: 2,013

Main Level Sq. Ft.: 1,323

Upper Level Sq. Ft.: 690

Bedrooms: 4

Bathrooms: 2½

Foundation: Slab

Materials List Available: No

Price Category: E

Images provided by designer/architect.

This charming country home will make you feel right at home. Exquisite country trim gives it character, and the front dormers give it charm.

Features:

- **Living Room:** This large entertaining area, with its 10-ft.-high ceiling and corner fireplace, is open to the kitchen and breakfast nook.

- **Dining Room:** This formal room has a 10-ft.-high ceiling, bay window, and easy access to the kitchen.

- **Kitchen:** The pantry, raised bar, and cozy breakfast nook are three reasons why this large kitchen is a winner.

- **Master Suite:** This private area has a cozy sitting area and a luxurious bathroom with two large walk-in closets.

- **Bedrooms:** Upstairs you'll find three large bedrooms, which share a convenient hall bathroom.

Main Level Floor Plan

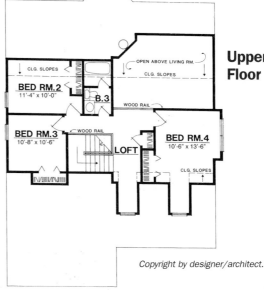

Upper Level Floor Plan

Copyright by designer/architect.

Plan #391001

Dimensions: 32' W x 40' D
Levels: 2
Square Footage: 2,015
Main Level Sq. Ft.: 1,280
Upper Level Sq. Ft.: 735
Bedrooms: 3
Bathrooms: 2½
Foundation: Crawl space
Materials List Available: Yes
Price Category: D

Images provided by designer/architect.

- Kitchen: This L-shaped kitchen features an expansive cooktop/lunch counter.

- Utility Areas: A utility room handles the laundry and storage, and a half bath with linen closet takes care of other necessities.

- Master Suite: This main-floor master suite is just that—sweet! The spa-style bath features a corner tub nestled against a greenhouse window. Plus, there are double sinks and a separate shower.

- Upstairs: The sun-washed loft overlooks the activity below while embracing two dreamy bedrooms and a sizable bath with double sinks.

Follow your dream to this home surrounded with decking. The A-frame front showcases bold windowing (on two levels), and natural lighting fills the house.

Features:

- Dining Room: This dining room and the family room are completely open to each other, perfect for hanging out in the warmth of the hearth.

Main Level Floor Plan

GREEN-HOUSE 8'-0"X10'-0"
BATH #1
MASTER BEDROOM 15'-3"X13'-3"
W D
UTIL
P
KITCHEN 15'-6"X10'-2"
DECK
FAMILY ROOM 15'-6" X 20'-0"
DINING ROOM 15'-6" X 12'-8"
DECK
PLAYHOUSE
DECK
32'-0"
40'-0"

Upper Level Floor Plan

BEDROOM #2 13'-0"X 13'-3"
B #2
BEDROOM #3 11'-4"X 13'-3"
LOFT 15'-9" X 12'-0"
DN
OPEN TO MAIN FLOOR

Copyright by designer/architect.

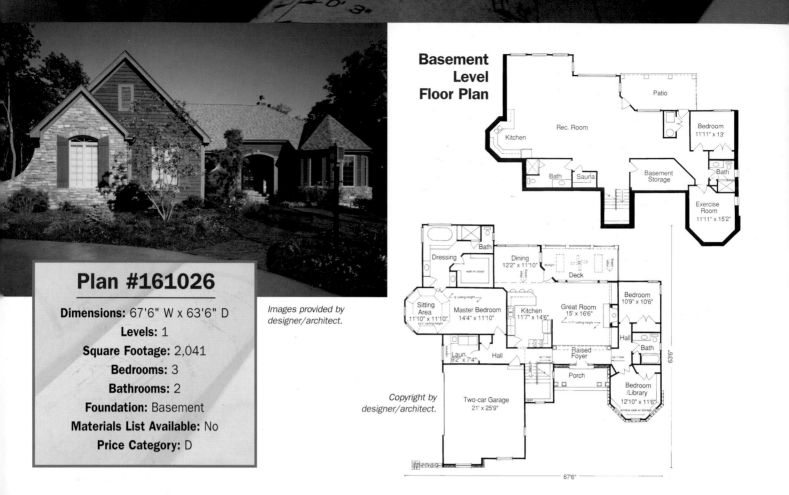

Basement Level Floor Plan

Images provided by designer/architect.

Copyright by designer/architect.

Plan #161026

Dimensions: 67'6" W x 63'6" D

Levels: 1

Square Footage: 2,041

Bedrooms: 3

Bathrooms: 2

Foundation: Basement

Materials List Available: No

Price Category: D

Plan #321030

Dimensions: 61' W x 51' D

Levels: 1

Square Footage: 2,029

Bedrooms: 4

Bathrooms: 2

Foundation: Crawl space, slab, basement, or walk-out

Materials List Available: Yes

Price Category: D

Images provided by designer/architect.

Copyright by designer/architect.

SMARTtip

Measuring Angles

A sure-fire way to accurately measure the wall-frame acute angle is to cut a piece of scrap lumber to emulate the angle, and then measure it.

Plan #151133

Dimensions: 66'4" W x 58'7" D

Levels: 1

Square Footage: 2,029

Bedrooms: 3

Bathrooms: 2

Foundation: Crawl space, slab, or basement

Materials List Available: No

Price Category: D

Optional Upper Level Floor Plan

Images provided by designer/architect.

Copyright by designer/architect.

Plan #111008

Dimensions: 43' W x 69' D

Levels: 2

Square Footage: 2,011

Main Level Sq. Ft.: 1,331

Upper Level Sq. Ft.: 680

Bedrooms: 3

Bathrooms: 2½

Foundation: Slab

Materials List Available: No

Price Category: D

Images provided by designer/architect.

Main Level Floor Plan

Upper Level Floor Plan

Copyright by designer/architect.

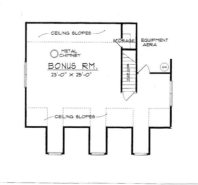

Plan #371056

Dimensions: 77'8" W x 60'1" D

Levels: 1

Square Footage: 2,043

Bedrooms: 3

Bathrooms: 2

Foundation: Slab

Materials List Available: No

Price Category: D

This classic country charmer has it all, large front porch, dormer windows, and beautiful bay windows.

Features:

• Dining Room: Once inside you will find a tiled entry that leads you into this elegant room set off by wood columns.

• Living Room: This large gathering area has a 9-ft.-high ceiling and a cozy fireplace, which opens into a cozy nook.

• Kitchen: This spacious island kitchen has plenty of counter space and a pantry with brick around the oven, making it a unique feature.

• Master Suite: This suite features a private bathroom with his and her walk-in closets and double vanities.

• Bedrooms: Two secondary bedrooms have large closets and share a hall bathroom.

Images provided by designer/architect.

Optional Upper Level Floor Plan

Plan #401001

Dimensions: 56' W x 43'4" D
Levels: 2
Square Footage: 2,071
Main Level Sq. Ft.: 1,204
Upper Level Sq. Ft.: 867
Bedrooms: 3
Bathrooms: 2½
Foundation: Basement
Materials List Available: Yes
Price Category: D

Images provided by designer/architect.

This transitional design carries the best of both worlds—popular details of both traditional and contemporary architecture. The high rooflines allow for dramatic full-height windows and vaulted ceilings in the formal areas.

Features:

• **Open Plan:** The open casual areas include the hearth-warmed family room, bayed breakfast nook, and island kitchen.

• **Den:** Located just off the foyer, this room is a well-appreciated haven for quiet time. Note the half-bath just beyond the den.

• **Master Suite:** This area has two walk-in closets and a full bath with a separate shower and tub.

• **Bedrooms:** Three bedrooms occupy the second floor and include two family bedrooms—one with a vaulted ceiling.

• **Utility Areas:** A laundry alcove leads to the two-car garage with extra storage space.

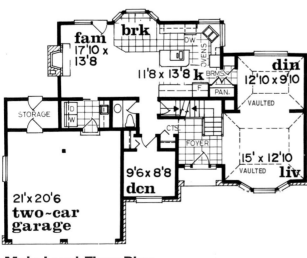

Main Level Floor Plan

Rear Elevation

Left Side Elevation

Upper Level Floor Plan

Right Side Elevation

Copyright by designer/architect.

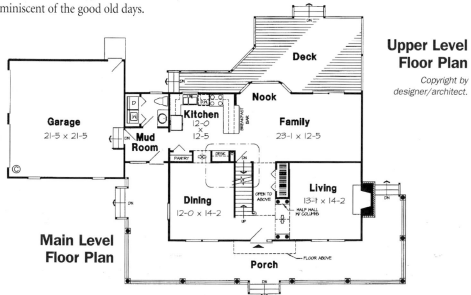

Plan #391007

Dimensions: 74' W x 41'6" D
Levels: 2
Square Footage: 2,083
Main Level Sq. Ft.: 1,113
Upper Level Sq. Ft.: 970
Bedrooms: 3
Bathrooms: 2½
Foundation: Crawl space, slab, or basement
Materials List Available: Yes
Price Category: D

Images provided by designer/architect.

With a wide-wrapping porch and a pretty Palladian window peeking from a sky-high dormer, this charming home is cheerfully reminiscent of the good old days.

Features:

- Dining and Living Rooms: Over the threshold, this dining room engages one side of the staircase and the living room with fireplace occupies the other to maintain balance.

- Kitchen: One section of this functional kitchen looks out at the deck, feeds into the breakfast area, and flows into the great-sized family room while the other leads to the laundry area, half bath, mudroom, and garage.

- Master Suite: The second level delivers the master suite, with its wide walk-in closet and a full bath with separate shower and tub areas, double sinks, and a bright window.

- Bedrooms: Each of the two equally spacious secondary bedrooms with wall-length closets and large windows shares a full-size bath uniquely outfitted with double sinks so that no one has to wait to primp.

Upper Level Floor Plan

Copyright by designer/architect.

Main Level Floor Plan

Crawl Space/Slab Option

Rear View

Rear View

Loft Area

Plan #321056

Dimensions: 40' W x 57'4" D

Levels: 2

Square Footage: 2,050

Main Level Sq. Ft.: 1,028

Upper Level Sq. Ft.: 1,022

Bedrooms: 3

Bathrooms: 2½

Foundation: Crawl space, slab, or basement

Materials List Available: Yes

Price Category: D

Images provided by designer/architect.

Main Level Floor Plan

Upper Level Floor Plan

Copyright by designer/architect.

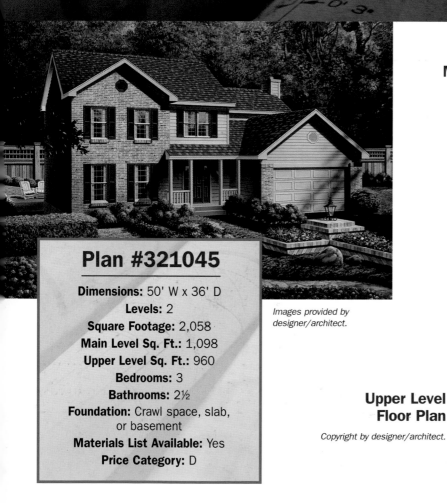

Plan #321045

Dimensions: 50' W x 36' D

Levels: 2

Square Footage: 2,058

Main Level Sq. Ft.: 1,098

Upper Level Sq. Ft.: 960

Bedrooms: 3

Bathrooms: 2½

Foundation: Crawl space, slab, or basement

Materials List Available: Yes

Price Category: D

Images provided by designer/architect.

Main Level Floor Plan

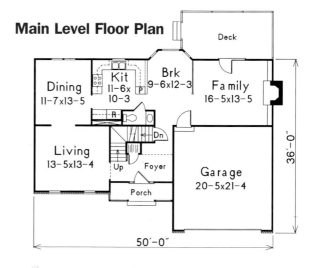

Upper Level Floor Plan

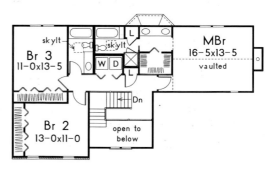

Copyright by designer/architect.

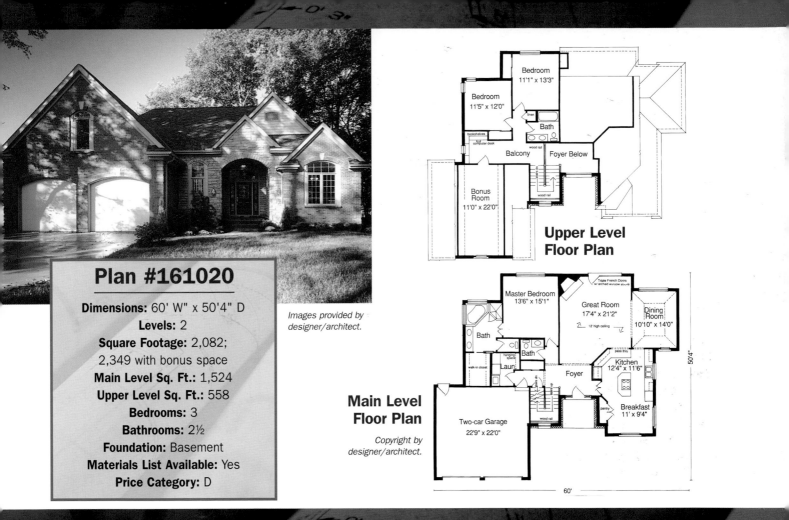

Plan #161020

Dimensions: 60' W" x 50'4" D
Levels: 2
Square Footage: 2,082;
2,349 with bonus space
Main Level Sq. Ft.: 1,524
Upper Level Sq. Ft.: 558
Bedrooms: 3
Bathrooms: 2½
Foundation: Basement
Materials List Available: Yes
Price Category: D

Images provided by designer/architect.

Upper Level Floor Plan

Main Level Floor Plan

Copyright by designer/architect.

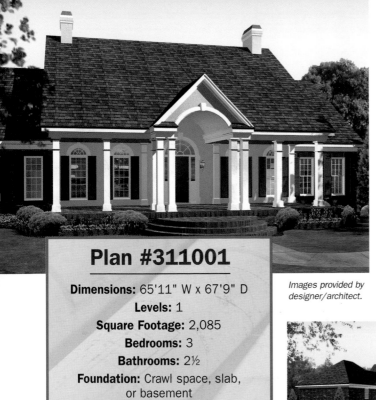

Plan #311001

Dimensions: 65'11" W x 67'9" D
Levels: 1
Square Footage: 2,085
Bedrooms: 3
Bathrooms: 2½
Foundation: Crawl space, slab, or basement
Materials List Available: No
Price Category: D

Images provided by designer/architect.

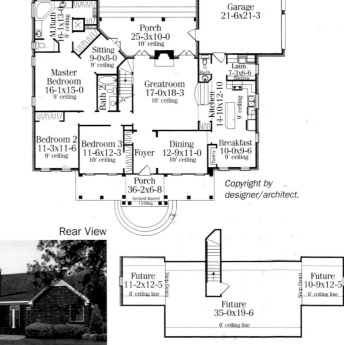

Rear View

Copyright by designer/architect.

Optional Bonus Area

Plan #181240

Dimensions: 40' W x 50' D
Levels: 2
Square Footage: 2,089
Main Level Sq. Ft.: 1,046
Upper Level Sq. Ft.: 1,043
Bedrooms: 3
Bathrooms: 2
Foundation: Basement
Materials List Available: Yes
Price Category: D

Images provided by designer/architect.

This stately home has grand presence in a compact size.

Features:

- Entry: Rising up two stories, this entry is breathtaking. On the left is the home office.

- Kitchen: This compact kitchen packs a powerful punch with its breakfast bar and access to the rear porch.

- Master Bedroom: This large sleeping area has a walk-in closet and an entry door with a side light.

- Bedrooms: The two secondary bedrooms have large closets. One room has a curved wall.

- Laundry Room: Located upstairs, this utility area is near all three bedrooms.

Main Level Floor Plan

Upper Level Floor Plan

Copyright by designer/architect.

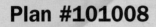

Plan #101008

Dimensions: 68' W x 53' D
Levels: 1
Square Footage: 2,088
Bedrooms: 3
Bathrooms: 2½
Foundation: Crawl space, slab, basement, or walk-out
Materials List Available: Yes
Price Category: D

This ranch sports an attractive brick-and-stucco exterior accented with quoins and layered trim.

Features:

- Ceiling Height: 11 ft. unless otherwise noted.

- Kitchen: You'll love cooking in this bright, airy kitchen, which is lit by an abundance of windows.

- Breakfast room: Off the kitchen is this breakfast room, the perfect spot for informal family meals.

- Master Suite: You'll look forward to retiring at the end of the day to this truly exceptional master suite, with its grand bath, spacious walk-in closet, and direct access to the porch.

- Morning Porch: Greet the day with your first cup of coffee on this porch, which is accessible from the master suite.

- Secondary Bedrooms: These bedrooms measure a generous 11 ft. x 14 ft. They share a compartmented bath.

Images provided by designer/architect.

Copyright by designer/architect.

SMARTtip
Accentuating Your Bathroom with Details

No matter how big or small the room, details will pull the style together. Some of the best details that you can include are the smallest—drawer pulls from an antique store or shells in a glass jar or just left on the countertop. Add period flavor with crown molding, or dress up contemporary fixtures with polished stone fittings.

Plan #371079

Dimensions: 51'4" W x 56'6" D

Levels: 2

Square Footage: 2,089

Main Level Sq. Ft.: 1,441

Upper Level Sq. Ft.: 648

Bedrooms: 3

Bathrooms: 2½

Foundation: Slab

Materials List Available: No

Price Category: D

Images provided by designer/architect.

This is an exquisite country house, which showcases a variety of materials, including stone, brick, wood siding, and copper.

Features:

- Living Room: This elegant formal room has a fireplace and a bay window looking onto the front yard.
- Dining Room: The spacious living room opens into this roomy space, which has a view of the backyard.

- Kitchen: This kitchen has an angular shape and a walk-in pantry near by. The peninsula counter is open to the breakfast nook.
- Master Suite: This master suite has a luxurious bathroom with walk-in his and her closets.
- Bedrooms: Upstairs you will find two additional large bedrooms that share a convenient Jack and Jill bathroom.

Copyright by designer/architect.

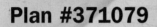

Main Level Floor Plan

Upper Level Floor Plan

Plan #211006

Dimensions: 61' W x 77' D

Levels: 1

Square Footage: 2,177

Bedrooms: 3

Bathrooms: 2

Foundation: Crawl space or slab

Materials List Available: Yes

Price Category: D

Images provided by designer/architect.

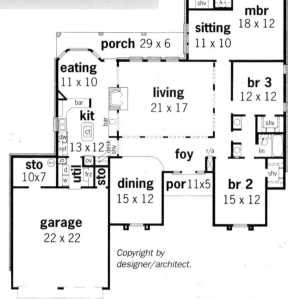

Copyright by designer/architect.

Plan #131022

Dimensions: 54'8" W x 43' D

Levels: 2

Square Footage: 2,092

Main Level Sq. Ft.: 1,152

Upper Level Sq. Ft.: 940

Bedrooms: 4

Bathrooms: 2½

Foundation: Crawl space, slab, or basement

Materials List Available: Yes

Price Category: E

Images provided by designer/architect.

Main Level Floor Plan

Upper Level Floor Plan

Copyright by designer/architect.

Plan #151050

Dimensions: 69'2" W x 74'10" D

Levels: 1

Square Footage: 2,096

Bedrooms: 3

Bathrooms: 2½

Foundation: Crawl space, slab, or basement

Materials List Available: No

Price Category: D

Copyright by designer/architect.

You'll love this spacious home for both its elegance and its convenient design.

Features:

- Ceiling Height: 8 ft.

- Great Room: A 9-ft. boxed ceiling complements this large room, which sits just beyond the front gallery. A fireplace and door to the rear porch make it a natural gathering spot.

- Kitchen: This well-designed kitchen includes a central work island and shares an angled eating bar with the adjacent breakfast room.

- Breakfast Room: This room's bay window is gorgeous, and the door to the garage is practical.

- Master Suite: You'll love the 9-ft. boxed ceiling in the bedroom and the vaulted ceiling in the bath, which also includes two walk-in closets, a corner whirlpool tub, split vanities, a shower, and a compartmentalized toilet.

- Workshop: A huge workshop with half-bath is ideal for anyone who loves to build or repair.

Plan #161016

Dimensions: 59'4" W x 58'8" D
Levels: 2
Square Footage: 2,101
Main Level Sq. Ft.: 1,626
Upper Level Sq. Ft.: 475
Bedrooms: 3
Bathrooms: 2½
Foundation: Basement
Optional crawl space
available for extra fee
Materials List Available: Yes
Price Category: D

Note: Home in photo reflects a modified garage entrance.

Images provided by designer/architect.

Features:

- **Great Room:** Made for relaxing and entertaining, the great room is sunken to set it off from the rest of the house. A balcony from the second floor looks down into this spacious area, making it easy to keep track of the kids while they are playing.

- **Kitchen:** Convenience marks this well laid-out kitchen where you'll love to cook for guests and for family.

- **Master Bedroom:** A vaulted ceiling complements the unusual octagonal shape

of the master bedroom. Located on the first floor, this room allows some privacy from the second floor bedrooms. It is also ideal for anyone who no longer wishes to climb stairs to reach a bedroom.

Rear Elevation

You'll love the exciting roofline that sets this elegant home apart from its neighbors as well as the embellished, solid look that declares how well-designed it is—from the inside to the exterior.

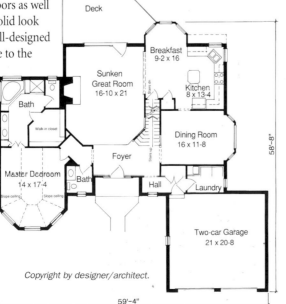

Main Level Floor Plan

Copyright by designer/architect.

Upper Level Floor Plan

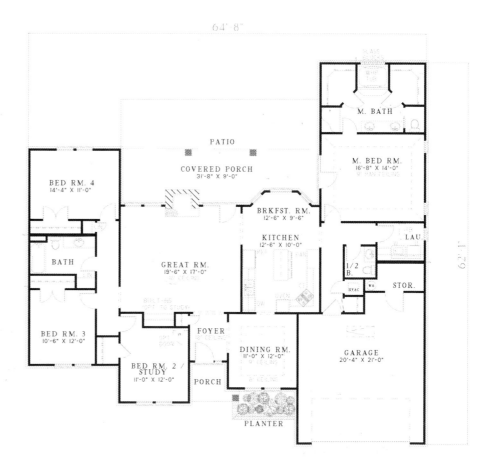

Plan #151004

Dimensions: 64'8" W x 62'1" D

Levels: 1

Square Footage: 2,107

Bedrooms: 4

Bathrooms: 2½

Foundation: Crawl space, slab, or basement

Materials List Available: No

Price Category: D

You'll love the spacious feeling in this comfortable home designed for a family.

Features:

- **Foyer:** A 10-ft. ceiling greets you in this home.

- **Great Room:** A 10-ft. ceiling complements this large room, with its fireplace, built-in cabinets, and easy access to the rear covered porch.

- **Dining Room:** The 9-ft. boxed ceiling in this large room helps to create a beautiful formal feeling.

- **Kitchen:** The island in this kitchen is open to the breakfast room for true convenience.

- **Breakfast Room:** Morning light will stream through the bay window here.

- **Master Suite:** A 9-ft. pan ceiling adds a distinctive note to this room with access to the rear porch. In the bath, you'll find a whirlpool tub, separate shower, double vanities, and two walk-in closets.

Plan #151034

Dimensions: 58'6" W x 64'6" D

Levels: 1

Square Footage: 2,133

Bedrooms: 3

Bathrooms: 2

Foundation: Crawl space, slab, or basement

Materials List Available: No

Price Category: D

Images provided by designer/architect.

This home, as shown in the photograph, may differ from the actual blueprints. For more detailed information, please check the floor plans carefully.

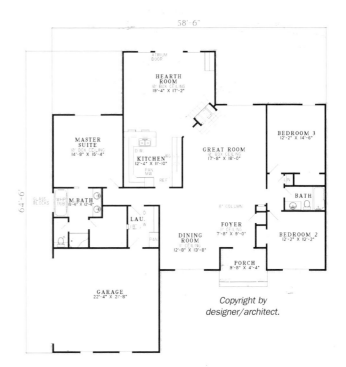

Copyright by designer/architect.

Plan #371044

Dimensions: 57'4" W x 63'8" D

Levels: 1

Square Footage: 2,094

Bedrooms: 4

Bathrooms: 2½

Foundation: Slab

Materials List Available: No

Price Category: D

Images provided by designer/architect.

Copyright by designer/architect.

Plan #401010

Dimensions: 62'6" W x 40' D

Levels: 2

Square Footage: 2,094

Main Level Sq. Ft.: 1,098

Upper Level Sq. Ft.: 996

Bedrooms: 4

Bathrooms: 2½

Foundation: Basement

Materials List Available: Yes

Price Category: D

Images provided by designer/architect.

Upper Level Floor Plan

This farmhouse deluxe is decorated with a covered, railed veranda and shuttered windows.

Features:

- **Foyer:** Flanking this foyer are the den, with double-door entry, and the living room/dining room combination with fireplace.

- **Kitchen:** This L-shaped kitchen can be reached from either the central hall or an entry at the dining room. An island work counter and planning desk add to its efficiency.

- **Breakfast Room:** This light-filled room provides a place for casual meals.

Copyright by designer/architect.

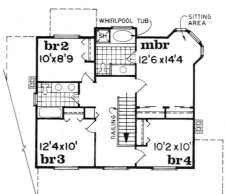

Main Level Floor Plan

Rear Elevation

Left Side Elevation

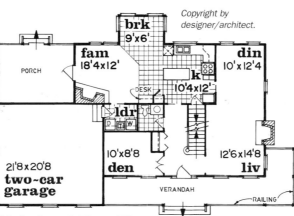

Right Side Elevation

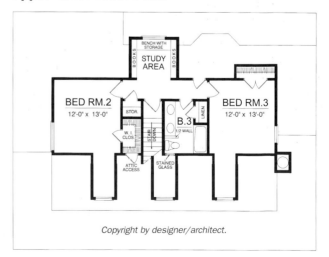

Plan #371081

Dimensions: 54'6" W x 41'10" D
Levels: 2
Square Footage: 2,143
Main Level Sq. Ft.: 1,535
Upper Level Sq. Ft.: 608
Bedrooms: 4
Bathrooms: 3
Foundation: Slab or basement
Materials List Available: No
Price Category: D

Features:

- **Family Room:** This large gathering area features a wonderful fireplace and is open to the dining room.
- **Kitchen:** The island cabinet in this fully functional kitchen brings an open feel to this room and the adjoining dining room.
- **Master Suite:** Mom and Dad can relax downstairs in this spacious master suite, with their luxurious master bathroom, which has double walk-in closets and a marble tub.
- **Bedrooms:** The kids will enjoy these two large secondary bedrooms and the study area with bookcases upstairs.

The cozy wraparound front porch of this beautiful country home invites you to stay awhile.

Rear Elevation

Upper Level Floor Plan

Main Level Floor Plan

Copyright by designer/architect.

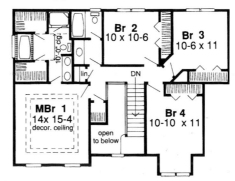

Plan #391043

Dimensions: 48' W x 36' D
Levels: 2
Square Footage: 2,143
Main Level Sq. Ft.: 1,086
Upper Level Sq. Ft.: 1,057
Bedrooms: 4
Bathrooms: 2½
Foundation: Crawl space, slab, or basement
Materials List Available: Yes
Price Category: D

Images provided by designer/architect.

This clapboard beauty brings back memories with a bright balance of multi-paned windows, covered porch, sun-catching dormer, and rear deck.

Features:

- Open Layout: Openness is "in," from the wide foyer to the open layout of the living and dining rooms, which share one entire side of the home.

- Kitchen: This kitchen, in close association with the dining room, pairs up with the breakfast area and hearth room for optimal family togetherness.

- Master Suite: This suite, with its decorative tray ceiling and charming windows at the front of the house, features two walk-in closets and a private bath with double sinks and spa-style tub tucked beneath a window.

- Bedrooms: The three secondary bedrooms, all with wall-length closets, enjoy a full bath room with two private chambers, one with a sink-vanity and the other with a tub and toilet.

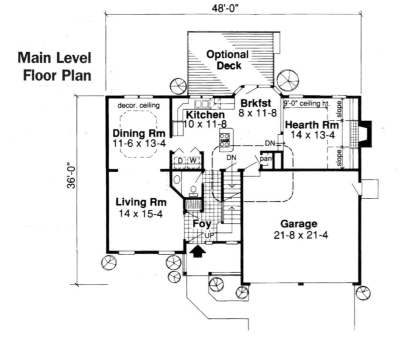

Main Level Floor Plan

Upper Level Floor Plan

Copyright by designer/architect.

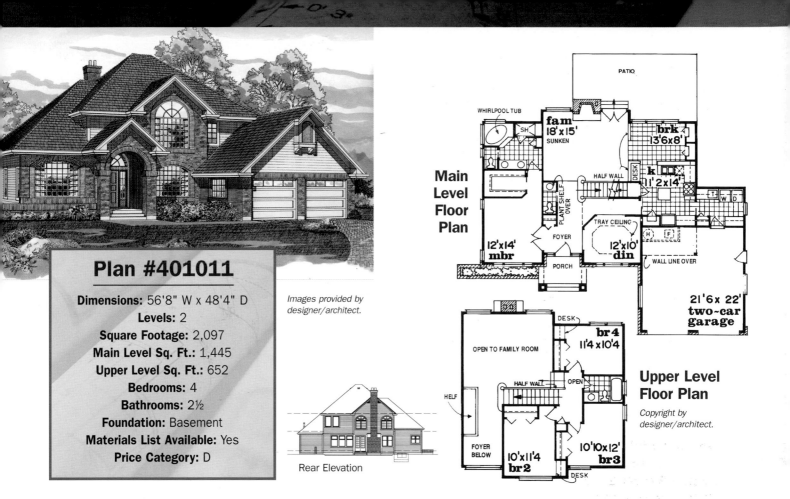

Plan #401011

Dimensions: 56'8" W x 48'4" D
Levels: 2
Square Footage: 2,097
Main Level Sq. Ft.: 1,445
Upper Level Sq. Ft.: 652
Bedrooms: 4
Bathrooms: 2½
Foundation: Basement
Materials List Available: Yes
Price Category: D

Images provided by designer/architect.

Main Level Floor Plan

PATIO

WHIRLPOOL TUB

fam 18'x15' SUNKEN

SH

brk 13'6x8'

HALF WALL

DESK

k 11'2x14'

T W D

PLANT SHELF OVER

TRAY CEILING

12'x10' din

12'x14' mbr

FOYER

PORCH

WALL LINE OVER

H F

21'6 x 22' two~car garage

Rear Elevation

Upper Level Floor Plan

OPEN TO FAMILY ROOM

DESK

br 4 11'4 x10'4

HALF WALL

OPEN

HELF

FOYER BELOW

10'x11'4 br 2

10'10x12' br 3

DESK

Copyright by designer/architect.

Plan #151206

Dimensions: 62'6" W x 62'4" D
Levels: 1
Square Footage: 2,151
Bedrooms: 3
Bathrooms: 2
Foundation: Crawl space or slab
Materials List Available: No
Price Category: D

Images provided by designer/architect.

62'-6"

62'-4"

MASTER SUITE 18'-8" X 14'-6" 9' BOX'D CEILING

GRILLING PORCH 27'-8" X 11'-0"

12" COLUMNS

BREAKFAST ROOM 11'-10" X 10'-6"

M. BATH 9'-6" X 13'-6"

GLASS SHWR

BEDROOM 3 11'-0" X 12'-4"

BUILT-INS

GREAT ROOM 15'-0" X 23'-7" 9' BOX CEILING

KITCHEN 11'-10" X 15'-0"

LAUNDRY 8'-10" X 6'-10"

OFFICE 7'-8" X 9'-8"

BATH 7'-0" X 7'-8"

LIN

OVEN

REF

WHP TUB

GARAGE 20'-8" X 20'-0"

BEDROOM 2 13'-4" X 11'-8"

FOYER 7'-6" X 7'-0"

FORMAL DINING 11'-10" X 12'-0"

ENTRY 10'-0" X 4'-0"

Copyright by designer/architect.

Plan #401038

Dimensions: 47' W x 48' D

Levels: 2

Square Footage: 2,142

Main Level Sq. Ft.: 1,092

Upper Level Sq. Ft.: 1,050

Bedrooms: 4

Bathrooms: 2½

Foundation: Basement

Materials List Available: Yes

Price Category: D

There is much to recommend this charming home. It begins with a quaint front porch opening to a raised foyer.

Features:

- **Living/Dining Room:** On the left side of the plan are this dining room with buffet space and living room with a tray ceiling and fireplace.

- **Kitchen:** This practical kitchen opens to the breakfast nook, which has double doors to the rear porch.

- **Family Room:** Open to the kitchen and breakfast nook to form one great gathering space, this room is warmed by a fireplace.

- **Utility Areas:** Access the two-car garage is through the laundry room and mudroom, near the half-bath at the entry.

- **Master Suite:** This area boasts a vaulted ceiling, a large walk-in closet, and a lavish full bathroom with twin vanities and a whirlpool spa.

- **Bedrooms:** Three additional bedrooms share a skylighted bathroom that includes a soaking tub.

Images provided by designer/architect.

Upper Level Floor Plan

Rear Elevation

Main Level Floor Plan

Right Side Elevation

Left Side Elevation

![Front view of house]

Plan #391012

Dimensions: 54' W x 46' D
Levels: 2
Square Footage: 2,157
Main Level Sq. Ft.: 1,590
Upper Level Sq. Ft.: 567
Bedrooms: 3
Bathrooms: 2½
Foundation: Crawl space, slab, or basement
Materials List Available: Yes
Price Category: D

This home, as shown in the photograph, may differ from the actual blueprints. Images provided by designer/architect. For more detailed information, please check the floor plans carefully.

Creativity comes home to roost in this two-story ultra-comfortable abode, with its covered porch and welcoming entrance.

Features:

- Dining Room: Located on the opposite side of the kitchen, this room opens into formal living space that makes room for large-scale entertaining.

- Family and Breakfast Rooms: These rooms share a double-sided fireplace. An exterior deck draws folks outdoors. Laundry facilities and a powder room are tucked away neatly.

- Master Suite: This main-floor master suite features a tray ceiling, deep walk-in closet, and private bath with double sinks.

- Bedrooms: Upstairs along the open mezzanine, two secondary bedrooms nestle near a shared bath, and a loft-style media room with window overlooks the front of the house.

Rear View

Family Hearth Room/Kitchen

Copyright by designer/architect.

Main Level Floor Plan

Upper Level Floor Plan

Living Room

Plan #401029

Dimensions: 37'6" W x 48'4" D
Levels: 2
Square Footage: 2,163
Main Level Sq. Ft.: 832
Upper Level Sq. Ft.: 1,331
Bedrooms: 3
Bathrooms: 2½
Foundation: Basement
Materials List Available: No
Price Category: D

Images provided by designer/architect.

This two-level plan has a bonus—a roof deck with hot tub! A variety of additional outdoor spaces makes this one wonderful plan.

Features:

- First Level: Family bedrooms, a full bath room, and a cozy den are on the first level, along with a two-car garage.

- Living Area: The living spaces are on the second floor and include a living/dining room combination with a deck and fireplace. The dining room has buffet space.

- Family Room: Featuring a fireplace and a built-in entertainment center, the gathering area is open to the breakfast room and sky lighted kitchen.

- Master Bedroom: This room features a private bath with a whirlpool tub and two-person shower, a walk-in closet, and access to still another deck.

Master Bathroom

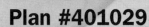

Rear View

Rear Elevation

Upper Level
Floor Plan

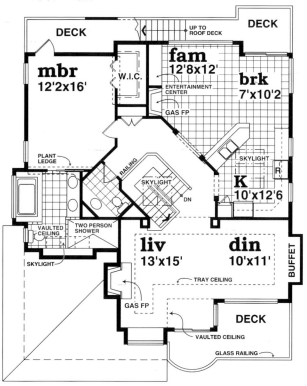

DECK

UP TO ROOF DECK

DECK

mbr
12'2x16'

W.I.C.

fam
12'8x12'

ENTERTAINMENT CENTER

GAS FP

brk
7'x10'2

PLANT LEDGE

RAILING

SKYLIGHT

SKYLIGHT

K
10'x12'6

R

DN

VAULTED CEILING

TWO PERSON SHOWER

SKYLIGHT

liv
13'x15'

din
10'x11'

BUFFET

GAS FP

TRAY CEILING

DECK

VAULTED CEILING

GLASS RAILING

Copyright by designer/architect.

Main Level
Floor Plan

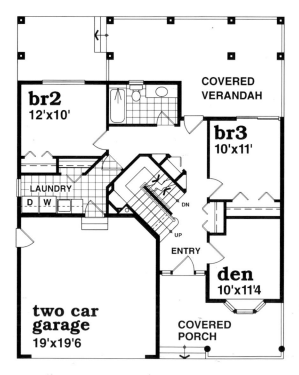

br2
12'x10'

COVERED VERANDAH

LAUNDRY

D W

br3
10'x11'

DN

UP

ENTRY

den
10'x11'4

two car garage
19'x19'6

COVERED PORCH

Dining Room/Kitchen

Family Room

Living Room

Plan #371057

Dimensions: 69' W x 47'8" D

Levels: 2

Square Footage: 2,168

Main Level Sq. Ft.: 1,647

Upper Level Sq. Ft.: 521

Bedrooms: 3

Bathrooms: 2½

Foundation: Crawl space, slab, or basement

Materials List Available: No

Price Category: D

Images provided by designer/architect.

This charming country home with optional bonus room is country living at its finest.

Features:

- Family Room: This large open family room, with its cozy fireplace, is great for entertaining.

- Dining Room: A large front window seat graces this formal room.

- Kitchen: This large kitchen has a pantry and a raised bar, and is open to a cozy breakfast nook with a window seat.

- Master Suite: This suite has a large window with window seat and a luxurious bathroom with a spacious walk-in closet.

- Bedrooms: Upstairs are two additional bedrooms with walk-in closets that share a convenient bathroom with two vanities.

Main Level Floor Plan

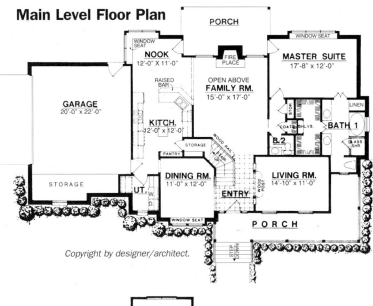

Copyright by designer/architect.

Upper Level Floor Plan

Main Level Floor Plan

PATIO

GARAGE
23'-4"
X
23'-4"

KITCHEN
11'-10"
X
13'-4"

LAUN.

DINING
12'-0"
X
15'-8"

LIVING ROOM
19'-8"
X
20'-4"
(10'-9" CLG.)

SCREENED
PORCH
10'-0"
X
10'-8"

FOYER

LIBRARY
10'-4"
X
13'-4"

BOOKCASE

MASTER
BEDROOM
16'-0"
X
15'-4"

Copyright by designer/architect.

Images provided by designer/architect.

Upper Level Floor Plan

BEDROOM 2
11'-8"
X
9'-10"

CEDAR CLOS.

BALCONY

BEDROOM 3
11'-8"
X
13'-2"

FOYER BELOW

Plan #391017

Dimensions: 77' W x 41'6" D
Levels: 2
Square Footage: 2,176
Main Level Sq. Ft.: 1,671
Upper Level Sq. Ft.: 505
Bedrooms: 3
Bathrooms: 2½
Foundation: Crawl space, slab, or basement
Materials List Available: Yes
Price Category: D

Rear View

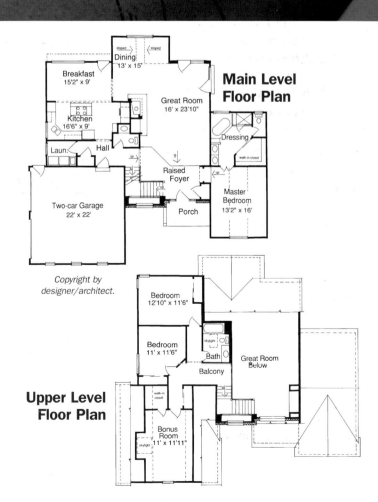

Main Level Floor Plan

Dining
13' x 15'

Breakfast
15'2" x 9'

Kitchen
16'6" x 9'

Great Room
16' x 23'10"

Laun.

Hall

Dressing

walk-in closet

Two-car Garage
22' x 22'

Raised Foyer

Porch

Master Bedroom
13'2" x 16'

Copyright by designer/architect.

Images provided by designer/architect.

Upper Level Floor Plan

Bedroom
12'10" x 11'6"

Bedroom
11' x 11'6"

Bath

Balcony

Great Room Below

walk-in closet

Bonus Room
11' x 11'11"

Plan #161034

Dimensions: 56' W x 53' D
Levels: 2
Square Footage: 2,156
Main Level Sq. Ft.: 1,605
Upper Level Sq. Ft.: 551
Bedrooms: 3
Bathrooms: 2½
Foundation: Basement
Materials List Available: No
Price Category: D

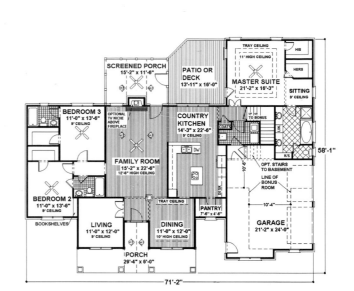

Copyright by designer/architect.

Plan #101011

Dimensions: 71'2" W x 58'1" D

Levels: 1

Square Footage: 2,184

Bedrooms: 3

Bathrooms: 3

Foundation: Crawl space, slab, basement, walkout

Materials List Available: Yes

Price Category: D

Images provided by designer/architect.

Main Level Floor Plan

Upper Level Floor Plan

Images provided by designer/architect.

Copyright by designer/architect.

Plan #271070

Dimensions: 70'3" W x 60' D

Levels: 2

Square Footage: 2,144

Main Level Sq. Ft.: 1,156

Upper Level Sq. Ft.: 988

Bedrooms: 4

Bathrooms: 2½

Foundation: Basement, crawl space

Materials List Available: No

Price Category: D

Plan #371058

Dimensions: 67'6" W x 53' D

Levels: 1

Square Footage: 2,195

Bedrooms: 4

Bathrooms: 2

Foundation: Slab

Materials List Available: No

Price Category: D

Images provided by designer/architect.

This traditionally classic brick four-bedroom home is loaded with charm.

Features:

- Living Room: The tiled entry takes you into this spacious room with a view of the backyard.

- Family Room: The living room's see-through fireplace opens into this large room with a double-stepped-up ceiling.

- Kitchen: A charming breakfast nook leads to this gourmet kitchen.

- Dining Room: Just off the kitchen, this formal room boasts a 10-foot-high ceiling.

- Master Suite: This massive sleeping suite has a sloped ceiling. The private bath has his and her vanities and two walk-in closets.

- Bedrooms: The three additional large bedrooms, all with sloped ceilings, share a common bathroom.

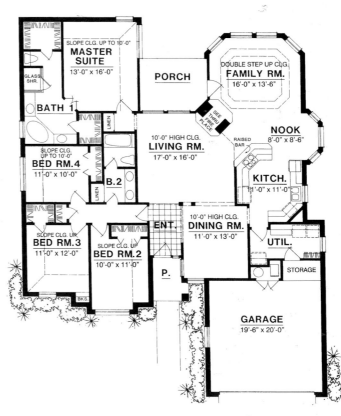

Copyright by designer/architect.

Accessorizing Your Landscape

Your new cottage home won't be complete until the lawns and plants in the landscape are established. That takes time, but one way to move the design along and to provide some design punch in the established garden is to include landscape accessories, such as trellises, arbors, distinctive planters, and landscape lighting.

Trellises

Trellises were a key element in Renaissance gardens and continued in popularity through the eighteenth century. Trellises enjoyed a resurgence of popularity in the late-nineteenth century, but never to the extent of earlier times.

Trellises can lend an air of magic and mystery to a cottage garden. Generally we think of trellises in terms of the prefabricated sheets of diamond- or square-grid lattice and the fan-shaped supports for training climbers, both of which are readily available at home and garden centers in both wood and plastic. Lacking a pattern book, most gardeners are unaware of the incredible variety of designs, patterns, and optical illusions that can be created with trellises.

Uses for Trellises

A trellis screen is a wonderfully airy way to achieve privacy or to partition off a space. The lath slats of lattice interrupt the view without totally obscuring it, creating the effect of a transparent curtain. Left bare, the pretty design of diamonds or squares makes an attractive effect. Covered in vines a trellis screen is enchanting.

Cover a Wall with a Trellis. The art of treillage, as the French call it, is not limited to screens. You can cover a bare wall or unattractive fence with a trellis pattern. Arrange the trellis pieces to create an optical illusion of an archway in the wall. Use a trellis for the walls of a gazebo to provide enclosure without being claustrophobic. Put a trellis screen with a pleasing, intricate pattern at the end of a walkway.

A metal trellis adorns a blank brick wall.

This stand-alone trellis provides interest even without plants.

Installing a ready-made trellises is a good way to jump-start your cottage landscape design.

Arbors and Pergolas

Arbors and pergolas can play a vital role in elevating the design and use of space from the ordinary to something special. The differences between an arbor and a pergola are somewhat technical, and you'll find people using the terms interchangeably. An arbor is a sheltered spot in which to sit. A pergola is generally a tunnel-like walkway or seating area created with columns or posts that support an open "roof" of beams or trelliswork. An arch (whether or not it has a curved top) is a structure through which you can walk. Usually all three structures are covered with vines.

Designing with Arbors and Pergolas

Because they stand tall, they add drama and importance to the scenery, especially if the rest of the garden features are predominantly horizontal. Take advantage of the upright supports to indulge in vertical gardening, growing climbing vines—preferably ones that flower profusely—up and over the structure. In addition, an arbor or pergola creates a shady, private retreat.

Create Transitions. Arches, arbors, and pergolas are stylish ways to mark the transition from one part of the cottage garden to another. Place an arch or arbor around the gate into the garden, or to mark the entrance from one garden room to another. Design the garden with reference to the arch or arbor so that it works like a picture window, framing a vista or a pretty vignette. Another idea is to nestle an arbor on the edge of the property to give the illusion that there is a passageway to another section. Place a bench beneath the arch for a protected, private place to sit. Design it so there is an appealing view from the arbor seat into the rest of the garden.

The English language is rich with synonyms for garden structures. Pergolas are also known as colonnades, galleries, piazzas, or porticos. Whatever you call them, these structures play a valuable role in the landscape design. In addition to being a walkway leading from one place to another, a pergola or gallery also can function as a garden wall, dividing two spaces. Instead of using a pergola as a walkway, you might place one across the far side of a patio so it serves as a partition, dividing the paved space from the planted area beyond. In addition to being a handsome architectural feature, the vine-covered structure will provide a shady retreat where people can comfortably sit, and if the central support posts are spaced properly, they can frame the view into the rest of the garden.

Integrate Arbors into the Cottage Landscape

Proper siting of an arbor or pergola is essential to its success in the design. All too often people plunk down an arbor in the middle of a lawn or garden space with no reference to the rest of the environment. Instead of being a beautiful feature, such an oddly placed structure is a curious anomaly, looking uncomfortably out of place.

Arches, arbors, and pergolas must be

An arbor or pergola placed along a path anchors the path and creates a destination for someone walking in the garden. It allows you to engage in vertical gardening.

connected to the overall design. For example, a path should lead to an arch or arbor. Place an arbor on the edge of the property, and then enhance the illusion that it is leading to additional grounds by camouflaging the property boundary with shrubs. Be sure to have a path leading to the arbor to anchor its position and to encourage people to stroll over and enjoy it.

Position Pergolas Over Paths. The best location for a pergola is over an important path. Ideally a pergola should not lead to a dead end. Even a small garden can have room for a pergola. Instead of running it down the center of the property, set it along the property line. Plant shade-loving plants under its protected canopy, and place a bench underneath to create a shady retreat. A vine-covered pergola gives much-valued privacy from the upper stories of adjacent houses.

Although a pergola often covers a straight walkway, there is no rule that says a pergola cannot cover a curving path. In such a case, the curve prompts curiosity.

The curving top of an arbor is a good shape to copy for other structures, such as the fence above, in a cottage garden.

A pergola and trellis combine to provide shade and a certain level of privacy to the patio shown below.

A pergola-like structure, right, supported by a deck railing provides dappled shade for the benches below it.

Near the house it is wise to choose a design for your arbor or pergola that complements the design of the building. For a traditional-style house like a cottage you may want to support your arbor or pergola with classical columns made of concrete, fiberglass, or stone. Augment a brick house with brick support posts. Cast-iron or aluminum posts could echo other wrought-iron features, such as a balcony, railing, or gate. Farther from the house, you can have more leeway.

Scale Pergolas to Garden Size. In a small cottage garden, make a pergola less architecturally domineering by building the support posts and rafters out of thinner material such as metal or finer-cut lumber. In a large garden where you need the extra mass, opt for columns built of brick, stone, or substantial pieces of lumber.

Place arbors and pergolas so that they become a destination in the yard, left.

An unusual shape draws attention to this arbor and the property beyond, above.

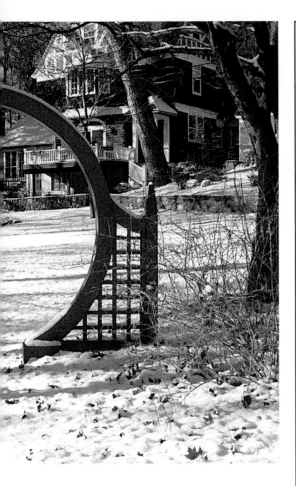

Plants for Arches, Arbors, and Pergolas

BOTANICAL NAME	COMMON NAME	ZONE
Aristolochia macrophylla	Dutchman's pipe	4–8
Bignonia capreolata	cross vine	6–9
Bougainvillea cultivars		10
Campsis radians	trumpet creeper	4–9
Clematis species and cultivars		
	'Comtesse de Bouchard'	4–9
	'Duchess of Albany'	4–9
	'Ernest Markham'	4–9
	'Gypsy Queen'	4–9
	'Gravetye Beauty'	4–9
	'Hagley Hybrid'	4–9
	'Henryi'	4–9
	'Horn of Plenty',	4–9
	C. x jackmanii 'Superba'	3–9
	C. montana	6–9
	C. tangutica 'Bill MacKenzie'	5–7
	C. terniflora sweet autumn clematis	5–9
Hydrangea petiolaris	climbing hydrangea	4–9, 4–10 in west
Lonicera species	honeysuckle	zones vary with species
Parthenocissus tricuspidata	Boston ivy	4–9
Rosa cultivars	climbing rose	
	'Alberic Barbier'	4–10
	'Albertine'	4–10
	'Blaze'	4–10
	'Chaplin's Pink Companion'	4–10
	'Felicite Perpetue'	4–10
	R. filipes 'Kiftsgate'	5–10
	'Mme. Gregoire Staechelin'	4–10
	'New Dawn'	4–10
	'Veilchenblau'	4–10
Schizophragma hydrangeoides	Japanese hydrangea vine	5–9
Trachelospermum jasminoides	star jasmine	8–10
Vitis coignetiae	crimson glory vine	6–9
Vitis vinifera 'Purpurea'	purpleleaf grape	6–9
Wisteria species	wisteria	5–10

Pergolas should always be somewhat higher than they are wide. A minimum width of about 5 feet allows two people to walk through the pergola abreast. The structure should be high enough to allow a tall adult to walk underneath comfortably. The upright support posts also need to be in proportion to the roof. If the supports are hefty, the overhead beams also should be substantial. How far apart you space the roof beams depends on the final effect you want. Wide spacing creates a skylight. Close spacing of the beams makes the pergola more tunnel-like.

Bear in mind that an arbor or pergola covered in vines must bear a lot of weight. The upright posts should be strong and properly rooted in a solid foundation, and the roof structure should be well built.

You can build your own or purchase ready-made units from a home center or garden-supply outlet. In most cases, large trellises, arbors, and pergolas come unassembled. Check with the local building department (or your house builder may know) for code requirements for foundations and construction.

Tips for Containers and Hanging Baskets

- To keep down the weight of containers filled with soil, fill the lower half of large pots with foam peanuts, perlite, or any other lightweight material that will not compact over time. Put potting mix in the remaining space, and plant as usual.

- To keep up with the heavy feeding most container-grown plants need, add compost to the planting mix or add liquid seaweed or a fish emulsion/liquid seaweed combination to the water every few weeks to ensure a well-balanced supply of all essential micronutrients.

- To remoisten peat moss if it becomes dry, fill a tub with water and add a drop of liquid detergent to help the water stick to the peat moss. Set the basket in the water, and leave it for several hours until the potting soil and peat moss mix is saturated with water.

- Pinch off dead blossoms regularly to keep container plants bushy and full of flowers.

- Cluster your pots together in a sheltered spot if you will be away for several days. The plants will need watering less frequently, and it will be easier to water if the containers are all in one place.

- To automatically water containers, bury one end of a long wick (such as those sold with oil-fueled lanterns) near the plant's roots. Insert the other end in a bucket of water. The wick will gradually soak up the water and provide a slow, continuous source of water for the plant.

- If a plant is root-bound, prune the roots by cutting back the outer edges of the root ball instead of transplanting it to a larger container. Then repot it in the same container with fresh soil.

- Consider watering many containers with an automatic drip irrigation system; install a line to each container.

- To reduce moisture loss, top the soil in your containers with mulch.

Containers for Plants

People have been gardening in containers at least since King Nebuchadnezzar built the Hanging Gardens of Babylon in 600 BC. While most people do not attempt container gardening on the massive scale achieved by Nebuchadnezzar, containers still play an important role in enhancing a garden. There are many advantages to container gardening.

Container Gardens are Versatile.
Container gardens can be moved when they are past their prime. You can grow tropical plants in containers by keeping them outside in the summer and moving them indoors to overwinter where winters are harsh. If your soil is alkaline, you can grow acid-loving plants in pots. Containers add color and excitement to patios. Cluster a group of containers to create a pleasing composition of shapes, sizes, and colors.

Attach baskets of cascading plants to pergolas, arbors, and eaves to bring color up high.

Designing with Containers
Choose your containers with the same care as you would a sculpture or any other garden ornament. In addition to finding pots that complement your garden style, think about which plants to put in them.

Match Plants to Containers. Showy plants such as palms, Dracaena, and shrubs pruned as standards look best in traditionally designed planters such as classic urns or white planter boxes. Rustic barrels or half barrels are inexpensive and unpretentious containers in an informal setting.

Try Unusual Containers. Fill an old wheelbarrow with potted plants, or give new life to a leaky metal watering can by turning it into a planter. Or plant an old shoe with shallow-rooted succulents.

Use your imagination and have fun. Whatever container you use, however, make sure it has drainage holes in the bottom. Unless you're growing bog plants, they'll be short-lived if their roots are sitting permanently in water.

Plant containers can be as distinctive or as simple as you like. The decorative planters shown top left look good on a porch or patio. The tall white bucket above add height to an arrangement of planters. A copper-finish planter on a table, left, decorates an entrance.

Maintaining Container Plants

Plants growing in containers need special care. Small containers dry out quickly and need frequent watering. In dry climates or on windy days, some containers should be watered at least once, if not twice, daily. However, frequent watering leaches out soil nutrients, so container-grown plants should be fertilized regularly.

Use Light, Well-Draining Soil. The soil in containers should be light and nutritious. Soil collected from the garden is too heavy. But soilless container mixes are often so light they dry out quickly. As a compromise, combine 2 parts potting mix with 1 part compost. The compost will give more body to the mix, as well as provide important nutrients.

Choice of Fertilizer Depends on What's Growing. The type and frequency of fertilizing depends on what's growing in the container. Some experts recommend fertilizing with half-strength fish emulsion every time you water. This makes it easier to remember when you last fed the plants. Or fertilize your plants with organic slow-release fertilizer pellets every 4 to 6 weeks. Mix the pellets with the potting mix at planting time; a good dose should feed annuals for the entire season.

Create a theme, such as the frogs shown left, if you are looking for an easy way to add some whimsy to a cottage garden.

Hide small sculptures or other items throughout the garden. The frog above would be at home near a water feature.

To highlight an arbor, string small lights over it. The arbor shown opposite left is covered with blanket lights.

A candle in a lantern, opposite right, isn't for everyday lighting, but it does make an interesting accent for special occasions.

Humor in the Landscape

A touch of levity adds to the pleasure of a cottage garden. Even in a formal landscape, there is room for a subtle, sophisticated joke—or some broad humor.

A childlike enthusiasm is often a factor in successful whimsy. Treehouses, in addition to being wonderful places for children to play, suggest a gardener who remembers the wonders of climbing trees for a bird's-eye view of the territory. Garden animal sculptures can be elevated to whimsy with careful placement. For example, concrete stalking cat sculptures with marble eyes are readily available and inexpensive. Stuck in plain view, these cats lack subtlety. But try placing one where it is partially hidden by arching shrubbery or cascading plants. Now you have a creature of the jungle on the prowl, glimpsed but not completely seen.

Be True to Yourself. Don't be daunted by the views of others. Be true to yourself, and express your own personality and sense of humor. With some thought and creativity, you can create a whimsical vignette or two in your garden that will lift your heart and tickle your funny bone.

Outdoor Lighting

First decide how much light you need and where it should go. Besides general overall illumination, locate fixtures near activity zones: the food preparation and cooking area, the wet bar, or wherever you plan to set up drinks, snacks, or a buffet when you entertain. Be sure that there is adequate light near the dining table, conversation areas, and recreational spots, such as the hot tub, if you plan to use them in the evening. You may want separate switches for each one, and you might consider dimmers; you don't need or want the same intensity of light required for barbecuing as you do for relaxing in the hot tub.

Lighting the Way

Walkways and staircases need lighting for safety. There are a number of practical options: path lights (if the walkway is ground level), brick lights that can be inserted into your walls near the steps, and railing fixtures that can be tucked under deck railings or steps. Less-functional but more-decorative lighting such as post lamps can provide illumination for high traffic areas; sconces can be effective on stair landings or near doors. Walk lights also provide a needed measure of safety. Be sure to pick fixtures that look as good during the day as they do at night.

Don't forget about areas that may call for motion-sensitive floodlights, such as entrances into the house and garage, underneath a raised deck, and deep yards are all excellent locations for floodlights. Keep these fixtures on separate switches so that they don't interfere with the atmosphere you want to create while you are using the deck.

Adding Accent Light

Are there any noteworthy plantings or objects in your garden that you can highlight? By using in-ground accent lighting or spotlights, you can create dramatic nighttime effects or a focal point. Artful lighting can enhance the ambiance of your deck by drawing attention to the shape of a handsome tree, a garden statue, a fountain or pond, or an outdoor pool.

Depending on the lighting system you buy, you may be able to install the fixtures yourself. But working with electricity does pose technical, code, and safety concerns. It's probably best to hire a qualified professional for the installation. For complex projects, you may also want to consult a landscape lighting professional. Home centers sometimes provide this type of expertise. If you decide to plot a design yourself, remember not to overlight the deck.

Other Considerations

As you plan to install deck lighting, think about the space's other electrical or wiring needs. If there is an outdoor kitchen, a grill area, or a bar, you may want outlets for a refrigerator or small appliances. You might include additional outlets for a stereo or speakers, or even a TV. Don't overlook a

phone jack for the modem on your laptop computer. Some decking systems come prewired and are ready to be hooked up.

So with forethought, you can incorporate everything you need into your outdoor living plans.

Decorative Lighting

Add another dimension to your yard or garden, and get more use out of it as well, by installing decorative lighting. Start by covering a garden arch with small decorative lights. You can use multicolor lights, or for a more sophisticated look, use single-color strands or blankets. Supplement the arch lights with lanterns and torches. When selecting lights, pick those that look as good during the day as they do at night.

Stairs and walkways, opposite, require lighting for safety.

Create drama by uplighting arbors, pergolas, and plantings on your property, right.

Outdoor lighting, below, consists of standard line-voltage or low-voltage lights. A low-voltage system is easier to install.

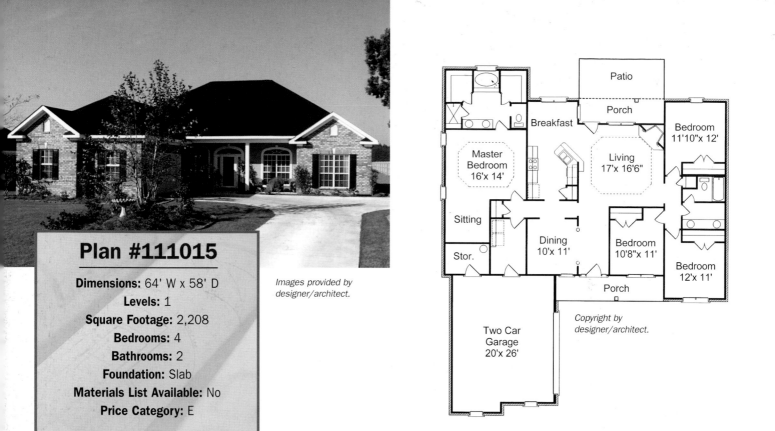

Plan #111015

Dimensions: 64' W x 58' D

Levels: 1

Square Footage: 2,208

Bedrooms: 4

Bathrooms: 2

Foundation: Slab

Materials List Available: No

Price Category: E

Images provided by designer/architect.

Copyright by designer/architect.

Patio

Porch

Breakfast

Master Bedroom 16'x 14'

Living 17'x 16'6"

Bedroom 11'10"x 12'

Sitting

Dining 10'x 11'

Bedroom 10'8"x 11'

Bedroom 12'x 11'

Stor.

Porch

Two Car Garage 20'x 26'

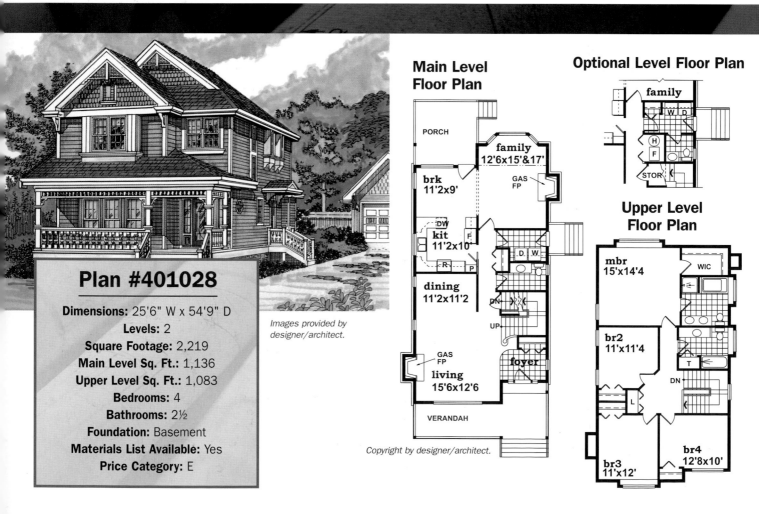

Plan #401028

Dimensions: 25'6" W x 54'9" D

Levels: 2

Square Footage: 2,219

Main Level Sq. Ft.: 1,136

Upper Level Sq. Ft.: 1,083

Bedrooms: 4

Bathrooms: 2½

Foundation: Basement

Materials List Available: Yes

Price Category: E

Images provided by designer/architect.

Main Level Floor Plan

Optional Level Floor Plan

Upper Level Floor Plan

family

PORCH

family 12'6x15'&17'

GAS FP

brk 11'2x9'

DW

kit 11'2x10'

dining 11'2x11'2

DN

UP

GAS FP

living 15'6x12'6

foyer

VERANDAH

mbr 15'x14'4

WIC

br2 11'x11'4

DN

br3 11'x12'

br4 12'8x10'

Copyright by designer/architect.

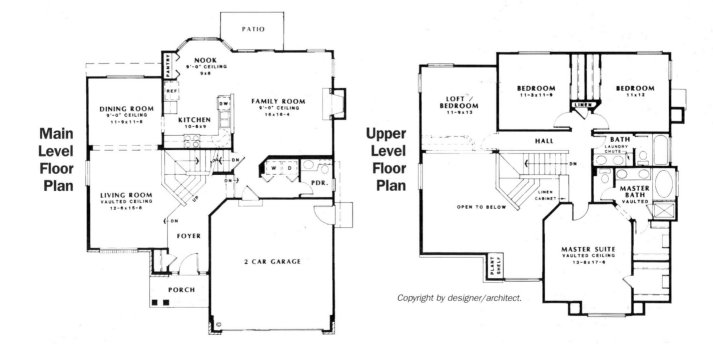

Plan #391023

Dimensions: 41'4" W x 47'4" D

Levels: 2

Square Footage: 2,244

Main Level Sq. Ft.: 1,115

Upper Level Sq. Ft.: 1,129

Bedrooms: 4

Bathrooms: 2½

Foundation: Crawl space, slab, or basement

Materials List Available: Yes

Price Category: E

Images provided by designer/architect.

This great four-bedroom home is perfect for your neighborhood.

Features:

- Living Room: Step down from the entry to this vaulted-ceiling gathering area.

- Dining Room: This special area has a 9-ft.-high ceiling and is open to the living room.

- Family Room: This casual, relaxing area has a fireplace and a sliding glass door to the patio.

- Master Suite: This oasis has a vaulted ceiling, his and her closets, and a private master bath.

- Bedrooms: The two secondary bedrooms share a hall bathroom. The loft can be converted to a fourth bedroom.

Main Level Floor Plan

Upper Level Floor Plan

Copyright by designer/architect.

Plan #371045

Dimensions: 56' W x 57'7" D

Levels: 2

Square Footage: 2,225

Main Level Sq. Ft.: 1,678

Upper Level Sq. Ft.: 547

Bedrooms: 3

Bathrooms: 2½

Foundation: Slab

Materials List Available: No

Price Category: E

Images provided by designer/architect.

With its spectacular brick gables and stunning windows, this French-style home will treat you to the lifestyle you deserve.

Features:

- **Living Room:** A 10-ft.-high ceiling, warm two-way fireplace, and generous windows give this large living room a touch of class.

- **Family Room:** French doors that provide access to the rear porch, a two-way fireplace with bookshelves on both sides, and a 10-ft.-high ceiling combine to create a warm and relaxing room the whole family will enjoy.

- **Dining Room:** This formal room has a 10-ft.-high ceiling and is open to the living room.

- **Kitchen:** In addition to easy access to the dining room, breakfast nook, and family room, this kitchen has a walk-in pantry and large central island.

- **Master Suite:** This large secluded retreat boasts an elegant bath with a marble tub and his and her walk-in closets.

- **Bedrooms:** Upstairs are two additional bedrooms with walk-in closets, and they share a hall bathroom with a dressing room.

Main Level Floor Plan

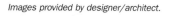

Upper Level Floor Plan

Copyright by designer/architect.

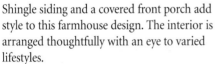

Plan #401042

Dimensions: 47' W x 48' D
Levels: 2
Square Footage: 2,239
Main Level Sq. Ft.: 1,092
Upper Level Sq. Ft.: 1,147
Bedrooms: 3
Bathrooms: 2½
Foundation: Basement
Materials List Available: Yes
Price Category: E

Images provided by designer/architect.

Features:

- **Living Room:** This formal room has a tray ceiling and a fireplace.
- **Dining Room:** This second formal room is separated from the living room by columns.
- **Kitchen:** This island kitchen connects directly to the breakfast room and the family room with a fireplace. Note the double doors in the breakfast room to the rear covered porch.

- **Master Suite:** This area has a vaulted ceiling and walk-in closet; it features a luxurious bath with a separate tub and shower.
- **Bedrooms:** The second floor provides space for three additional bedrooms.

Shingle siding and a covered front porch add style to this farmhouse design. The interior is arranged thoughtfully with an eye to varied lifestyles.

Right Side Elevation

Left Side Elevation

Main Level Floor Plan

din 10'x13'
brk 9'6x13'8
fam 16'x13'
k 10'2x13'6
liv 12'x15'
PORCH
DN
UP ENTRY
DN
DN
D W
TRAY CEILING
garage 20'6x23'6

Copyright by designer/architect.

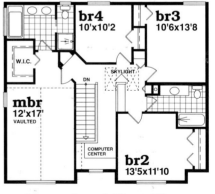

Upper Level Floor Plan

br4 10'x10'2
br3 10'6x13'8
W.I.C.
SKYLIGHT
mbr 12'x17' VAULTED
DN
COMPUTER CENTER
br2 13'5x11'10

Rear Elevation

Plan #371059

Dimensions: 77'8" W x 56'6" D

Levels: 1

Square Footage: 2,240

Bedrooms: 4

Bathrooms: 2½

Foundation: Slab

Materials List Available: No

Price Category: E

This beautiful brick home achieves one-of-a-kind styling with a unique roofline.

Features:

- Dining Room: Once inside you will find a tiled entry that steps into this elegant room with an 11-ft.-high ceiling.

- Living Room: This large gathering area has an 11-ft.-high ceiling, built-in bookcases, and a grand fireplace.

- Kitchen: This kitchen is open to the breakfast nook and meets the garage entrance.

- Master Suite: This suite, with stepped-up ceiling, features a private bathroom with his and her walk-in closets and double vanities.

- Bedrooms: Three secondary bedrooms have large closets and share a hall bathroom.

Images provided by designer/architect.

Copyright by designer/architect.

3 CAR GARAGE 21'-0" x 31'-0"

BATH 1

MASTER SUITE 14'-0" x 17'-0"

PORCH

BED RM.2 12'-0" x 11'-0"

UTIL.

LIVING RM. 20'-0" x 16'-0" — 11'-0" HIGH CLG.

B.2

NOOK 8'-0" X 8'-0"

BED RM.3 12'-0" x 11'-0"

KITCH. 12'-0" x 11'-0"

DINING RM. 11'-0" x 15'-0" — 11'-0" HIGH CLG.

ENT.

BED RM.4 11'-8" x 10'-0" — 10'-0" HIGH CLG.

BONUS RM. 21'-4" x 14'-0"

Bonus Area

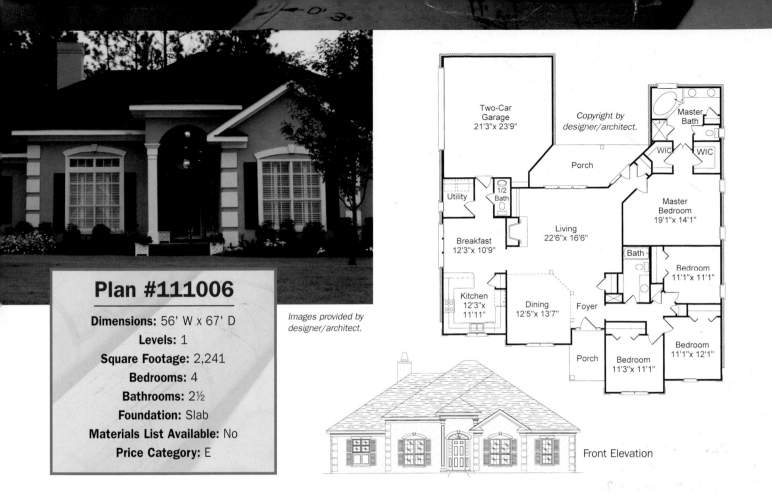

Copyright by designer/architect.

Two-Car Garage
21'3"x 23'9"

Porch

Utility

1/2 Bath

Breakfast
12'3"x 10'9"

Living
22'6"x 16'6"

Kitchen
12'3"x 11'11"

Dining
12'5"x 13'7"

Foyer

Porch

Master Bath

WIC WIC

Master Bedroom
19'1"x 14'1"

Bath

Bedroom
11'1"x 11'1"

Bedroom
11'1"x 12'1"

Bedroom
11'3"x 11'1"

Images provided by designer/architect.

Plan #111006

Dimensions: 56' W x 67' D
Levels: 1
Square Footage: 2,241
Bedrooms: 4
Bathrooms: 2½
Foundation: Slab
Materials List Available: No
Price Category: E

Front Elevation

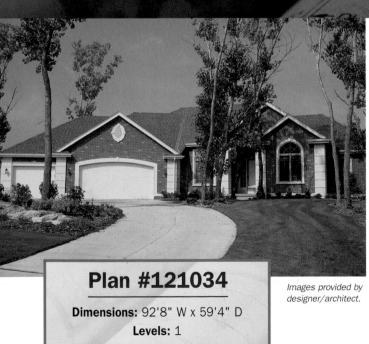

Plan #121034

Dimensions: 92'8" W x 59'4" D
Levels: 1
Square Footage: 2,223
Bedrooms: 1
Bathrooms: 1½
Foundation: Basement
Materials List Available: Yes
Price Category: E

Images provided by designer/architect.

Copyright by designer/architect.

COVERED DECK

Eating Area

Hearth Room
9'0" x 10'

Great Room
19'0" x 16'
12'-0" CEILING

Mbr.
13' x 16'
12'-0" CEILING

Workshop
14' x 11'

Garage
33' x 30'

Dining Room
12'3" x 13'
11'-0" CEILING

Covered Stoop

Flex Room
12'-0" CEILING

59'-4"

92'-8"

Optional Basement Level Floor Plan

Recreation Room
34' x 15'

Exercise
12'3" x 12'10"

Br.2
14' x 11'

Br.3
14' x 10'

UNFINISHED STORAGE

UP

Plan #351055

Dimensions: 73'8" W x 58'4" D

Levels: 1

Square Footage: 2,251

Bedrooms: 3

Bathrooms: 2½

Foundation: Crawl space, slab, or basement

Materials List Available: Yes

Price Category: E

Images provided by designer/architect.

Main Level Floor Plan

Bonus Area Floor Plan

Copyright by designer/architect.

Plan #101017

Dimensions: 57' W x 51' D

Levels: 2

Square Footage: 2,253

Main Level Sq. Ft.: 1,719

Upper Level Sq. Ft.: 534

Opt. Upper Level Bonus Sq. Ft.: 247

Bedrooms: 4

Bathrooms: 3

Foundation: Basement

Materials List Available: No

Price Category: E

Images provided by designer/architect.

Main Level Floor Plan

Upper Level Floor Plan

Copyright by designer/architect.

Main Level Floor Plan

- Mbr. 13⁸ x 15⁰
- Grt. Rm. 14⁰ x 18⁴ 18'-0" CEILING
- Bfst. 10¹⁰ x 14⁸
- RECYCLE SNACK BAR
- Kit. 10⁸ x 15¹¹
- P.
- UP
- DN
- W. D.
- E.
- WHIRLPOOL
- Din. Rm. 11⁰ x 12⁴
- Gar. 22⁰ x 22⁴
- Study 13⁸ x 11⁰
- COVERED PORCH

45'-4"
54'-8"

Images provided by designer/architect.

Upper Level Floor Plan

- OPEN TO GRT. RM. 18'-0" CEILING
- Br.3 10⁰ x 12⁶
- Br.2 11² x 14¹⁰
- DN
- L.
- OPEN TO ENTRY
- Br.4 12⁰ x 10⁰
- Storage 10⁰ x 21⁸

Copyright by designer/architect.

Plan #121032

Dimensions: 54'8" W x 45'4" D
Levels: 2
Square Footage: 2,339
Main Level Sq. Ft.: 1,665
Upper Level Sq. Ft.: 674
Bedrooms: 4
Bathrooms: 2½
Foundation: Basement
Materials List Available: Yes
Price Category: E

Main Level Floor Plan

- Raised Hearth
- Family Rm 15-0 x 17-4
- Deck (Optional)
- Brkfst 9-9 x 14-10
- Kitchen 12-1 x 13-4
- Lndry
- Garage 23-8 x 35-4
- Flat Clg @ 4'
- Shelves
- Pantry
- Br.
- Parlor 12-1 x 12-4
- Flat Clg @ 8'
- Dining 11-7 x 12-4
- UP
- Porch

Upper Level Floor Plan

- Attic Space (Optional)
- WLP. Tub
- Skylt
- Skylt
- Br #3 11-7 x 9-10
- MBr #1 12-1 x 15-10 8' Clg
- DN
- Railing
- Li.
- Plant Shelf
- Br #2 11-7 x 11-10
- Flat Clg @ 10'
- Open to Below

Copyright by designer/architect.

Images provided by designer/architect.

Alternate Crawl Space/Slab

- D
- W
- LT
- Furn
- WH
- Br.

Plan #391002

Dimensions: 76'4" W x 45'10" D
Levels: 2
Square Footage: 2,281
Main Level Sq. Ft.: 1,260
Upper Level Sq. Ft.: 1,021
Bedrooms: 3
Bathrooms: 2½
Foundation: Crawl space, slab, or basement
Materials List Available: Yes
Price Category: E

Images provided by designer/architect.

Plan #181151

Dimensions: 50' W x 46' D
Levels: 2
Square Footage: 2,283
Main Level Sq. Ft.: 1,274
Second Level Sq. Ft.: 1,009
Bedrooms: 3
Bathrooms: 2½
Foundation: Basement
Materials List Available: Yes
Price Category: E

- Kitchen: This efficient and well-designed kitchen has double sinks and offers a separate eating area for those impromptu family meals.

- Master Bedroom: This master retreat has a walk-in closet and its own sumptuous bath.

- Home Office: Whether you work at home or just need a place for the family computer and keeping track of family finances, this home office fills the bill.

Multiple porches, stately columns, and arched multi-paned windows adorn this country home.

Features:

- Ceiling Height: 8 ft. unless otherwise noted.

- Great Room: The second-floor mezzanine overlooks this great room. With its soaring ceiling, this dramatic room is the centerpiece of a spacious and flowing design that is just as suited to entertaining as it is to family life.

- Dining Area: Guests will naturally flow into this dining area when it is time to eat. After dinner they can step directly out onto the porch to enjoy coffee and dessert when the weather is fair.

Main Level Floor Plan

21'-0" X 20'-8"
6,30 X 6,20

17'-0" X 11'-8"
5,10 X 3,50

9'-8" X 8'-8"
2,90 X 2,60

9'-0" X 10'-0"
2,70 X 3,00

10'-0" X 12'-0"
3,00 X 3,60

9'-8" X 9'-4"
2,90 X 2,80

12'-0" X 20'-8"
3,60 X 6,20

46'-0"
13,8 m

50'-0"
15,0 m

Upper Level Floor Plan

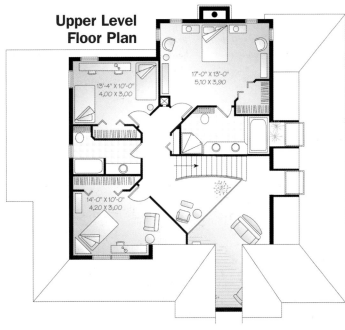

13'-4" X 10'-0"
4,00 X 3,00

17'-0" X 13'-0"
5,10 X 3,90

14'-0" X 10'-0"
4,20 X 3,00

Copyright by designer/architect.

SMARTtip

Coping Chair Rails

If the teeth of your rasp tend to break out thin edges of the cope, try wrapping the rasp with sandpaper to make fine adjustments.

Dining Room

Living Room

Master Bath

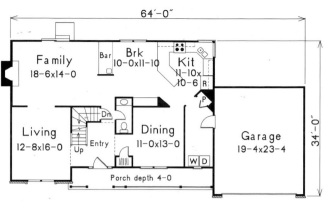

Main Level Floor Plan

Upper Level Floor Plan

Copyright by designer/architect.

Plan #321041

Dimensions: 64' W x 34' D

Levels: 2

Square Footage: 2,286

Main Level Sq. Ft.: 1,283

Upper Level Sq. Ft.: 1,003

Bedrooms: 4

Bathrooms: 2½

Foundation: Crawl space, slab, or basement

Materials List Available: Yes

Price Category: E

Images provided by designer/architect.

Plan #121021

Dimensions: 46' W x 48' D

Levels: 2

Square Footage: 2,270

Main Level Sq. Ft.: 1,150

Upper Level Sq. Ft.: 1,120

Bedrooms: 4

Bathrooms: 2½

Foundation: Basement

Materials List Available: Yes

Price Category: E

Images provided by designer/architect.

This home, as shown in the photograph, may differ from the actual blueprints. For more detailed information, please check the floor plans carefully.

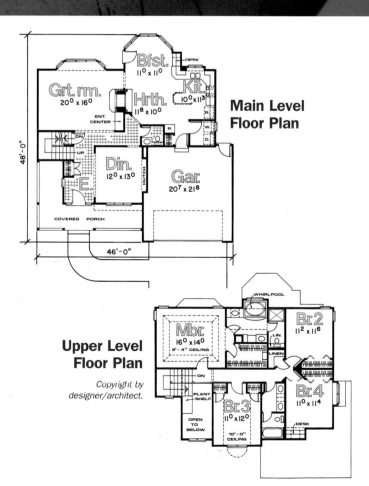

Main Level Floor Plan

Upper Level Floor Plan

Copyright by designer/architect.

Plan #371060

Dimensions: 70'9" W x 59' D

Levels: 1

Square Footage: 2,296

Bedrooms: 4

Bathrooms: 2

Foundation: Basement

Materials List Available: No

Price Category: E

Images provided by designer/architect.

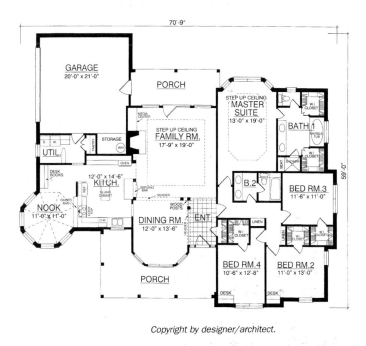

Copyright by designer/architect.

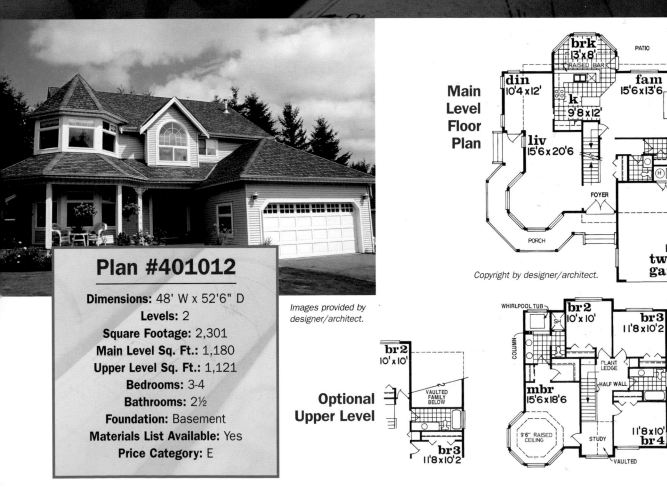

Plan #401012

Dimensions: 48' W x 52'6" D

Levels: 2

Square Footage: 2,301

Main Level Sq. Ft.: 1,180

Upper Level Sq. Ft.: 1,121

Bedrooms: 3-4

Bathrooms: 2½

Foundation: Basement

Materials List Available: Yes

Price Category: E

Images provided by designer/architect.

Copyright by designer/architect.

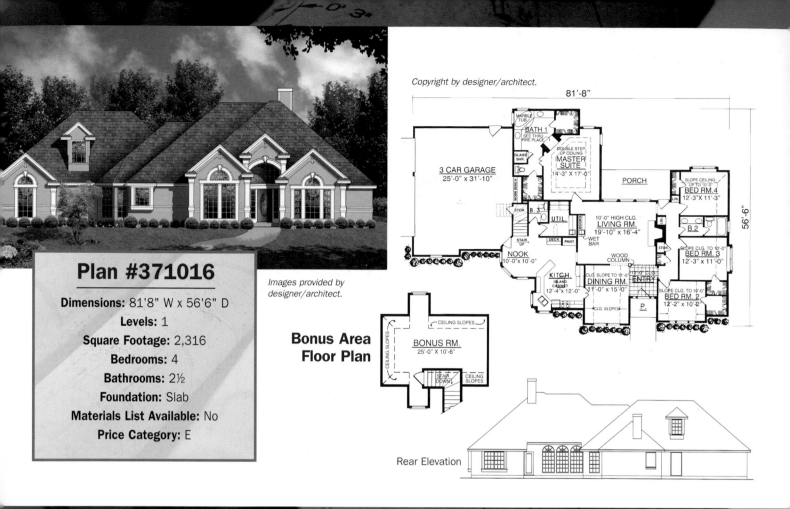

Plan #371016

Dimensions: 81'8" W x 56'6" D

Levels: 1

Square Footage: 2,316

Bedrooms: 4

Bathrooms: 2½

Foundation: Slab

Materials List Available: No

Price Category: E

Images provided by designer/architect.

Copyright by designer/architect.

81'-8"

3 CAR GARAGE
25'-0" x 31'-10"

BATH 1
SEE THRU
FIRE PLACE

MARBLE TUB

GLASS SHR.

DOUBLE STEP UP CEILING
MASTER SUITE
14'-3" X 17'-0"

PORCH

SLOPE CEILING UP TO 10'-0"
BED RM.4
12'-3" X 11'-3"

WORK BENCH

STOR.

B.3

UTIL.

10'-0" HIGH CLG.
LIVING RM.
19'-10" x 16'-4"

B.2

56'-6"

STAIR UP

DECK

PANT.

WET BAR

SLOPE CLG. TO 10'-0"
BED RM. 3
12'-3" X 11'-0"

NOOK
10'-0" x 10'-0"

WOOD COLUMN

ENTRY

STOR.

KITCH.
ISLAND CABINET
12'-4" x 12'-0"

CLG. SLOPE TO 11'-0"
DINING RM.
11'-0" x 15'-0"

SLOPE CLG. TO 10'-0"
BED RM. 2
12'-2" x 10'-2"

P.

Bonus Area Floor Plan

CEILING SLOPES

CEILING SLOPES

BONUS RM.
25'-0" X 10'-6"

STAIR DOWN

CEILING SLOPES

Rear Elevation

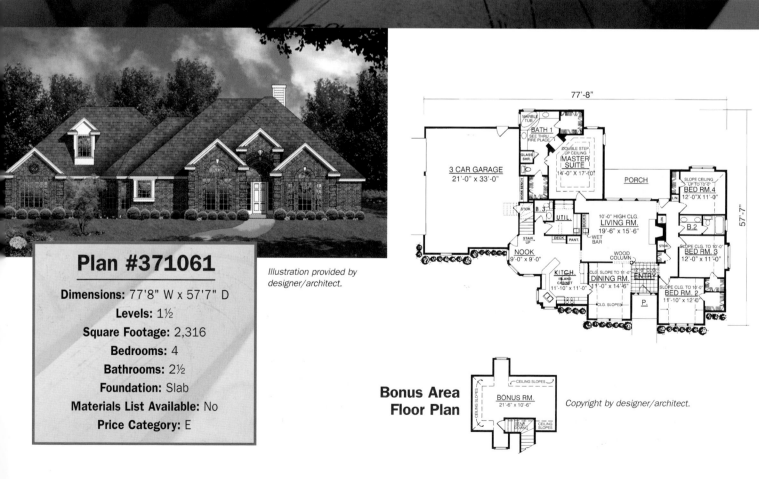

Plan #371061

Dimensions: 77'8" W x 57'7" D

Levels: 1½

Square Footage: 2,316

Bedrooms: 4

Bathrooms: 2½

Foundation: Slab

Materials List Available: No

Price Category: E

Illustration provided by designer/architect.

77'-8"

BATH 1
SEE THRU
FIRE PLACE

MARBLE TUB

GLASS SHR.

DOUBLE STEP UP CEILING
MASTER SUITE
14'-0" X 17'-0"

3 CAR GARAGE
21'-0" x 33'-0"

PORCH

SLOPE CEILING UP TO 10'-0"
BED RM.4
12'-0" X 11'-0"

WORK BENCH

STOR.

B.3

UTIL.

10'-0" HIGH CLG.
LIVING RM.
19'-6" x 15'-6"

B.2

57'-7"

STAIR UP

DECK

PANT.

WET BAR

SLOPE CLG. TO 10'-0"
BED RM. 3
12'-0" X 11'-0"

NOOK
9'-0" x 9'-0"

WOOD COLUMN

ENTRY

STOR.

KITCH.
ISLAND CABINET
11'-0" x 11'-0"

CLG. SLOPE TO 11'-0"
DINING RM.
11'-0" x 14'-6"

SLOPE CLG. TO 10'-0"
BED RM. 2
11'-10" x 12'-0"

P.

Bonus Area Floor Plan

CEILING SLOPES

BONUS RM.
21'-6" x 10'-6"

STAIR DOWN

CEILING SLOPES

Copyright by designer/architect.

Main Level Floor Plan

Bonus Area Floor Plan

Copyright by designer/architect.

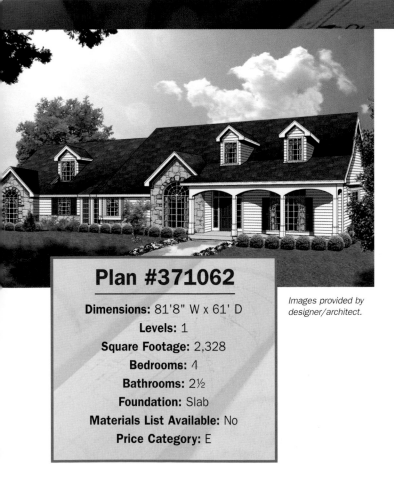

Plan #371017

Dimensions: 77'8" W x 58'7" D

Levels: 1½

Square Footage: 2,320

Bedrooms: 4

Bathrooms: 2½

Foundation: Slab

Materials List Available: No

Price Category: E

Images provided by designer/architect.

Copyright by designer/architect.

Bonus Area Floor Plan

Plan #371062

Dimensions: 81'8" W x 61' D

Levels: 1

Square Footage: 2,328

Bedrooms: 4

Bathrooms: 2½

Foundation: Slab

Materials List Available: No

Price Category: E

Images provided by designer/architect.

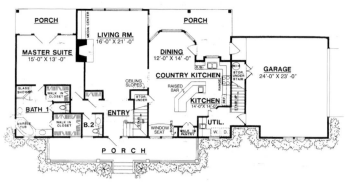

Main Level Floor Plan

Copyright by designer/architect.

Upper Level Floor Plan

Plan #371063

Dimensions: 81' W x 40'6" D

Levels: 2

Square Footage: 2,330

Main Level Sq. Ft.: 1,605

Upper Level Sq. Ft.: 725

Bedrooms: 3

Bathrooms: 2½

Foundation: Slab

Materials List Available: No

Price Category: E

Images provided by designer/architect.

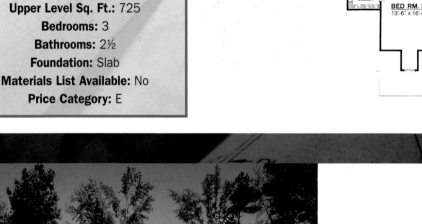

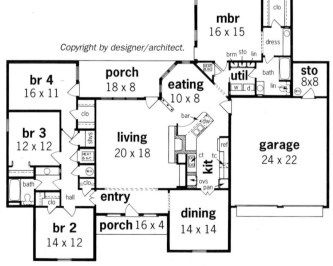

Copyright by designer/architect.

Plan #211007

Dimensions: 72' W x 60' D

Levels: 1

Square Footage: 2,252

Bedrooms: 4

Bathrooms: 2

Foundation: Slab

Materials List Available: Yes

Price Category: E

Images provided by designer/architect.

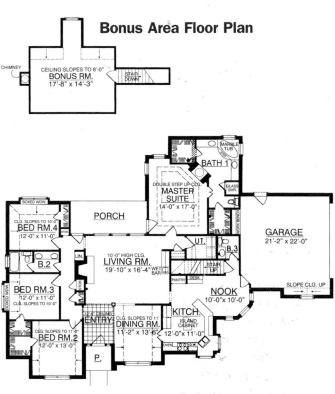

Bonus Area Floor Plan

CHIMNEY

CEILING SLOPES TO 8'-0"
BONUS RM.
17'-8" x 14'-3"

STAIR DOWN

Plan #371018

Dimensions: 77'8" W x 58'7" D

Levels: 1

Square Footage: 2,333

Bedrooms: 4

Bathrooms: 2½

Foundation: Slab

Materials List Available: No

Price Category: E

Images provided by designer/architect.

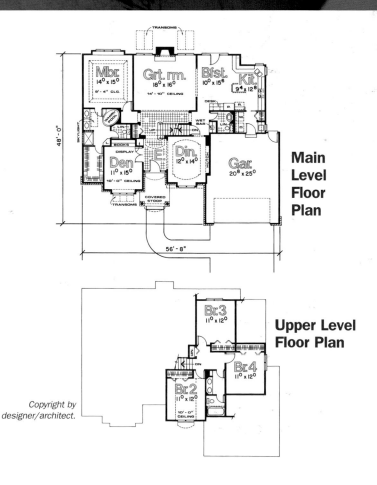

Main Level Floor Plan

Upper Level Floor Plan

Plan #121088

Dimensions: 56'8" W x 48' D

Levels: 2

Square Footage: 2,340

Main Level Sq. Ft.: 1,701

Upper Level Sq. Ft.: 639

Bedrooms: 4

Bathrooms: 2½

Foundation: Basement

Materials List Available: Yes

Price Category: E

Images provided by designer/architect.

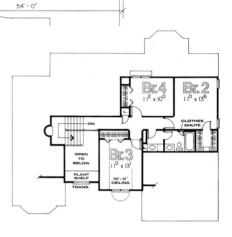

Main Level Floor Plan

Images provided by designer/architect.

Upper Level Floor Plan

Copyright by designer/architect.

Plan #121017

Dimensions: 54' W x 50' D
Levels: 2
Square Footage: 2,353
Main Level Sq. Ft.: 1,653
Upper Level Sq. Ft.: 700
Bedrooms: 4
Bathrooms: 2½
Foundation: Basement
Materials List Available: Yes
Price Category: E

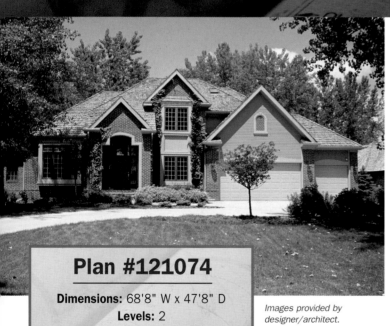

Main Level Floor Plan

Images provided by designer/architect.

Upper Level Floor Plan

Copyright by designer/architect.

Plan #121074

Dimensions: 68'8" W x 47'8" D
Levels: 2
Square Footage: 2,486
Main Level Sq. Ft.: 1,829
Upper Level Sq. Ft.: 657
Bedrooms: 4
Bathrooms: 2½
Foundation: Basement
Materials List Available: Yes
Price Category: E

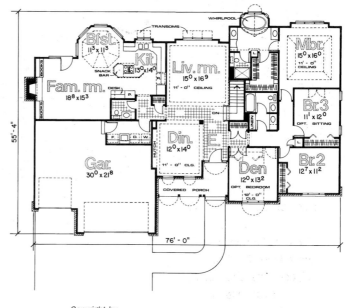

Plan #121003

Dimensions: 76' W x 55'4" D

Levels: 1

Square Footage: 2,498

Bedrooms: 4

Bathrooms: 2½

Foundation: Basement

Materials List Available: Yes

Price Category: E

Images provided by designer/architect.

Copyright by designer/architect.

Main Level Floor Plan

FIRST FLOOR

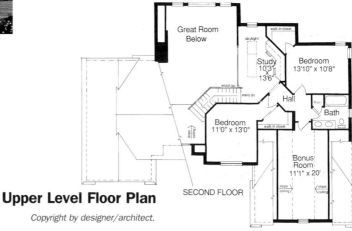

Upper Level Floor Plan

Copyright by designer/architect.

Plan #161038

Dimensions: 58'6" W x 49' D

Levels: 2

Square Footage: 2,209

Main Level Sq. Ft.: 1,542

Upper Level Sq. Ft.: 667

Bedrooms: 3

Bathrooms: 2½

Foundation: Basement

Materials List Available: No

Price Category: E

Images provided by designer/architect.

Plan #131030

Dimensions: 51' W x 41'10" D
Levels: 2
Square Footage: 2,470
Main Level Sq. Ft.: 1,290
Upper Level Sq. Ft.: 1,180
Bedrooms: 4
Bathrooms: 2½
Foundation: Crawl space, slab, basement, or walk-out basement
Materials List Available: Yes
Price Category: F

Images provided by designer/architect.

Master Bedroom

Master Bathroom

Entry

If high ceilings and spacious rooms make you happy, you'll love this gorgeous home.

Features:

- Family Room: An 18-ft. vaulted ceiling that's open to the balcony above, a corner fireplace, and a wall of windows make this room feel special.

- Dining Room: This formal room, which flows into the living room, also opens to the front porch and optional backyard deck.

- Kitchen: A bright breakfast room joins with this kitchen and opens to the backyard deck.

- Master Suite: You'll smile when you see the 11-ft. vaulted ceiling, stunning arched window, and two walk-in closets in the bedroom. A skylight lets natural light into the private bath, with its spa tub, separate shower, and dual-sink vanity.

- Bedrooms: To reach these three charming bedrooms, you'll admire the view into the family room below as you walk along the balcony hall.

Main Level Floor Plan

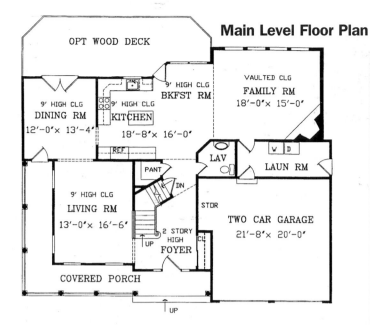

OPT WOOD DECK

9' HIGH CLG
DINING RM
12'-0" x 13'-4"

9' HIGH CLG
KITCHEN
18'-8" x 16'-0"

9' HIGH CLG
BKFST RM

VAULTED CLG
FAMILY RM
18'-0" x 15'-0"

REF

PANT

DN

LAV

W D

LAUN RM

9' HIGH CLG
LIVING RM
13'-0" x 16'-6"

UP

2 STORY
HIGH
FOYER

STOR

CL

TWO CAR GARAGE
21'-8" x 20'-0"

COVERED PORCH

UP

Upper Level Floor Plan

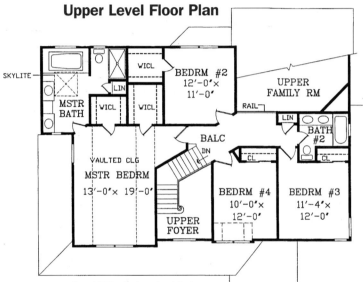

SKYLITE

WICL

LIN

MSTR
BATH

WICL

WICL

BEDRM #2
12'-0" x
11'-0"

UPPER
FAMILY RM

RAIL

LIN

BATH
#2

CL

VAULTED CLG
MSTR BEDRM
13'-0" x 19'-0"

BALC

DN

UPPER
FOYER

BEDRM #4
10'-0" x
12'-0"

BEDRM #3
11'-4" x
12'-0"

CL

Copyright by designer/architect.

Kitchen/Breakfast Area

Dining Room

Living Room

Kitchen/Breakfast Area

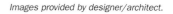

Plan #401039

Dimensions: 69'8" W x 49' D

Levels: 2

Square Footage: 2,462

Main Level Sq. Ft.: 1,333

Upper Level Sq. Ft.: 1,129

Bedrooms: 4

Bathrooms: 2½

Foundation: Basement

Materials List Available: Yes

Price Category: E

Images provided by designer/architect.

A large wraparound porch graces the exterior of this home and gives it great outdoor livability.

Features:

- **Foyer:** This raised foyer spills into a hearth-warmed living room and the bay-windowed dining room beyond; French doors open from the breakfast and dining rooms to the spacious porch.

- **Family Room:** Built-ins surround a second hearth in this cozy gathering room.

- **Study:** Located in the front, this room is adorned by a beamed ceiling and, like the family room, features built-ins.

- **Bedrooms:** You'll find three family bedrooms on the second floor.

- **Master Suite:** This restful area, located on the second floor, features a walk-in closet and private bath.

- **Garage:** Don't miss the workshop area in this garage.

Main Level Floor Plan

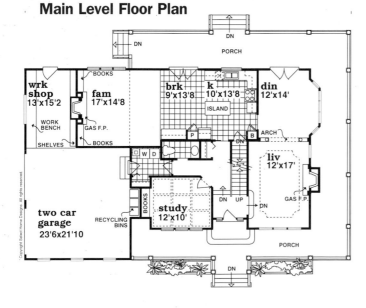

Upper Level Floor Plan

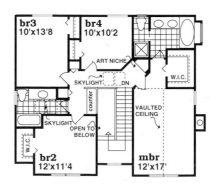

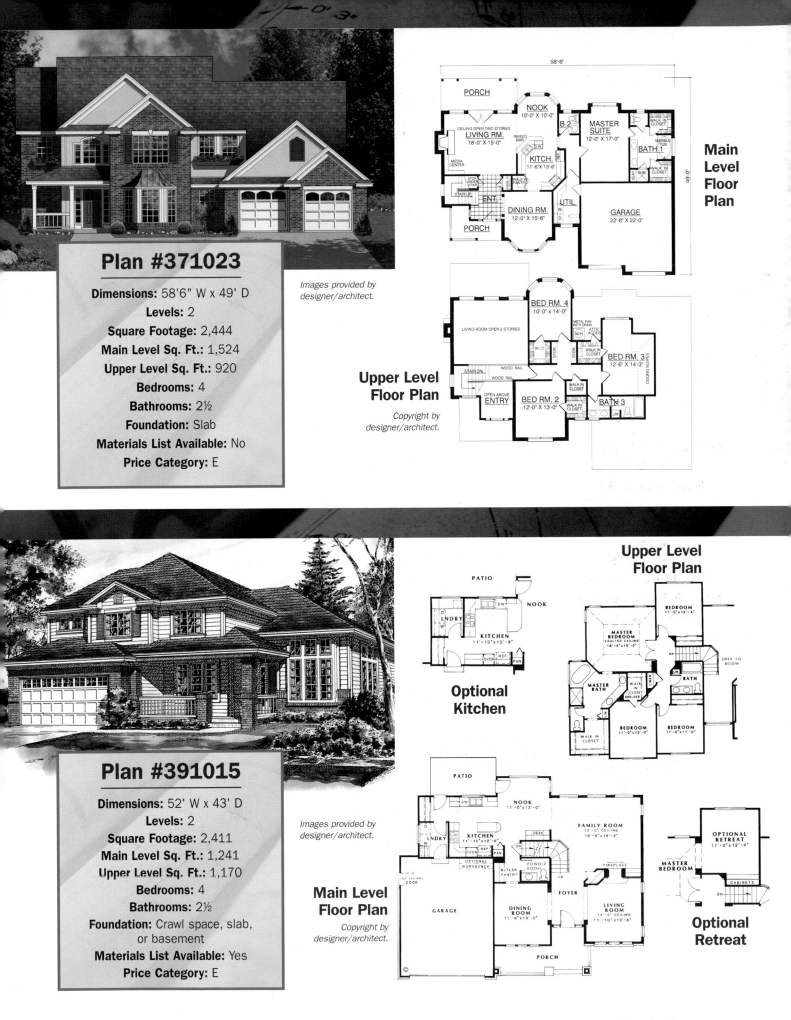

Plan #371023

Dimensions: 58'6" W x 49' D

Levels: 2

Square Footage: 2,444

Main Level Sq. Ft.: 1,524

Upper Level Sq. Ft.: 920

Bedrooms: 4

Bathrooms: 2½

Foundation: Slab

Materials List Available: No

Price Category: E

Images provided by designer/architect.

Main Level Floor Plan

Upper Level Floor Plan

Copyright by designer/architect.

Plan #391015

Dimensions: 52' W x 43' D

Levels: 2

Square Footage: 2,411

Main Level Sq. Ft.: 1,241

Upper Level Sq. Ft.: 1,170

Bedrooms: 4

Bathrooms: 2½

Foundation: Crawl space, slab, or basement

Materials List Available: Yes

Price Category: E

Images provided by designer/architect.

Upper Level Floor Plan

Optional Kitchen

Main Level Floor Plan

Copyright by designer/architect.

Optional Retreat

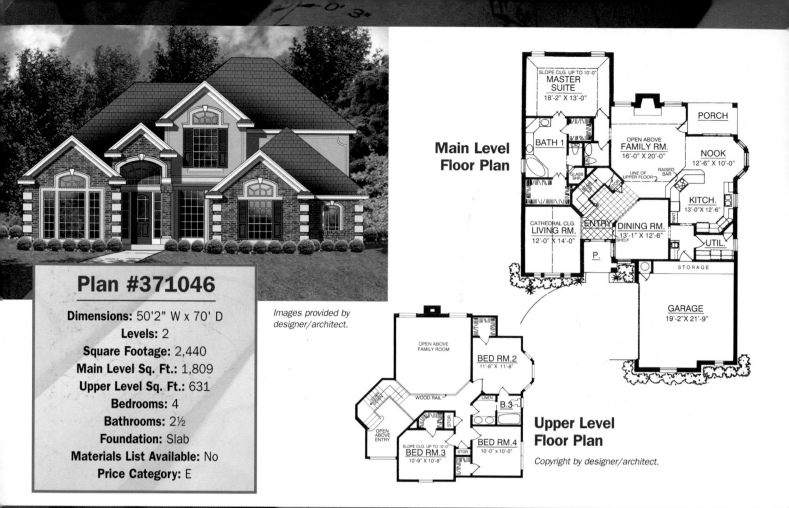

Main Level Floor Plan

SLOPE CLG. UP TO 10'-0"
MASTER SUITE
18'-2" X 13'-0"

PORCH

BATH 1

OPEN ABOVE
FAMILY RM.
16'-0" X 20'-0"

NOOK
12'-6" X 10'-0"

GLASS SHR.

LINE OF UPPER FLOOR

RAISED BAR

KITCH.
13'-0" X 12'-6"

CATHEDRAL CLG.
LIVING RM.
12'-0" X 14'-0"

ENTRY

DINING RM.
13'-1" X 12'-6"

UTIL.

STORAGE

GARAGE
19'-2" X 21'-9"

Images provided by designer/architect.

OPEN ABOVE FAMILY ROOM

BED RM.2
11'-8" X 11'-8"

WOOD RAIL

LINEN

B.3

OPEN ABOVE ENTRY

SLOPE CLG. UP TO 10'-0"
BED RM.3
10'-9" x 10'-8"

STOR.

BED RM.4
10'-0" x 10'-0"

STOR.

Upper Level Floor Plan

Copyright by designer/architect.

Plan #371046

Dimensions: 50'2" W x 70' D

Levels: 2

Square Footage: 2,440

Main Level Sq. Ft.: 1,809

Upper Level Sq. Ft.: 631

Bedrooms: 4

Bathrooms: 2½

Foundation: Slab

Materials List Available: No

Price Category: E

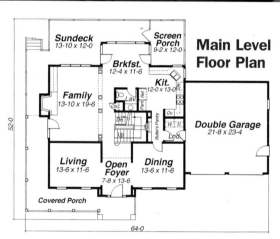

Sundeck
13-10 x 12-0

Screen Porch
9-2 x 12-0

Main Level Floor Plan

Brkfst.
12-4 x 11-6

Kit.
12-0 x 13-0

Family
13-10 x 19-6

Double Garage
21-8 x 23-4

Living
13-6 x 11-6

Open Foyer
7-8 x 13-6

Dining
13-6 x 11-6

Covered Porch

52-0

64-0

Images provided by designer/architect.

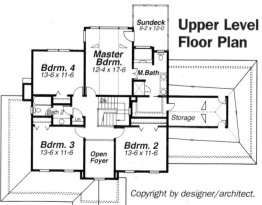

Sundeck
9-2 x 12-0

Upper Level Floor Plan

Bdrm. 4
13-6 x 11-6

Master Bdrm.
12-4 x 17-6

M.Bath

Storage

Bath 2

Lin

Bdrm. 3
13-6 x 11-6

Open Foyer

Bdrm. 2
13-6 x 11-6

Copyright by designer/architect.

Plan #141016

Dimensions: 64' W x 52' D

Levels: 2

Square Footage: 2,416

Main Level Sq. Ft.: 1,250

Upper Level Sq. Ft.: 1,166

Bedrooms: 4

Bathrooms: 2½

Foundation: Basement

Materials List Available: Yes

Price Category: E

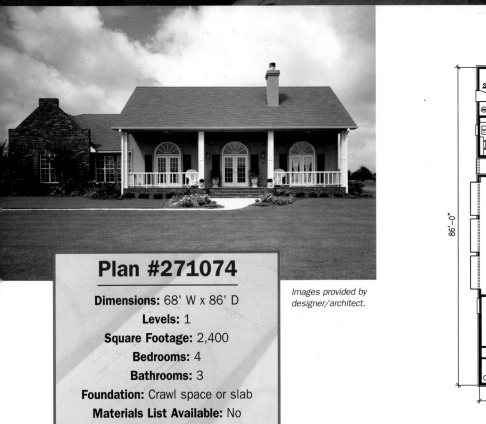

Plan #271074

Dimensions: 68' W x 86' D

Levels: 1

Square Footage: 2,400

Bedrooms: 4

Bathrooms: 3

Foundation: Crawl space or slab

Materials List Available: No

Price Category: E

Images provided by designer/architect.

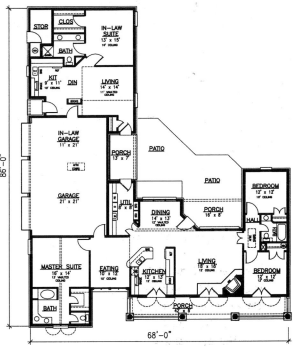

Copyright by designer/architect.

Plan #321037

Dimensions: 78'8" W x 50'6" D

Levels: 1

Square Footage: 2,397

Bedrooms: 3

Bathrooms: 2

Foundation: Walkout

Materials List Available: Yes

Price Category: E

Images provided by designer/architect.

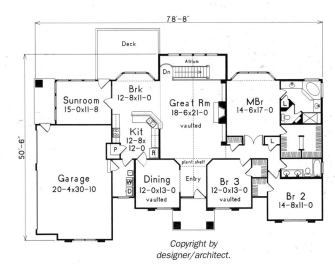

Copyright by designer/architect.

Optional Basement Level Floor Plan

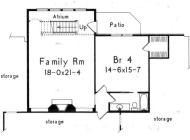

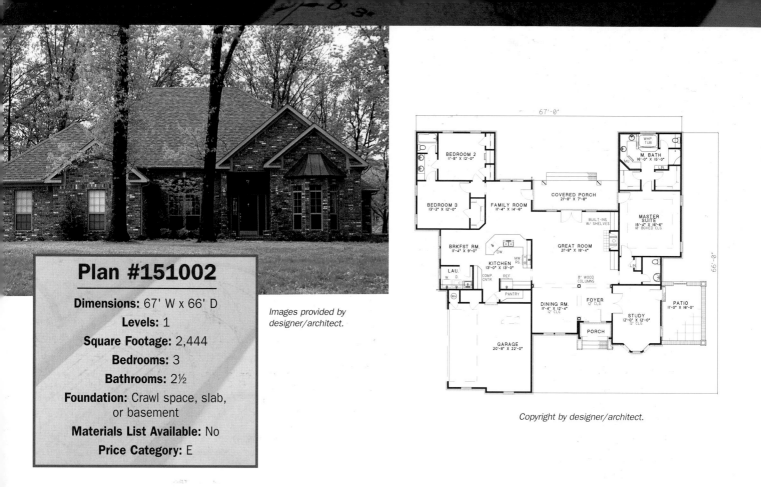

Plan #151002

Dimensions: 67' W x 66' D

Levels: 1

Square Footage: 2,444

Bedrooms: 3

Bathrooms: 2½

Foundation: Crawl space, slab, or basement

Materials List Available: No

Price Category: E

Images provided by designer/architect.

Copyright by designer/architect.

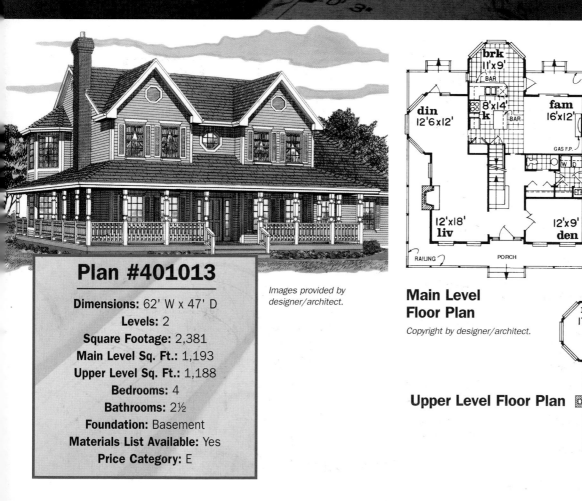

Plan #401013

Dimensions: 62' W x 47' D

Levels: 2

Square Footage: 2,381

Main Level Sq. Ft.: 1,193

Upper Level Sq. Ft.: 1,188

Bedrooms: 4

Bathrooms: 2½

Foundation: Basement

Materials List Available: Yes

Price Category: E

Images provided by designer/architect.

Main Level Floor Plan

Copyright by designer/architect.

Upper Level Floor Plan

Main Level Floor Plan

Copyright by designer/architect.

Upper Level Floor Plan

Plan #371021

Dimensions: 53' W x 48'10" D

Levels: 2

Square Footage: 2,384

Main Level Sq. Ft.: 1,542

Upper Level Sq. Ft.: 842

Bedrooms: 4

Bathrooms: 3½

Foundation: Slab

Materials List Available: No

Price Category: E

Images provided by designer/ architect.

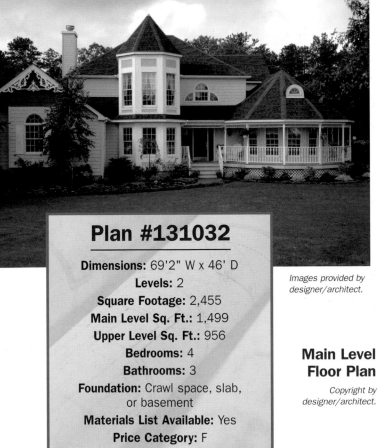

Plan #131032

Dimensions: 69'2" W x 46' D

Levels: 2

Square Footage: 2,455

Main Level Sq. Ft.: 1,499

Upper Level Sq. Ft.: 956

Bedrooms: 4

Bathrooms: 3

Foundation: Crawl space, slab, or basement

Materials List Available: Yes

Price Category: F

Images provided by designer/architect.

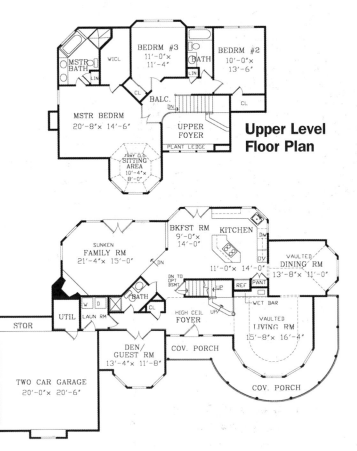

Upper Level Floor Plan

Main Level Floor Plan

Copyright by designer/architect.

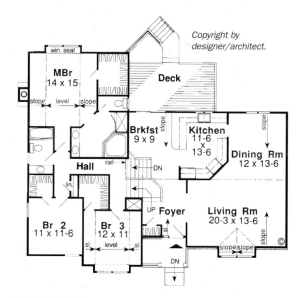

Copyright by designer/architect.

Plan #391020

Dimensions: 54' W x 50' D

Levels: 1

Square Footage: 2,387

Bedrooms: 3

Bathrooms: 2½

Foundation: Basement

Materials List Available: Yes

Price Category: E

Images provided by designer/architect.

Plan #371022

Dimensions: 76'10" W x 54'3" D

Levels: 1

Square Footage: 2,390

Bedrooms: 4

Bathrooms: 2

Foundation: Slab

Materials List Available: No

Price Category: E

Images provided by designer/architect.

Copyright by designer/architect.

Plan #141031

Dimensions: 58'4" W x 30' D
Levels: 2
Square Footage: 2,367
Main Level Sq. Ft.: 1,025
Upper Level Sq. Ft.: 1,342
Bedrooms: 4
Bathrooms: 2½
Foundation: Basement
Materials List Available: No
Price Category: E

This inviting home combines traditional exterior lines, luxurious interior amenities, and innovative design to present a package that will appeal to all members of your family.

Features:

- Foyer: Formal living and dining rooms flank this impressive two-story foyer, which welcomes you to this delightful home with a staircase leading to a balcony.

- Command Center: You will enjoy the open flow of the main floor from the family room to this command center, beyond the kitchen, where you can plan your family activities.

- Master Suite: This master bedroom with optional window seat features a stepped tray ceiling. The master bath with cathedral ceiling offers an optional radius window.

- Additional Bedrooms: The secondary bedroom, next to the master, offers an over look to the foyer, well suited for a sitting room or study.

Images provided by designer/architect.

Main Level Floor Plan

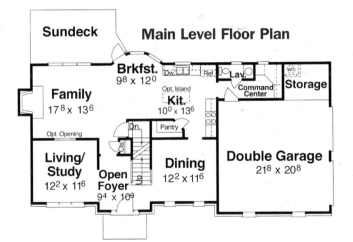

Upper Level Floor Plan

Copyright by designer/architect.

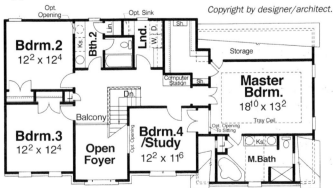

Plan #121080

Dimensions: 56' W x 49' D
Levels: 2
Square Footage: 2,384
Main Level Sq. Ft.: 1,616
Upper Level Sq. Ft.: 768
Bedrooms: 4
Bathrooms: 2½
Foundation: Slab
Materials List Available: Yes
Price Category: E

Images provided by designer/architect.

This design is ideal if you want a generously sized home now and room to expand later.

Features:

• Living Room: Your eyes will be drawn towards the ceiling as soon as you enter this lovely room. The ceiling is vaulted, giving a sense of grandeur, and a graceful balcony from the second floor adds extra interest to this room.

• Kitchen: Designed with lots of counter space to make your work convenient, this kitchen also shares an eating bar with the breakfast nook.

• Breakfast Nook: Eat here or go out to the adjoining private porch where you can enjoy your meal in the morning sunshine.

• Master Suite: The bayed area in the bedroom makes a picturesque sitting area. French doors in the bedroom open to a private bath that's fitted with a whirlpool tub, separate shower, two vanities, and a walk-in closet.

Main Level Floor Plan

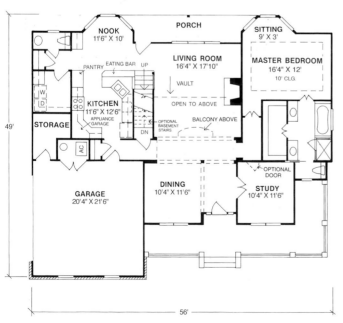

Upper Level Floor Plan

Copyright by designer/architect.

Plan #151240

Dimensions: 67' W x 59'2" D
Levels: 1
Square Footage: 2,395
Bedrooms: 4
Bathrooms: 2
Foundation: Crawl space or slab
Materials List Available: No
Price Category: E

Images provided by designer/architect.

The round-top windows help to set the tone for this traditional brick home.

Features:

- **Foyer:** This entry hall features a high ceiling and opens to the formal dining room.

- **Great Room:** This room warms up with a fireplace and is open to the kitchen.

- **Kitchen:** This kitchen features a peninsula with a raised bar, creating more seating space for the adjacent breakfast room.

- **Master Suite:** This suite, located on the opposite side of the home from the secondary bedrooms, features a private bathroom with a walk-in closet and double vanities.

- **Bedrooms:** Three secondary bedrooms have large closets and share a hall bathroom.

Copyright by designer/architect.

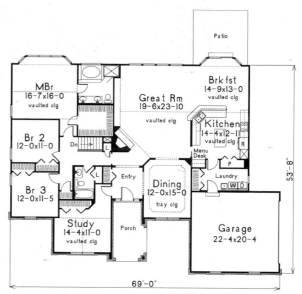

Copyright by designer/architect.

Plan #321005

Dimensions: 69' W x 53'8" D

Levels: 1

Square Footage: 2,483

Bedrooms: 3

Bathrooms: 2

Foundation: Basement

Materials List Available: Yes

Price Category: E

Images provided by designer/architect.

SMARTtip

Art in Pools

The tiled walls and floor of a pool make great canvases for art, so incorporate a serious or whimsical design. Also, make the stairs wide and shallow to form a wading area for kids.

Copyright by designer/architect.

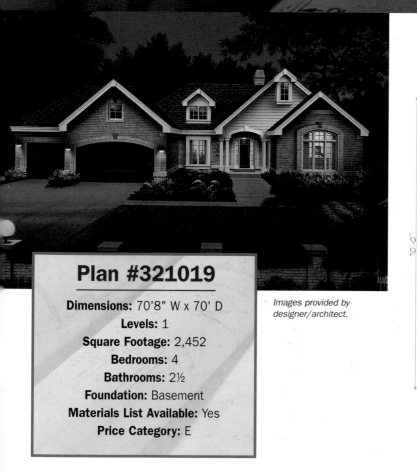

Plan #321019

Dimensions: 70'8" W x 70' D

Levels: 1

Square Footage: 2,452

Bedrooms: 4

Bathrooms: 2½

Foundation: Basement

Materials List Available: Yes

Price Category: E

Images provided by designer/architect.

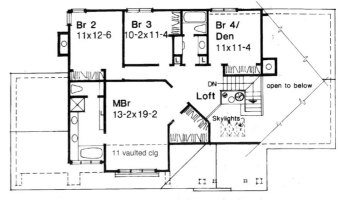

Plan #271018

Dimensions: 67' W x 37' D
Levels: 2
Square Footage: 2,445
Main Level Sq. Ft.: 1,290
Upper Level Sq. Ft.: 1,155
Bedrooms: 4
Bathrooms: 2½
Foundation: Basement
Materials List Available: Yes
Price Category: E

This traditional home re-creates the charm and character of days gone by.

Features:

• Living Room: A dramatic skylighted entry preludes this formal, sunken living room, which includes a stunning corner fireplace, a vaulted ceiling, and an adjoining formal dining room.

• Dining Room: This quiet space offers a built-in hutch beneath a vaulted ceiling.

• Kitchen: A built-in desk and a pantry mark this smartly designed space, which opens to a breakfast room and the family room beyond.

• Family Room: Sunken and filled with intrigue, this gathering room features a fireplace flanked by windows, plus French doors that open to a backyard deck.

• Master Suite: This luxurious upper-floor retreat boasts a vaulted ceiling, an angled walk-in closet, and a private bath.

Main Level Floor Plan

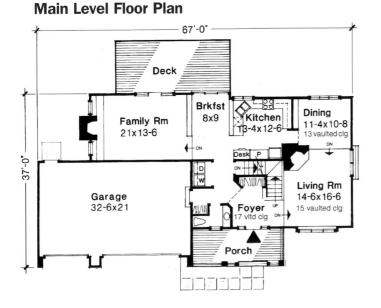

Upper Level Floor Plan

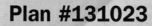

Plan #131023

Dimensions: 78'8" W x 36'2" D
Levels: 2
Square Footage: 2,460
Main Level Sq. Ft.: 1,377
Upper Level Sq. Ft.: 1,083
Bedrooms: 4
Bathrooms: 3½
Foundation: Crawl space, slab, or basement
Materials List Available: Yes
Price Category: F

Images provided by designer/architect.

You'll love the modern floor plan inside this traditional two-story home, with its attractive facade.

Features:

- Ceiling Height: 8 ft.

- Living Room: The windows on three sides of this room make it bright and sunny. Choose the optional fireplace for cozy winter days and the wet bar for elegant entertaining.

- Family Room: Overlooking the rear deck, this spacious family room features a fireplace and a skylight.

- Dining Room: The convenient placement of this large room lets guests flow into it from the living room and allows easy to access from the kitchen.

- Kitchen: The island cooktop and built-in desk make this space both modern and practical.

Rear Elevation

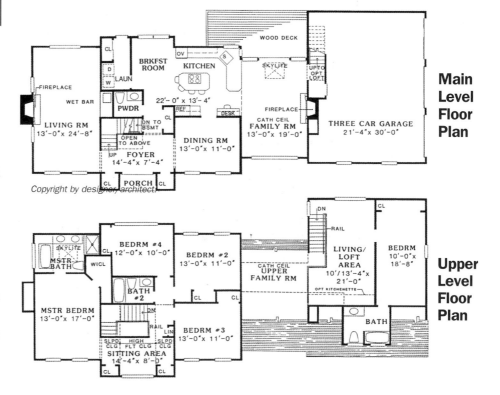

Main Level Floor Plan

Upper Level Floor Plan

Copyright by designer/architect.

Plan #271049

Dimensions: 74' W x 44' D
Levels: 2
Square Footage: 2,464
Main Level Sq. Ft.: 1,288
Upper Level Sq. Ft.: 1,176
Bedrooms: 4
Bathrooms: 2½
Foundation: Basement, crawl space
Materials List Available: Yes
Price Category: E

Images provided by designer/architect.

This classic farmhouse design features a wraparound porch for enjoying conversation on warm afternoons.

Features:

- Living Room: A central fireplace warms this spacious gathering place, while French doors offer porch access.
- Dining Room: On formal occasions, this room is perfect for hosting elegant meals.

- Country Kitchen: An island workstation and a handy pantry keep the family chef organized and productive.
- Family Room: The home's second fireplace warms this cozy area, which is really an extension of the kitchen. Set up a kitchen table here, and enjoy casual meals near the crackling fire.
- Master Suite: The master bedroom is certainly vast. The walk-in closet is large as well. The private, compartmentalized bath offers a sit-down shower and a separate dressing area.

Main Level Floor Plan

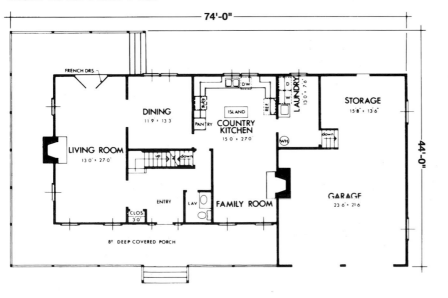

Upper Level Floor Plan

Copyright by designer/architect.

Plan #131051

Dimensions: 64'4" W x 53'4" D

Levels: 2

Square Footage: 2,431

Main Level Sq. Ft.: 1,293

Upper Level Sq. Ft.: 1,138

Bedrooms: 4

Bathrooms: 2½

Foundation: Crawl space, slab, or basement

Materials List Available: Yes

Price Category: F

Gracious and charming with a wraparound front porch and a backyard terrace, this home also has a ready-to-finish third floor all-purpose room and a full bath.

Features:

- Main Level Ceiling Height: 8 ft.

- Family Room: A comfortable space for the entire family to gather, this delightful room can be warmed by a heat-circulating fireplace.

- Dining Room: A cozy dinette boasts a sliding glass door with access to a gorgeous backyard terrace with an optional calm reflecting pool.

- Kitchen: Adjoining the dining area, the kitchen offers plenty of storage and counter space. The laundry room and half-bath are nearby for convenience.

- Garage: The garage is tucked way back to keep it from intruding into the traditional facade.

Main Level Floor Plan

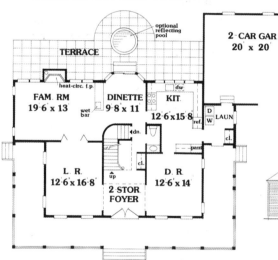

Rear Elevation

Upper Level Floor Plan

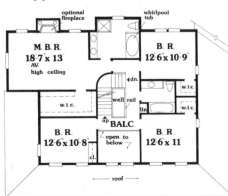

Optional 3rd Level Floor Plan

Plan #391011

Dimensions: 46' W x 45' D
Levels: 2
Square Footage: 2,483
Main Level Sq. Ft.: 1,361
Upper Level Sq. Ft.: 1,122
Bedrooms: 4
Bathrooms: 2½
Foundation: Crawl space, slab, or basement
Materials List Available: Yes
Price Category: E

Images provided by designer/architect.

Features:

- Sloped Ceilings: These ceilings raise the character of the living room and hearth area. Even the foyer has special ceiling effects.

- Hearth Room: This room snuggles by a fireplace and opens to the breakfast room, exterior deck, and adjoining kitchen.

- Bedrooms: The second level features two secondary bedrooms, one with a sloped ceiling. Both open to a view of the balcony and a convenient bathroom.

- Master Suite: Located over the garage, this suite features a sitting area with arched window, room-sized closet with window, and a skylighted full bath.

Rear Elevation

Striking Palladian windows, large dormers, streamlined living space deem this home — gorgeous! The main level brings living, dining, hearth room, kitchen, and den into stylish L-shaped alignment.

Upper Level Floor Plan

Copyright by designer/architect.

Main Level Floor Plan

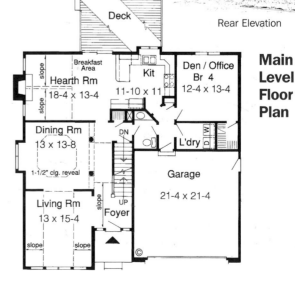

Plan #271069

Dimensions: 63'5" W x 51'8" D

Levels: 2

Square Footage: 2,376

Main Level Sq. Ft.: 1,248

Upper Level Sq. Ft.: 1,128

Bedrooms: 4

Bathrooms: 2½

Foundation: Basement, crawl space

Materials List Available: No

Price Category: E

This home's Federal-style facade has a simple elegance that is still popular among today's homeowners.

Features:

• Living Room: This formal space is perfect for serious conversation or thoughtful reflection. Optional double doors would open directly into the family room beyond.

• Dining Room: You won't find a more elegant room than this for hosting holiday feasts.

• Kitchen: This room has everything the cook could hope for—a central island, a handy pantry, and a menu desk. Sliding glass doors in the dinette let you step outside for some fresh air with your cup of coffee.

• Family Room: Here's the spot to spend a cold winter evening. Have hot chocolate in front of a crackling fire!

• Master Suite: With an optional vaulted ceiling, the sleeping chamber is bright and spacious. The private bath showcases a splashy whirlpool tub.

Main Level Floor Plan

Upper Level Floor Plan

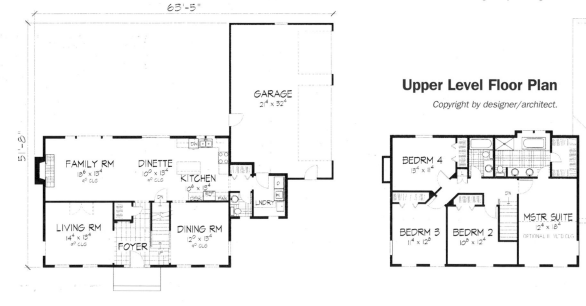

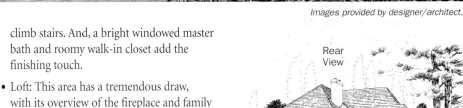

Plan #391014

Dimensions: 64' W x 52' D
Levels: 2
Square Footage: 2,372
Main Level Sq. Ft.: 1,752
Upper Level Sq. Ft.: 620
Bedrooms: 3
Bathrooms: 2½
Foundation: Crawl space, slab, or basement
Materials List Available: Yes
Price Category: E

This home sets the imagination in motion, with its showcase vaulted ceilings, open entry, two-way fireplace, and more.

Features:

- **Kitchen:** In this kitchen and dinette area, a built-in desk lines up along a wall of shelving and cabinetry, and a pantry and half-bath line the back wall.

- **Master Bedroom:** The main-floor master bedroom is a treat for mom and dad who prefer not to climb stairs. And, a bright windowed master bath and roomy walk-in closet add the finishing touch.

- **Loft:** This area has a tremendous draw, with its overview of the fireplace and family room below.

- **Bedrooms:** Two secondary bedrooms with walk-in closets flank opposite ends of the upper level. Each bedroom also has a private vanity sink and a separate entrance to the shared toilet, tub, and linen closet.

Images provided by designer/architect.

Rear View

Living Room

Main Level Floor Plan

Deck

Family Rm
15-6 x 19-2
vaulted

MBr 1
15 x 13-2
pan vault

Dinette/Kitchen
22 x 13-8
bench

Balcony above

desk

pantry

spa

UP DN

Living Rm
13 x 13-8
vaulted

Foyer
vaulted

Dining Rm
11 x 13-8

Garage
21-4 x 31-4

Copyright by designer/architect.

Br 2
13-2 x 13-10
shelves

Loft

linen

DN

Br 3
12-6 x 10-8

Upper Level Floor Plan

Plan #271068

Dimensions: 72' W x 36' D

Levels: 2

Square Footage: 2,214

Main Level Sq. Ft.: 1,150

Upper Level Sq. Ft.: 1,064

Bedrooms: 4

Bathrooms: 2½

Foundation: Basement

Materials List Available: No

Price Category: E

Images provided by designer/architect.

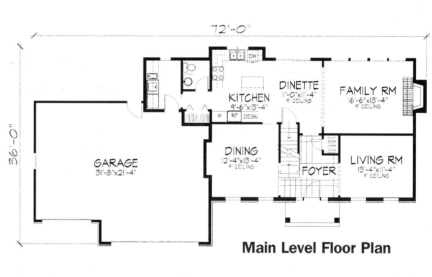

Main Level Floor Plan

This traditional home is reminiscent of the Federal styling of a bygone era.

Features:

- **Living Room:** To the right of the foyer, this room is a perfect spot for adults to chat while the kids are playing elsewhere.

- **Dining Room:** Imagine hosting holiday feasts here! This room is quiet, but is also nicely situated near the kitchen for ease of service.

- **Kitchen:** A central work island, a useful menu desk, and a handy pantry equip the family chef for culinary successes. The casual dinette offers sliding glass doors to your prize-winning garden.

- **Family Room:** This space is large enough for a game of charades. The fireplace will be a welcome feature when the family comes inside after playing in the snow.

- **Master Suite:** A tray ceiling makes the sleeping chamber seem special. The private bath flaunts a whirlpool tub to soak away the cares of the day.

Copyright by designer/architect.

Upper Level Floor Plan

Let Us Help You Plan Your Dream Home

Whether you've always dreamed of building your own home or you can't find the right house from among the dozens you've toured, our collection of affordable plans can help you achieve the home of your dreams.

You could have an architect create a one-of-a-kind home for you, but the design services alone could end up costing up to 15 percent of the cost of construction—a hefty premium for any building project. Isn't it a better idea to select from among the hundreds of unique designs shown in our collection for a fraction of the cost?

What does Creative Homeowner Offer?

In this book, Creative Homeowner provides hundreds of home plans from the country's best architects and designers. Our designs are among the most popular available. Whether your taste runs from traditional to contemporary, Victorian to early American, you are sure to find the best house design for you and your family. Our plans packages include detailed drawings to help you or your builder construct your dream house. **(See page 280.)**

Can I Make Changes to the Plans?

Creative Homeowner offers three ways to help you achieve a truly unique home design. Our customizing service allows for extensive changes to our designs. **(See page 281.)** We also provide reverse images of our plans, or we can give you and your builder the tools for making minor changes on your own. **(See page 282.)**

Can You Help Me Stay on Budget?

Building a house is a large financial investment. To help you stay within your budget, Creative Homeowner can provide you with general construction costs based on your zip code. **(See page 282.)** Also, many of our plans come with the option of buying detailed materials lists to help you price out construction costs.

Is There Anything I Missed?

A typical construction crew consists of a number of skilled professionals. If you plan on doing all or part of the work yourself, or you want to keep tabs on your builder, we offer best-selling building and design books at attractive prices. (See our company Web site at www.creativehomeowner.com.) Our home-building book package covers all phases of home construction, from framing and drywalling to wiring and plumbing. **(See page 288.)**

Our Plans Packages Offer:

Our home plans are the result of many hours of work by leading architects and professional designers. Most of our home plans include each of the following.

Frontal Sheet

This artist's rendering of the front of the house gives you an idea of how the house will look once it is completed and the property landscaped.

Detailed Floor Plans

These plans show the size and layout of the rooms. They also provide the locations of doors, windows, fireplaces, closets, stairs, and electrical outlets and switches.

Foundation Plan

A foundation plan gives the dimensions of basements, walk-out basements, crawl spaces, pier foundations, and slab construction. Each house design lists the type of foundation included. If the plan you choose does not have the foundation type you require, our customer service department can help you customize the plan to meet your needs.

Roof Plan

In addition to providing the pitch of the roof, these plans also show the locations of dormers, skylights, and other elements.

Exterior Elevations

These drawings show the front, rear, and sides of the house as if you were looking at it head on. Elevations also provide information about architectural features and finish materials.

Interior Elevations and Details

Interior elevations show specific details of such elements as fireplaces, kitchen and bathroom cabinets, built-ins, and other unique features of the design.

Cross Sections

These show the structure as if it were sliced to reveal construction requirements, such as insulation, flooring, and roofing details.

Frontal Sheet

Floor Plan

Foundation Plan

Roof Plan

Elevation

Stair Details

Cross Sections

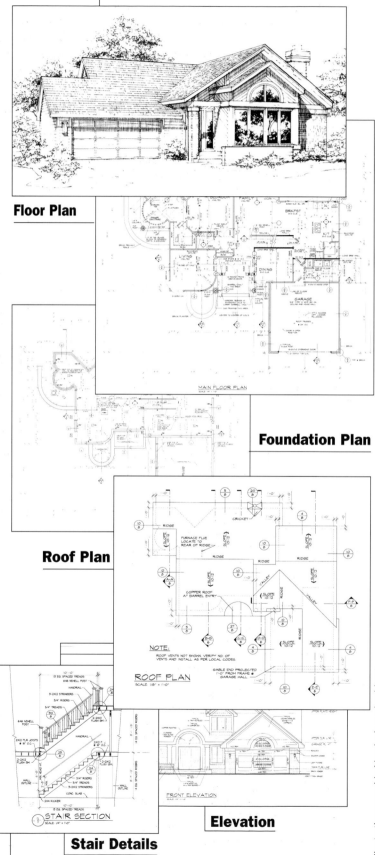

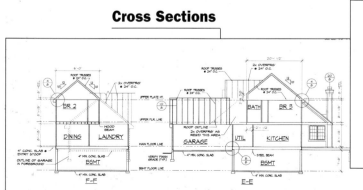

Illustrations provided by designer/architect

Customize Your Plans in 4 Easy Steps

1 **Select the home plan** that most closely meets your needs. Purchase of a reproducible master is necessary in order to make changes to a plan.

2 **Call 1-800-523-6789 to place your order.** Tell our sales representative you are interested in customizing your plan. To receive your customization cost estimate, we will send you a checklist (via fax or email) for you to complete indicating the changes you would like to make to your plan. There is a $50 nonrefundable consultation fee for this service. If you decide to continue with the custom changes, the $50 fee is credited to the total amount charged.

3 **Fax the completed checklist** to 1-201-760-2431 or email it to us at customize@creativehomeowner.com. Within three business days of receipt of your checklist, a detailed cost estimate will be provided to you.

4 **Once you approve the estimate,** a 75% retainer fee is collected and customization work begins. Preliminary drawings typically take 10 to 15 business days. After approval, we will collect the balance of your customization order cost before shipping the completed plans. You will receive five sets of blueprints or a reproducible master, plus a customized materials list if desired.

Modification Pricing Guide

Categories	Average Cost For Modification
Add or remove living space	Quote required
Bathroom layout redesign	Starting at $120
Kitchen layout redesign	Starting at $120
Garage: add or remove	Starting at $400
Garage: front entry to side load or vice versa	Starting at $300
Foundation changes	Starting at $220
Exterior building materials change	Starting at $200
Exterior openings: add, move, or remove	$65 per opening
Roof line changes	Starting at $360
Ceiling height adjustments	Starting at $280
Fireplace: add or remove	Starting at $90
Screened porch: add	Starting at $280
Wall framing change from 2x4 to 2x6	Starting at $200
Bearing and/or exterior walls changes	Quote required
Non-bearing wall or room changes	$65 per room
Metric conversion of home plan	Starting at $400
Adjust plan for handicapped accessibility	Quote required
Adapt plans for local building code requirements	Quote required
Engineering stamping only	Quote required
Any other engineering services	Quote required
Interactive illustrations (choices of exterior materials)	Quote required

Note: Any home plan can be customized to accommodate your desired changes. The average prices above are provided only as examples of the most commonly requested changes, and are subject to change without notice. Prices for changes will vary according to the number of modifications requested, plan size, style, and method of design used by the original designer. To obtain a detailed cost estimate, please contact us.

Terms & Copyright

These home plans are protected under the terms of United States Copyright Law and may not be copied or reproduced in any way, by any means, unless you have purchased reproducible masters, which clearly indicate your right to copy or reproduce. We authorize the use of your chosen home plan as an aid in the construction of one single-family home only. You may not use this home plan to build a second or multiple dwellings without purchasing another blueprint or blueprints, or paying additional home plan fees.

Architectural Seals

Because of differences in building codes, some cities and states now require an architect or engineer licensed in that state to review and "seal" a blueprint, or officially approve it, prior to construction. Delaware, Nevada, New Jersey, and New York require that all plans for houses built in those states be redrawn by an architect licensed in the state in which the home will be built. We strongly advise you to consult with your local building official for information regarding architectural seals.

Before Customization

After

Decide What Type of Plan Package You Need

How many Plans Should You Order?

Standard 8-Set Package. We've found that our 8-set package is the best value for someone who is ready to start building. Once the process begins, a number of people will require their own set of blueprints. The 8-set package provides plans for you, your builder, the subcontractors, mortgage lender, and the building department.
Minimum 4-Set Package. If you are in the bidding process, you may want to order only four sets for the bidding round and reorder additional sets as needed.
1-Set Study Package. The 1-set package allows you to review your home plan in detail. The plan will be marked as a study print, and it is illegal to build a house from a study print alone. It is a violation of copyright law to reproduce a blueprint without permission.

Buying Additional Sets

If you require additional copies of blueprints for your home construction, you can order additional sets within 60 days of the original order date at a reduced price. The cost is $45.00 for each additional set. For more information, contact customer service.

Reproducible Masters

If you plan to make minor changes to one of our home plans, you can purchase reproducible masters. Printed on vellum paper, an erasable paper that you can reproduce in a copying machine, reproducible masters allow an architect, designer, or builder to alter our plans to give you a customized home design. This package also allows you to print as many copies of the modified plans as you need for construction.

Mirror-Reverse Sets

Plans can be printed in mirror-reverse—we can "flip" plans to create a mirror image of the design. This is useful when the house would fit your site or personal preferences if all the rooms were on the opposite side than shown. As the image is reversed, the lettering and dimensions will also be reversed, meaning they will read backwards. Therefore, when ordering mirror-reverse drawings, you must order at least one set of right-reading plans. A $50.00 fee per order will be charged for mirror-reverse (regardless of the number of mirror-reverse sets ordered).

EZ Quote: Home Cost Estimator

EZ Quote is our response to one of the most frequently asked questions we hear from customers: "How much will the house cost me to build?" EZ Quote: Home Cost Estimator will enable you to obtain a calculated building cost to construct your new home, based on labor rates and building material costs within your zip code area. This summary is useful for those who want to know the total construction costs before purchasing sets of home plans. It will also provide a level of comfort when you begin soliciting bids from builders. The cost is $29.95 for the first EZ Quote and $14.95 for each additional one. Available only in the U.S. and Canada.

CompleteCost Estimator

CompleteCost Estimator is a valuable tool for use in planning and constructing your new home. It combines the detail of a materials list with line-by-line cost estimating. The result is a complete, detailed estimate—similar to a bid—that will act as a checklist for all the items you will need to select or coordinate during our building process. CompleteCost Estimator is only available for certain plans (please see Plan Index) and may only be ordered with the purchase of at least four sets of home plans. The cost is $125 for CompleteCost Estimator.

Materials List

Available for most of our plans, the Materials List provides you an invaluable resource in planning and estimating the cost of your home. Each Materials List outlines the quantity, dimensions, and type of materials needed to build your home (with the exception of mechanical systems). You will get faster, more-accurate bids from your contractors and building suppliers—and avoid paying for unused materials. A Materials List may only be ordered with the purchase of at least four sets of home plans.

Order Toll Free by Phone
1-800-523-6789
By Fax: 201-760-2431

Regular office hours are
8:30AM–7:00PM ET, Mon–Fri

Orders received 3PM ET, will be
processed and shipped within two
business days.

Order Online
www.ultimateplans.com

Mail Your Order
Creative Homeowner
Attn: Home Plans
24 Park Way
Upper Saddle River, NJ 07458

Canadian Customers
Order Toll Free 1-800-393-1883

Mail Your Order (Canada)
Creative Homeowner Canada
Attn: Home Plans
113-437 Martin St., Ste. 215
Penticton, BC V2A 5L1

Before You Order

Our Exchange Policy

Blueprints are nonrefundable. However, should you find that the plan you have purchased does not fit your needs, you may exchange that plan for another plan in our collection within 60 days from the date of your original order. The entire content of your original order must be returned before an exchange will be processed. You will be charged a processing fee of 20% of the amount of the original plan set, the cost difference between the new plan set and the original plan set (if applicable), and all related shipping costs for the plans. Contact our customer service department for more information. Please note: reproducible masters may only be exchanged if the package is unopened.

Building Codes and Requirements

At the time of creation, our plans meet the buliding code requirements published by the Building Officials and Code Administrators International, the Southern Building Code Congress International, the International Conference of Building Officials, or the Council of American Building Officials. Because building codes vary from area to area, some drawing modifications and/or the assistance of a professional designer or architect may be necessary to comply with your local codes or to accommodate specific building site conditions. We strongly advise you to consult with your local building official for information regarding codes governing your area.

Blueprint Price Schedule

Price Code	1 Set	4 Sets	8 Sets	Reproducible Masters	Materials List
A	$290	$330	$380	$510	$60
B	$360	$410	$460	$580	$60
C	$420	$460	$510	$610	$60
D	$470	$510	$560	$660	$70
E	$520	$560	$610	$700	$70
F	$570	$610	$670	$750	$70
G	$620	$670	$720	$850	$70
H	$700	$740	$800	$900	$70
I	$810	$850	$900	$940	$80

Note: Prices subject to change

Shipping & Handling

	1-4 Sets	5-7 Sets	8+ Sets or Reproducibles
US Regular (7–10 business days)	$15	$20	$25
US Priority (3–5 business days)	$25	$30	$35
US Express (1–2 business days)	$40	$45	$50
Canada Regular (8–12 business days)	$35	$40	$45
Canada Express (1–2 business days)	$60	$70	$80
Worldwide Express (2–5 business days)	$80	$80	$80

Note: *All delivery times are from date the blueprint package is shipped (typically within 1-2 days of placing order).*

Order Form

Please send me the following:

Plan Number: _____

Price Code: _____ (see Plan Index)

Indicate Foundation Type: (Select ONE. See plan page for availability.)
❑ Slab ❑ Crawl space ❑ Basement ❑ Walk-out basement

Basic Blueprint Package	Cost
❑ Reproducible Masters	$_____
❑ 8-Set Plan Package	$_____
❑ 4-Set Plan Package	$_____
❑ 1-Set Study Package	$_____
❑ Additional plan sets: __ sets at $45.00 per set	$_____
❑ Print in mirror-reverse: $50.00 per order __ sets printed in mirror-reverse	$_____

Important Extras

❑ Materials List	$_____
❑ CompleteCost Materials Report at $125	$_____
❑ Zip Code of Home/Building Site_____	
❑ EZ Quote for Plan #_____ at $29.95	$_____
❑ Additional EZ Quotes for Plan #s_____ at $14.95 each	$_____
Shipping (see chart above)	$_____
SUBTOTAL	$_____
Sales Tax (NJ residents only add 6%)	$_____
TOTAL	$_____

Order Toll Free: 1-800-523-6789   By Fax: 201-760-2431
Creative Homeowner
24 Park Way
Upper Saddle River, NJ 07458

Name _____
(Please print or type)

Street _____
(Please do not use a P.O. Box)

City _____ State _____

Country _____ Zip _____

Daytime telephone ( )_____

Fax ( )_____
(Required for reproducible orders)

E-Mail _____

Payment ❑ Check/money order *Make checks payable to Creative Homeowner*

❑ VISA   ❑ MasterCard   ❑ AMERICAN EXPRESS Cards   ❑ DISCOVER

Credit card number _____

Expiration date (mm/yy) _____

Signature _____

Please check the appropriate box:
❑ Licensed builder/contractor   ❑ Homeowner   ❑ Renter

SOURCE CODE **CA650**

Copyright Notice

Index

Plan #	Price Code	Page	Total Finished Area Square Feet	Materials List	CompleteCost
101004	C	132	1,787	Yes	No
101005	D	180	1,992	Yes	No
101006	D	179	1,982	Yes	No
101008	D	209	2,088	Yes	No
101011	D	226	2,184	Yes	No
101017	E	246	2,253	No	No
111006	E	245	2,241	No	No
111008	D	201	2,011	No	No
111015	E	240	2,208	No	No
111047	D	157	1,863	No	No
121001	D	169	1,911	Yes	No
121003	E	257	2,498	Yes	No
121004	C	101	1,666	Yes	No
121006	C	123	1,762	Yes	No
121008	C	89	1,651	Yes	No
121009	B	36	1,422	Yes	No
121015	D	182	1,999	Yes	No
121017	E	256	2,353	Yes	No
121021	E	250	2,270	Yes	No
121027	C	101	1,660	Yes	No
121031	C	128	1,772	Yes	No
121032	E	247	2,339	Yes	No
121034	E	245	2,223	Yes	No
121050	D	181	1,996	Yes	No
121051	D	160	1,808	Yes	No
121055	C	89	1,622	Yes	No
121064	D	160	1,846	Yes	No
121074	E	256	2,486	Yes	No
121080	E	268	2,384	Yes	No
121086	D	181	1,998	Yes	No
121088	E	255	2,340	Yes	No
121089	D	177	1,976	Yes	No
121092	D	159	1,887	Yes	No
131001	D	102	1,615	Yes	No
131002	D	143	1,709	Yes	No
131003	B	13	1,466	Yes	No
131004	B	39	1,097	Yes	No
131005	C	72	1,595	Yes	No
131005	C	73	1,595	Yes	No
131007	D	84	1,595	Yes	No
131007	D	85	1,595	Yes	No
131014	B	34	1,380	Yes	No
131014	B	35	1,380	Yes	No
131022	E	211	2,092	Yes	No
131023	F	272	2,460	Yes	No
131030	F	258	2,470	Yes	No
131030	F	259	2,470	Yes	No
131032	F	265	2,455	Yes	No
131047	C	129	1,793	Yes	No
131051	F	274	2,431	Yes	No

Plan #	Price Code	Page	Total Finished Area Square Feet	Materials List	CompleteCost
141016	E	262	2,416	Yes	No
141031	E	267	2,367	No	No
151002	E	264	2,444	No	Yes
151003	C	103	1,680	No	Yes
151004	D	214	2,107	No	Yes
151005	D	176	1,940	No	Yes
151007	C	133	1,787	No	Yes
151008	D	158	1,892	No	Yes
151010	B	36	1,379	No	Yes
151016	C	128	1,783	No	Yes
151034	D	215	2,133	No	Yes
151037	C	145	1,538	No	Yes
151050	D	212	2,096	No	Yes
151089	D	156	1,921	No	Yes
151117	D	176	1,957	No	Yes
151133	D	201	2,029	No	Yes
151205	C	177	1,969	No	Yes
151206	D	219	2,151	No	Yes
151210	C	113	1,716	No	Yes
151211	C	137	1,797	No	Yes
151212	B	55	1,462	No	Yes
151213	B	26	1,231	No	Yes
151215	C	71	1,519	No	Yes
151218	B	17	1,008	No	Yes
151219	C	112	1,712	No	Yes
151220	B	40	1,325	No	Yes
151240	E	269	2,395	No	Yes
151243	D	183	1,923	No	Yes
151244	D	171	1,923	No	Yes
151245	D	152	1,923	No	Yes
161002	D	157	1,860	Yes	No
161015	C	123	1,768	Yes	No
161016	D	213	2,101	Yes	No
161020	D	207	2,082	Yes	No
161024	C	142	1,698	No	No
161026	D	200	2,041	No	No
161034	D	225	2,156	No	No
161038	E	257	2,209	No	No
181151	E	248	2,283	Yes	No
181151	E	249	2,283	Yes	No
181215	A	11	929	Yes	No
181216	A	10	910	Yes	No
101217	C	83	1,588	Yes	No
181218	A	12	946	No	No
181219	B	38	1,311	Yes	No
181220	C	86	1,597	Yes	No
181222	C	140	1,670	Yes	No
181223	B	53	1,440	Yes	No
181225	C	118	1,746	Yes	No
181226	B	58	1,485	Yes	No

Index

Plan #	Price Code	Page	Total Finished Area Square Feet	Materials List	CompleteCost
181230	D	175	1,943	Yes	No
181232	B	40	1,325	Yes	No
181233	B	56	1,482	Yes	No
181235	B	20	1,077	Yes	No
181240	D	208	2,089	Yes	No
181242	D	172	1,826	Yes	No
211002	C	134	1,792	Yes	No
211003	D	158	1,865	Yes	No
211006	D	211	2,177	Yes	No
211007	E	254	2,252	Yes	No
221015	D	169	1,926	No	No
271018	E	271	2,445	Yes	No
271038	D	153	1,820	No	No
271049	E	273	2,464	Yes	No
271068	E	278	2,214	No	No
271069	E	276	2,376	No	No
271070	D	226	2,144	No	No
271074	E	263	2,400	No	No
271077	C	134	1,786	No	No
301005	D	153	1,930	Yes	No
311001	D	207	2,085	No	No
321001	C	122	1,721	Yes	No
321002	B	45	1,400	Yes	No
321003	C	133	1,791	Yes	No
321005	E	270	2,483	Yes	No
321006	D	178	1,977	Yes	No
321008	C	122	1,761	Yes	No
321012	D	159	1,882	Yes	No
321013	B	41	1,360	Yes	No
321014	C	102	1,676	Yes	No
321015	C	103	1,501	Yes	No
321019	E	270	2,452	Yes	No
321021	C	68	1,708	Yes	No
321022	B	23	1,140	Yes	No
321023	B	21	1,092	Yes	No
321024	B	45	1,403	Yes	No
321025	A	13	914	Yes	No
321026	C	144	1,712	Yes	No
321030	D	200	2,029	Yes	No
321033	B	41	1,268	Yes	No
321035	B	55	1,384	Yes	No
321037	E	263	2,397	Yes	No
321038	B	54	1,452	Yes	No
321039	B	23	1,231	Yes	No
321040	B	21	1,084	Yes	No
321041	E	250	2,286	Yes	No
321045	D	206	2,058	Yes	No
321053	D	179	1,985	Yes	No
321056	D	206	2,050	Yes	No
321057	C	68	1,524	Yes	No
321058	C	144	1,700	Yes	No
351001	D	154	1,855	Yes	No
351001	D	155	1,855	Yes	No
351009	B	46	1,400	Yes	No
351013	A	8	800	Yes	No
351014	B	15	1,000	Yes	No
351016	B	16	1,002	Yes	No
351018	B	29	1,251	Yes	No
351019	B	50	1,427	Yes	No
351021	C	61	1,500	Yes	No
351022	C	69	1,503	Yes	No
351023	C	87	1,600	Yes	No
351029	C	88	1,606	Yes	No
351030	C	70	1,503	Yes	No
351033	C	96	1,654	Yes	No
351035	C	143	1,701	Yes	No
351036	D	138	1,799	Yes	No
351038	D	139	1,800	Yes	No
351045	E	170	2,000	Yes	No
351055	E	246	2,251	Yes	No
351065	D	196	2,005	Yes	No
371005	B	28	1,250	No	No
371006	B	42	1,374	No	No
371009	B	24	1,223	No	No
371010	B	51	1,429	No	No
371011	C	142	1,681	No	No
371012	C	114	1,720	No	No
371013	C	132	1,791	No	No
371014	D	166	1,908	No	No
371016	E	252	2,316	No	No
371017	E	253	2,320	No	No
371018	E	255	2,333	No	No
371021	E	265	2,384	No	No
371022	E	266	2,390	No	No
371023	E	261	2,444	No	No
371028	B	43	1,376	No	No
371029	B	44	1,394	No	No
371030	B	52	1,434	No	No
371031	C	86	1,599	No	No
371032	C	99	1,659	No	No
371033	C	115	1,724	No	No
371034	C	120	1,753	No	No
371035	C	121	1,758	No	No
371036	C	124	1,764	No	No
371037	C	127	1,774	No	No
371038	D	162	1,896	No	No
371039	D	163	1,898	No	No
371040	D	168	1,913	No	No
371041	D	175	1,950	No	No
371042	D	182	1,999	No	No

order direct: 1-800-523-6789